About this Edition

In the Name of Osama bin Laden was originally published in France, the week of September 11, 2001. Ours is the first English-language edition, translated from the French and then modified considerably.

This revised, updated, and partially rewritten edition includes extensive new material, including: new, previously unpublished documents, including a proclamation by bin Laden on September 24, 2001; an interview conducted by the author with bin Laden; and an excerpt from Ayman al-Zawahiri's book, *Knights under The Flag of the Prophet,* which was smuggled out of Afghanistan in October 2001; a preface tracing the evolution of terrorist movements in the second half of the twentieth century; an extensive introduction situating the bin Laden organization in the broader context of the global rise in religious fundamentalism in general, and the political developments in the Middle East and the world that served as backdrop and catalyst for the development of the movement over the last decade; an epilogue bringing the reader up to date on unconventional weapons threats and the future of the Bin Laden Brotherhood; an afterword debating the clash of civilization discourse that dominates in the aftermath of September 11 and exploring the role of new communications technology in the war for public opinion, with particular focus on the role of al-Jazeera, the Arab satellite TV station.

In addition, there has been comprehensive annotation of Islamic terms and references to sects, additional biographical material on al-Qaeda leadership added, and new material translated from the Arabic documents, with excerpts that were not available in the French edition.

Praise for In the Name of Osama bin Laden

For the English edition:

"Bin Laden's genesis and genius are all chronicled in Jacquard's sweeping account of the Saudi-born terrorist and his brotherhood. The book rightfully brings into focus the role of modern media, especially satellite TV and the Internet, in bin Laden's cunning wager that he could defeat the U.S. as a world power. A chilling read, a must read for all who continue to grapple with the twin legacy of hatred and hope from September 11."—Bruce B. Lawrence, author of *Shattering the Myth: Islam Beyond Violence*

For the French edition:

"Remarkably documented and prescient. . . . Citing confidential reports from intelligence agencies the world over, [Jacquard] unveils the secret plan of the man who has declared holy war against the Americans, the Jews, and Christians."—*Le Figaro Magazine* (September 15, 2001)

"This biography of Osama bin Laden by Roland Jacquard could not have come at a better moment."—*Le Monde* (September 22, 2001)

"Remarkable and essential."—*France-Soir*
(September 21, 2001)

IN THE NAME OF OSAMA BIN LADEN

Global Terrorism & the Bin Laden Brotherhood

Roland Jacquard

Samia Serageldin, Consulting Editor   *George Holoch, Translator*

DUKE UNIVERSITY PRESS *Durham and London* 2002

Printed in the United States of America on acid-free paper
An earlier edition was published in French with the title
Au Nom D'Oussama Ben Laden

Typeset in Galliard
Library of Congress Cataloging-in-Publication Data appear
on the last printed page of this book.

Contents

Preface

"Would terrorists resort to using conventional weapons, including missiles, when it is in the very nature of terrorism to resort only to unforeseeable methods or techniques, if necessary calling on fanatical fighters ready to give up their lives to reach their target?"

When I wrote these lines for the French edition of this book, before the events of September 11, 2001, I could not have imagined just how tragically prophetic they would prove to be. Since the apocalyptic events of that day, the same urgent questions are on everyone's mind: Were these attacks in any way predictable or preventable? What motivates the fanatic ready to give his life to accomplish a mission so doomed and nihilistic by all rational calculations?

This is where the history of terrorist movements and their evolution over the past thirty years proves instructive. Those who take part in Islamist extremist movements are different from the violent activists of earlier times and have a modus operandi that makes them elusive and extraordinarily difficult to track. The European terrorists of the far Left in the 1980s were organized around a small number of clandestine cells, making it easier for the police and security services to keep a close watch on them. Moreover, these organizations, inspired by Marxist ideological motives, eagerly sought publicity, and their leaders had a visceral need to brag about their actions, even at the risk of exposing themselves. Their demands were an integral part of an attack and revealed the state of mind of the terrorists, who almost always said or wrote more than was needed to locate and break them up. For the Bin Laden Brotherhood, by contrast, demands were not a concern; they took it for granted that the destruction of what they hated would be handed to them without their needing to ask for it. The press came to bin Laden, not he to it, and he held it at arm's length to increase the value of the infrequent messages he usually sent by fax or through spokesmen.

The European terrorist movements were limited both in power and range and were eradicated because they were fragile. Informers and moles rarely had to go outside Europe to follow a trail, and drug cartels had not yet become the bankers for terror. The world was made up of villages, but was not yet a global village. The leaders of these movements and their accomplices are serving long prison terms in France, Germany, and Italy. How many young people remember now the Red Brigades, Action Directe, or the Red Army? The "heroic deeds" of these once feared organizations have been turned by history into minor jolts or hiccups in the confrontation between Marxism and capitalism.

The Arab and Palestinian activism that succeeded the European Marxist movements originated in a political ideal and not in a generalized ideology. In the Middle East, terror became a matter for professionals and mercenaries; it was supported by governments and millions of dollars of funding. Terrorists hid under diplomatic cover, used forged passports and remote training camps, and refined their "working" methods and their means of funding. Drugs from the Bekaa Valley in Lebanon and extortion, backed up by shrewd techniques for money laundering, entered the stage, and the frontiers of terrorism expanded. It was not uncommon for extremist Palestinians or affiliated Arab organizations to open offices in Stockholm or Madrid, thereby shifting their operational centers outside their natural and historic battleground, the Middle East. The global village was in the process of formation. Instead of quietly placing "bomblets" stuffed with defoliants outside the headquarters of a manufacturers' association in the small hours of the morning, as the Reds had done, terrorists began to hijack commercial airliners and divert them to airports in countries friendly to their cause. No one thought it necessary to go that far in order to be heard, because they were intent simply on being heard and not on carrying out justice in the name of some illusory fatwa. With the new terrorism, intelligence services began to lose ground. It became more and more difficult for the police to track down the Middle Eastern terrorists, who had access to significant financial resources and who crossed borders easily, thanks to the accomplices they had acquired in many countries, including countries in

Europe. Hence, the task of dismantling terrorist organizations and preventing further attacks was already becoming increasingly complex, to the great surprise of political authorities, who were able to see only the outward signs of terrorism but not its underlying causes.

Terrorist activity related to the Palestinian situation evolved in the 1990s into a political struggle. Though the Intifada continued to erupt at times, terrorist attacks generally faded and were replaced by Arab-Israeli dialogue. Danger had been temporarily removed from all sides, and veteran militant terrorists such as Abu Nidal, Georges Habbash, and Carlos "the Jackal" (arrested in Sudan in 1994) now appeared as retired figures and rebels without a cause, whereas the leader of them all, Yasser Arafat, became something close to a head of state.

Industry and capital became increasingly globalized, but the populations of the Third World did not share in the new prosperity of the West. The fundamentalist Islamic movement arose partly in response to this state of affairs—from global causes rather than a single, concrete issue like the Palestinian problem, which was rooted in the soil. When it passed into these new hands, terrorist violence also changed character.

In becoming the immediate enemy of the terrorist fundamentalist Islamists, the West had also of course become a target, and the global village of the new millennium, spreading its geographical and virtual locations to places as far apart as the crowded streets of Manila and New York, made life even more difficult for intelligence services and antiterrorism organizations, who were already partly disabled by their inability to adapt to the entirely new spiritual and irrational drive that had become the engine of worldwide terrorism.

This is why Osama bin Laden's terrorist networks were able to strike the World Trade Center towers and the Pentagon ruthlessly, easily, and at little cost: because they are dispersed or, more precisely, because they can emerge anywhere in a few hours or a few days, because they expect nothing material from their network or their leaders, neither financial assistance nor reward. They have no reason to be demanding because they believe they will be rewarded in a future life. These new terrorists move around in a shadowy and informal sprawling organization, unlike the cells of the Italian Red Brigades of the 1970s, which were hierarchically organized and carefully documented, by their leaders as well as by the police.

Osama bin Laden's strength was his belief that his combatants were immortal. When one of his admirers died, ten, twenty, thirty would arise to fund the battle with their own, often hard-earned money. And some of these militants would perhaps be much more anti-imperialist, much more anti-American, than Islamist, particularly in the Third World countries where Osama bin Laden frequently recruited and where, all things considered, "Osama the rebel" was seen in a favorable light. For them, the global village might then be submerged by a new "rejection front."

The heads of the principal intelligence services and political leaders have finally understood that terror has to be looked at in a new way in order for it to be eradicated: by identifying its causes and catalysts rather than by attempting to predict and limit the effects of terrorism in the short run. André Malraux, the centenary of whose birth is celebrated in 2001, wrote that the twenty-first century would be a mystical one, and he was not mistaken. The rise of religion as a force for good or for evil is a fact of the new millennium. The world has now been dragged by force into the mysteries of the irrational, and we will have to adapt to these new conditions.

In the Name of Osama bin Laden

Introduction / *Samia Serageldin*

In 1989, the Soviets retreated from Afghanistan, having failed to subdue the Afghan mujahedeen. Their retreat signaled the beginning of the end of the cold war; Zbigniew Brzezinski called it the turning point in the fall of the Soviet empire. Francis Fukuyama even went so far as to announce the end of history, in his article "The End of History?," published in 1989 in the *National Interest.* Fukuyama, a senior official at the State Department at the time, speculated that liberal democracy, then apparently in the ascendant, constituted the end point of humankind's ideological evolution and hence the final form of human government. His argument was somewhat premature, as it turns out, since in that victory for democracy against the Soviets on Afghan soil, the seeds were sown for the events that, over a decade later, would mark history indelibly in the first year of the new millennium.

The name of one man, Osama bin Laden, has come to be associated with these events more than any other. But what ideological trend is he emblematic of? What turned a Saudi billionaire into an international renegade? What is the larger context in which this drama unfolds?

Violence in the name of religion—of all religions—is as old as history, but it came to the forefront in the second half of the twentieth century. A global rise in religious terrorism has been documented; fundamentalists of all faiths have committed acts of violence in the name of religion and ethnic identity. Irish Catholic and Protestant nationalists in Britain; the Hindu-Buddhist Aum Shinri Kyo sect in Tokyo; Algerian Islamists in France; Christian militia and antiabortion activists in the United States; Palestinian suicide bombers and Jewish religious extremists in the Middle East; Sikh and Kashmiri separatists in India; Islamists in Egypt and the

United States. Homegrown or imported, all have contributed to the international toll of violence.

The religious activist who turns to violence does not typically fit the profile of the lone sociopath or psychopath bent on committing acts of terror in the name of one ideology or another, or none. The studies of the psychology of terrorism deal largely with social psychology. "Activists involved in religious terrorism . . . are people . . . caught up in extraordinary communities and share extreme world views."[1] Their vision of the world is that of a world at war in which violent acts may be regarded as legitimate. Justification can take the form of the perceived need for self-defense; a lesser act of violence can be argued to prevent a greater. Just as the state can legitimize violence in the name of nationalism, so a power that supercedes the state—religion—can be called upon to provide a divine mandate for destruction.

Beyond internal conviction, this vision of the world is validated by the shared support of the collectivity and by approval from a legitimizing ideology or authority. The lone gunman or bomber is backed by a community that tacitly or explicitly validates his action. In February 1998 Osama bin Laden proclaimed that the world was at war, a war he did not start, but rather the Americans, who, through their actions in the Middle East, had made "a clear declaration of war on God, his messenger and Muslims."[2]

For countless followers, Osama bin Laden came to represent the authoritative voice of ideological approval that inspired and validated their actions. He did not need to order, let alone to mastermind, an act, only to approve it ex post facto. Only after the fact did the perpetrators of these acts claim their allegiance in the name of Osama bin Laden. Bin Laden himself relied on the "doctors of jurisprudence," as he referred to his mentors, for the theological and ideological underpinnings: such men as Ayman al-Zawahiri, Hassan al-Turabi, and the works of Sayid Qutb. His own role was that of the charismatic leader, not the scholarly ideologue or the intellectual.

The network of training camps in Afghanistan, known as al-Qaeda or the Bin Laden Brotherhood, served a psychological and ideological purpose as much as a military or practical one. It provided the environment of a commune of deep trust, the brotherhood of a shared worldview. Originally brothers in arms in a just cause, the mujahedeen were hailed as freedom fighters in the West as well as in the Muslim world. But this legitimate fight produced a permanent war mentality among many of its veterans. Once armed, these veterans typically never abandon the fight. What might have started as a legitimate struggle against occupation, alongside other nationalist groups, can turn, especially if these causes fail, to other, less articulated, unsanctioned struggles. This mindset conforms to the pattern observed with other groups, such as Gulf War veterans Timothy McVeigh and Terry Nichols and others in the Michigan Militia.

National struggles and political ideologies can gradually take on the characteristics of a much wider conflict between religious or cultural paradigms. Both the Irish confrontation and the Palestinian struggle began as nationalist aspirations and only later took on the coloring of a sacred conflict as spiritual authorities infused it with religious significance.

In contrast to the strictly political agendas of the activists who resort to acts of terror with a specific, rational outcome in mind, the acts of violence committed by religious terrorists can seem senseless and desperate, doomed to failure by any rational calculation. They can only be understood as symbolic acts, temporarily alleviating feelings of extreme hopelessness and humiliation by lending an illusory sense of empowerment. The terrorists are finally taken seriously by the authorities. Their actions can be intended as warnings to the world that it is in a state of ultimate conflict, or as retaliation against perceived violence they have suffered, or as preemptive strikes in an ongoing battle.

One mindset that religious extremist movements seem to share is a fear of globalization, of an international political and economic conspiracy. Bin Laden, no less than Christian survivalist militia groups and their theories about the black helicopters of the United Nations, has expressed concerns about such a one-world conspiracy.

But if violence in the name of religion in general is symptomatic of our times, it is Islamist groups that are the most widespread and make the greatest impact. One feature of the culture of terrorism is that these activists share a vision of a world at war in which their communities are under attack and a violent response is seen as self-defense. In the second half of the twentieth century and into this century, the Muslim world has been and continues to be in turmoil. The overwhelming majority of the world's refugees are Muslim; that statistic alone is an indicator of the wars and political upheaval in that part of the world. Other socioeconomic factors are cited: the overwhelming poverty endemic to most of these societies and the unstable demographics of societies in which the majority of the population is under twenty-five years old. Whereas the foot soldiers of "cosmic war" tend to be young and poor, their leaders are often middle-aged and affluent. The Saudi Osama bin Laden was born into great wealth and privilege; his right-hand man, the Egyptian Ayman al-Zawahiri, was a well-connected, upper-middle-class physician before the two men headed the FBI's most-wanted list.

There is a widespread sense in these societies that Islam itself is under attack, from secular forces within and without the country. In addition there are specific grievances related to injustices, or perceived injustices, in particular countries. Political ideology and religion are a potent combination, whichever is at the service of the other. The condition for their intertwining to lead to violence is "the coalescence of a peculiar set of circumstances—political, social, and ideological—when religion becomes fused with violent expressions of social aspirations, personal pride, and movements for political change."[3]

Many parts of the Muslim world on the eve of the last decade of the second millennium presented a particularly combustible mix of religious and political grievances. The year 1990 was a pivotal year on the world stage, particularly in the Middle East. Not coincidentally, it was also the turning point in bin Laden's career. An honored Saudi citizen, he turned into a renegade, flouting his own government and the United States that he had served with in the struggle against the atheist Soviet invasion. But around the Middle East, that fateful year, many trajectories began that eventually, one way or another, converged on Afghanistan.

In 1990 the Americans, and the Saudis under American pressure, withdrew their support for the Afghan rebellion, leaving the native communist regime still in power in Kabul and the civil war still raging. The Soviet troops had retreated and the United States decided it no longer had a compelling stake in this war—a decision, it turned out, that would come back to haunt it. An outraged bin Laden traveled to Riyadh in Saudi Arabia to make a passionate personal appeal to the Saudi monarchy to rethink their decision and continue to support the mujahedeen rebels. He was rebuffed. His sense of betrayal was on the scale of the ten years of his life that he had devoted to the cause. He refused to disown the struggle of his companions in arms and continued to support the cause with his own means. This once solid Saudi citizen turned his animus against his own regime, accusing the Saudi monarchy of corruption and failure to live up to the true standards of puritan Wahhabi Islam that the Saudi dynasty has always espoused as a legitimizing principle of its rule. Osama the rebel burned his bridges and turned renegade.

Meanwhile, in Iraq, Saddam Hussein was massing his forces, and the Gulf War was about to begin, providing fresh fuel to bin Laden's list of grievances against the Saudi regime. American forces would be stationed permanently on Saudi soil, the home of the holiest sites in Islam, the cities of Mecca and Medina. This was a sacrilege to bin Laden, who openly opposed the legitimacy of the Saudi monarchy, the official "Protector of the Two Holy Places." Increasing his sense of bitterness was the fact that his overtures to help in the war against Saddam were rebuffed.

At the same time, in Egypt, nearly ten years after the assassination of Anwar Sadat in October 1981 by a little-known group called Islamic Jihad, the militant Islamist movement had gained in strength, and some of its leaders had found refuge in Afghanistan, chiefly Ayman al-Zawahiri. But the history of Islamic activism in Egypt harks back to the 1930s with the establishment of Hassan al-Banna's Ikhwan al-Muslimun, or Muslim Brethren, in 1929. Going beyond advocates of reform or revival of Islam, the Ikhwan advocated its restoration at the heart of Egyptian society, including the establishment of sharia, or Islamic law. This vision, however, is not to be confused with an Iranian-style theocracy; in Egypt, and in Sunni Islam generally, the ulema are religious functionaries or scholars with none of the rank or authority of Shii clerics.[4]

The tripartite power struggle in Egypt during the 1940s among the monarchy, the British, and the popular Wafd Party, in addition to the defeat of the 1948 war, contributed to the swelling of the ranks of the Ikhwan before the revolution of 1952. The new military regime, though not averse to coopting Islam as part of a nationalist veneer, was fundamentally secular, increasingly socialist and single-party in orientation. In 1954, an assassination attempt on President Gamal Abdel Nasser's life provided the catalyst for severe repression against the Ikhwan. One of the principal ideologues of the movement, Sayid Qutb, later executed by Nasser in 1966, posthumously inspired Osama bin Laden through his writings. Qutb advocated an Islamic alternative to what he perceived as the failed nationalisms and godless ideologies of the Middle East: nationalism would be recognized as belief, the homeland as Dar-al-Islam (the Muslim world), the ruler as God, and the constitution as the Quran.

Egypt's shocking defeat in the 1967 war, followed by Nasser's death in 1971 and the succession of Anwar Sadat, provided the opening for the Islamists to regroup. In the decade that followed, pressure mounted as Sadat's abrupt about-face to the West and his unilateral peace treaty with Israel were seen by the Islamists as betrayals of both Islam and Egypt. That their message found receptive ears among a growing number of supporters reflects the reality of economic exclusion of large segments of the population from the selective prosperity of the *infitah,* or economic open-door policy, followed by Sadat and exploited by his constituent elite.

This decade witnessed the birth of several militant groups that were far more radical than the superannuated Ikhwan; the most notable of these is the Gamaa Islamiya. On October 6, 1981, a little-known group called Islamic Jihad claimed responsibility for the assassination of Anwar Sadat as he stood in the stands reviewing the troops in commemoration of the 1973 war. In the scene of the attack, unforgettably captured on television, the perpetrator, a young officer by the name of Khalid Islambouli, calls out: "I have killed Pharaoh." One of the Islamic Jihad activists caught in the dragnet following the assassination was Ayman al-Zawahiri. After serving three years in prison, Zawahiri left Egypt and eventually found his way to Afghanistan, where he was to become one of bin Laden's mentors and chief lieutenants. Khalid Islambouli's brother was also to end up in Afghanistan in bin Laden's entourage.

The Hosni Mubarak regime that succeeded Sadat declared martial law and launched an all-out war against the Islamist groups. For their part these movements persisted in their goal of destabilizing the regime by mounting terrorist attacks against tourists, notably the Luxor massacre. Many of the Egyptian militants, under death sentences in their native Egypt, fled abroad; some made their way to Afghanistan.[5]

In May of that fateful year, 1990, the blind preacher Sheikh Omar Abdel Rahman of the Gamaa Islamiya entered the United States. Somehow he was granted an entry visa, although his past in Egypt was as notorious as it was long-standing: a known extremist, he had been tried for conspiracy in the assassination of Sadat, based on a *fatwa*[6] he issued that declared the president an infidel. Following a series of bloody clashes between his group and the Egyptian government, the blind preacher fled abroad; although he was on the State Department's terrorist watch list, he obtained an entry visa and eventually a green card. The key to this paradox points, again, to Afghanistan. The sheikh had traveled to Pakistan before arriving in New York; he had met with representatives of the Afghan mujahedeen, who were providing training for his underground terrorist group in Egypt. According to high-ranking Egyptian sources, when the sheikh moved to Brooklyn in May 1990, he worked closely with the CIA, helping to channel a steady flow of money, men, and guns to mujahedeen bases in Afghanistan and Pakistan. Although the United States and the Saudis had officially withdrawn from Afghanistan, the CIA still had an interest in overthrowing the Soviet-backed communist regime that remained in power. According to this intriguing hypothesis, Afghanistan had made strange bedfellows of the sheikh and the CIA.

Be that as it may, this relationship must have ended in 1993, when the sheikh was arrested and accused of conspiracy in the February 1993 bombing of the World Trade Center, the worst terrorist attack on U.S. soil at the time. In 1995, after an eight-month trial, Abdel Rahman and nine others known to have attended lectures at his mosque were convicted. Today, the sixty-three-year-old preacher is serving a life sentence in prison, isolated from much of the world, though his influence continues to spread in many circles around the Muslim world.

Two of his sons, Ahmed and Mohamed, at the time in their teens, had already joined the ranks of the mujahedeen fighters in Afghanistan in the late eighties. In late November 2001 at least one, Ahmed Abdel Rahman, had been captured by the Northern Alliance and was being interrogated by American officials on his links to the al-Qaeda.

On June 30, 1989, in the Sudan, against a background of the civil war between the north and south and internecine political battles, General Omar Hassan al-Beshir took over in a military coup and came to power with the help of Hassan al-Turabi's Islamic party. Al-Turabi, a lawyer by training, is as articulate and bilingual as he is radical in his advocacy of his own brand of African Islam. For him, Islam provides a sense of identity, a direction, and a common allegiance, shattered in Africa since colonialism. He was to become Osama bin Laden's mentor and protector in a crucial period of exile.

Meanwhile, in Algeria, the Islamic Salvation Front (FIS) came to the fore on the political scene in the regional and local elections held June 1990, thereby challenging the domination of the National Liberation Front (FLN). The FLN, which had monopolized power since the Algerian war of liberation from the French, was discredited by its failure to find credible solutions to the nation's economic problems, notwithstanding Algeria's substantial oil and gas reserves. As elsewhere in the Middle East, opponents of the FLN rallied under the banner of Islam largely because the ruling party tolerated no alternative secular platform. When the military regime belatedly revised the constitution to permit a multiparty system in response to the widespread riots of 1988, one of the most organized parties to emerge was Abbas Madani's Islamic Salvation Front. In the 1990 provincial and municipal elections, the FIS won handily. In the postponed parliamentary elections, eventually held in December 1991, the FIS won by an overwhelming majority in the first round. President Shazli bin Jedid stepped down to make way for Muammad abou Diaf. But the new president, strongly backed by the French, canceled the elections to prevent the Islamic Front from coming to power and outlawed the FIS in March 1992, bringing the democratic experiment in Algeria to an end. Abou Diaf was assassinated in June 1992, unleashing the beginning of a bloody conflict that has so far claimed scores of thousands of lives.

The Armed Islamic Group (GIA) made its appearance on the scene, initiating massacres and assassinating leaders. Further clouding the bloody picture in Algeria is that, while the military regime insisted that the extremist Islamists were responsible for the attacks, some of these groups accused the government or certain factions in the army of committing the massacres in order to incriminate the Islamists and consolidate their own grip on power. At the very least, the European Union expressed concern that the government did not seem to be actively trying to prevent these massacres. In the broader context, many analysts argue that the radicalization of the Islamic groups in Algeria is a direct result of denying them their legitimate electoral victory. Elsewhere, as in Turkey, when Necmettin Erbekan of the Islamist Welfare Party gained power, the Islamists showed a tendency to moderation, compromise, and power sharing.

The violence in Algeria reverberated in Europe when the GIA was held responsible for attacks in the Parisian metro, and as Algerians flocked to form part of the hard-core fighters of al-Qaeda.

Meanwhile, in Gaza and the West Bank, the Intifada, or popular uprising that broke out in 1987, was still raging, inflaming Arab public opinion and putting in question the role of the PLO leadership abroad. All around the Middle East, hotbeds of conflict swelled the ranks of activists who responded to bin Laden's call.

As the decade of the nineties unfolded, the conflict spread deeper into Europe. The centrifugal effect of the collapse of the Soviet empire led to fragmentation along atavistic lines of ethnic and religious identity. In the violent conflicts that ensued, the Muslim minorities of the Balkans and the former Soviet empire were particularly vulnerable. Ethnic cleansing against Bosnians and Kosovars and the brutal repression of Chechens reinforced the sense among many in the Islamic world that Muslims were victims of widespread violence. In the Middle East, Iraq continued to be subject to periodic bombing raids by American and British forces, and severe economic sanctions caused visible hardship to the population, especially children. To some, it appeared that the world was at war against Islam, and the call to jihad to fight in defense of Islam and Muslims did not fall on deaf ears. For these militants, all roads inevitably led to Afghanistan.

In the Name of Osama bin Laden guides the reader along the maze of these intertwining activist networks and introduces us to the main players in the drama that unfolds over the last decade, culminating in the apocalyptic events of September 11. The copious dossiers of Western intelligence reproduced here as an appendix, some heretofore confidential, reveal a tangled web of shifting alliances, strange bedfellows, and sudden betrayals, and acquaint us with the cast of mentors and followers that formed the Bin Laden Brotherhood and its armed wing, al-Qaeda.

1 / A Young Man from a Good Family

Osama bin Laden flew to Pakistan in January 1980, just a few days after the Soviet invasion of Afghanistan. In answering the call to jihad[1] in Afghanistan, bin Laden had given his life a purpose, but he had also irrevocably changed its direction. Who was this rich young Saudi, trained as an engineer, a businessman and pious Muslim, who later said, "One day in Afghanistan counted for more than a thousand days praying in a mosque"?

Osama bin Laden's father, Sheikh Mohammed bin Oud bin Laden, an engineer and architect according to some sources, a simple peasant according to others, left his native province of Hadramut in central Yemen in the early 1920s. He is thought to have settled in the Hejaz province of Saudi Arabia in 1932. There he made a fortune and a name for himself as a scrupulous and honest businessman. It is said that he began working as a laborer and porter before managing to establish, through sheer hard work, the small construction firm that would one day get the contract to build the first royal palace in the major Saudi port of Jedda.

Having become wealthy, the head of the bin Laden clan helped the monarchy financially when the Saudi Treasury encountered difficulties; it is said that he once came up with the funds to guarantee payment of the salaries of government employees. By way of thanks for his services, Mohammed bin Laden's company was given the contract to rebuild the Haram Sharif mosque in Mecca and to renovate the Masjid al-Nabawi mosque. Mohammed bin Laden, who had become a Saudi subject, was even for a time King Feisal's minister of public works, but he was also and above all his friend. The consortium of bin Laden enterprises, known as the Bin Laden Corporation, flourished on Saudi oil in the 1970s, and the king ultimately granted it exclusive rights for the construction and renovation of religious buildings. The elder bin Laden's company secured contracts in several countries in the Arab world, including a project in Jordan for which Mohammed bin Laden oddly required that his engineers submit a bid at cost. According to family legend, the head of the clan decided to reduce the price calculated by his experts even further in order to ensure that God was well served in this mosque in a friendly country.

The piety of Mohammed bin Laden, who was the father of more than fifty children, twenty-five of whom were boys (he had eleven wives in the course of his life), was of another era. For more than forty years, he awaited patiently and without losing hope the coming of the Hazrat Mahdi,[2] a messianic figure in many Muslim traditions. Mohammed bin Laden had even established a charitable fund of about $12 million to assist the Mahdi, were he to appear during bin Laden's lifetime, in restoring the grandeur and glory of Islam throughout the world.

When bin Laden died in 1972, King Feisal was still on the throne; the bin Laden family says that the king, who had wept only twice in his life, shed a third tear at the death of his friend.

The cordial relations between the royal family and Mohammed bin Laden benefited his children. This friendship was reinforced when bin Laden's sons attended the same schools as the numerous sons of King Abdelaziz, notably Victoria College in Alexandria, Egypt. Several of bin Laden's sons were classmates of the future King Hussein of Jordan or of the Khashoggi brothers, whose father was one of the doctors of the Saudi royal family.[3]

The elder bin Laden was not the only one in the family to enjoy the friendship of King Feisal, and later of King Fahd.[4] Bin Laden's son Salem was also very close to the king, and it is likely that he rendered significant services to the monarchy, in particular by carrying out secret missions. According to several witnesses, his mysterious death is evidence of this. In 1988, a BAC 111 plane piloted by Salem crashed in Texas.[5] His death gave rise to speculations about the exact role he played for King Fahd and the Saudi government in secret operations in the Middle East and Central America. For instance, there was an indication from American sources that he was connected to a secret meeting between Iranian and American emissaries in Paris in October 1980. Some felt that his death was not an accident.

In addition to being close to the king, the bin Ladens were also business and financial mentors to his children. Mohammed bin Fahd and Saud bin Nayef, two of the more enterprising princes in the royal family, became tycoons of finance and industry in the 1980s, under the tutelage of the bin Laden sons, often sitting together on the boards of powerful multinationals financed by petrodollars.

The relationship of trust between the two families was resilient despite a few serious crises. The most important was the seizure of the Great Mosque in Mecca on November 20, 1979. The bin Laden construction company had the exclusive contract for repairs to the Holy Places, and its trucks thus had the privilege of entering and leaving Mecca without inspection. It was precisely by using these trucks that the terrorists succeeded in smuggling arms into the mosque. The assault was traumatizing for the Saudis, as more than 50,000 pilgrims were caught inside the Great Mosque by a commando group. The terrorists were led by a man of about thirty, Juhayman al-Otaibi. Just as prayers had barely begun, he deployed nearly 200 armed "brothers" on the seven minarets of the mosque and, using a microphone he had seized, demanded of the faithful at prayer that they recognize one of his associates, Mohammed al-Qahtani, as the Mahdi. Unable to control 50,000 people, the commando group decided to hold only 130 of them hostage, during a siege lasting two weeks. The French police of the GIGN (Intervention Group of the National Gendarmes) brought about a resolution of the situation on December 5, which required some instant conversions to enable the elite gendarmes to enter precincts reserved for Muslims. However, it was by enlisting the bin Ladens, who were then the only ones to have precise plans of the Holy Places, that the Saudi police and the GIGN were able to find their way in the cellars and put down the rebellion.[6]

At the time of this crisis, one of the bin Laden sons, Mahrous, was arrested because of his ties with the Islamists involved in the assault but was later released. The terrorists had established contact with Mahrous several years earlier, when he was a student in London and when he counted among his friends the son of a Southern Yemeni dignitary, the leader of a very active fundamentalist group. Following this university connection, Mahrous bin Laden became involved with a group of Syrian Muslim Brotherhood activists exiled to Saudi Arabia. The Saudi secret service investigation ultimately declared Mahrous innocent. The investigation stated that by exploiting networks of the young Mahrous's former friendships, the terrorists had gained access to the bin Laden group's trucks to organize their attack without the young man's knowledge. Mahrous now heads the bin Laden group's subsidiary in Medina.

This tragic episode did not undermine the close ties of the bin Laden clan with the royal family, which consistently showed understanding when members of the bin Laden clan were involved in complex or shady affairs.

Osama bin Laden, born in the year 1377 of the Hegira (1957), in the al-Malazz neighborhood of Riyadh, is one of the youngest sons of the clan. His mother is said not to have been Mohammed's favorite wife, and Osama is said not to have been one of the favorite sons of the patriarch. Nonetheless, Osama grew up in the company of about fifty cousins—his uncles' children—and a few dozen aunts. He received a traditional education and finished his secondary education in a Jedda high school in 1973.

Like many well-off young Arabs, Osama bin Laden had the opportunity to travel and, according to reports, some of which come from American "profilers"[7] of international criminals, he was in Beirut from 1968 to 1970 along with his brothers Omar, Khaleb, and Bakri, enrolled in a school frequented primarily by students from Persian Gulf countries. There is some debate about Osama's character and behavior at this time. Some claim that, along with Bakri, Osama gave no evidence of exemplary piety, in contrast to his two other brothers, Omar and Khaleb, who were studious and serious, never missed a prayer, and finally alerted their father to the misdemeanors of Osama and Bakri. The stories of Osama's escapades are challenged by one of the older brothers, Abdelaziz; according to him, Osama was devout, self-effacing, and very attached to the values of Islam. According to relatives, moreover, Osama speaks neither English nor French, two languages that would have been indispensable in Beirut at the time for anyone wanting to live a life of pleasure. And if one were to judge by physical appearance, his ascetic figure and his meditative gaze do not argue in favor of a debauched history.

According to other sources, through an arranged marriage in about 1975, Osama bin Laden took as a first wife a young Syrian to whom he was distantly related. At about the same time he entered King Abdelaziz University.

Bin Laden's degree completed his formal education and prepared him for an upper-management position in the Bin Laden Corporation. This professional training was supplemented by a "moral rearmament." It hardly matters whether the piety was put on at the time for opportunistic reasons or whether it was sincere; from the time he graduated Osama bin Laden's religious commitment was vivid and explicit. His father, Sheikh Mohammed, was proud of his pious outlook and entrusted him with the contract for the enlargement of the Masjid al-Nabawi mosque.

On the death of Sheikh Mohammed in 1972, his children inherited an industrial and financial empire, but there were fifty-four of them. As a further complication in the division of the inheritance, the bin Laden brothers had different mothers and were of different nationalities (something they made use of to develop the family interests abroad). Bakr and Yehia represented the Syrian line of the family; Yeslam the Lebanese group; Abdelaziz was the standard bearer of the Egyptian circle and the largest employer of the family, with forty thousand employees. There was also a Jordanian branch, as well as the Saudi branch, of which Osama was the single representative. The clan was frequently in danger of exploding into conflict. What was at stake in these internecine battles was of course money, but also, and primarily, power in the financial empire.

After Sheikh Mohammed's death, continuity was in question. Management of the bin Laden group was taken over temporarily by Mohammed Baharath, brother of patriarch Mohammed bin Laden's first wife and the oldest of the uncles. Soon thereafter, the oldest son, Sheikh Salem bin Laden, took over the controls with the assistance of several of his brothers. After Salem's death in 1988, another brother, Bakr, with thirteen of his brothers, headed up the family group's board and took up the succession. Tensions began to appear. Ali bin Laden, Bakr's older brother, who had been dividing his time among Beirut, Damascus, and Paris, moved away from the others. He apparently felt stifled inside the family empire, but, in order not to quarrel with the clan, he claimed private reasons for his departure. This kind of discretion is the norm for the bin Ladens, who maintain a facade of solidarity despite any internal disputes.

The division of the group's dividends soon became a bone of contention, and Ali had great difficulty in securing his share from his brothers. Mahrous, marked for life by the tragic episode at the Mecca mosque, remained discreetly in the background. Another brother, Yeslam,[8] also distanced himself, but without conflict; he manages the group's international activities between Geneva and Paris. He is the most Westernized of the bin Laden sons, perhaps because of his marriage to a Francophone Iranian princess. He travels frequently and, like his brother Salem, flies his own business planes. Within this prosperous and diversified group, Osama bin Laden could choose how to occupy himself and earn money.

In 1976, four years after the death of the father, the group modernized itself in order to deal with the new requirements of business it had secured in almost every sector, diversifying from construction through imports to industry. The company adopted the name Bin Laden Brothers for Contracting and Industry. Its headquarters was in Jedda. The bin Laden group ranked thirty-second for revenues in Saudi Arabia at the time. It built several tens of thousands of housing units; it constructed roads, such as a major thoroughfare between Mecca and Medina; it developed farms and undertook irrigation work. The group also represented major European companies in Saudi Arabia, including Audi and Porsche automobiles. The brothers were associated with distributors of luxury products, such as the Dutch company Pander Projects, but also with the British enterprise Hunting Surveys Ltd. for the construction of prefabricated buildings.

The bin Laden family was known around the world not only for its financial and industrial power but also for its good reputation. At a lunch given by President Jacques Chirac on July 7, 1996, in the course of his official visit to Saudi Arabia, Yahya bin Laden, number two in the family hierarchy, was among the guests.

Through its financial investments, the activities of the bin Laden group extend well beyond what is publicly known. As a purely family enterprise without external or institutional shareholders, the group is very discreet about its investments and its policy of diversification; in light of its privileged relations with the king, no one has taken the risk of expressing unhealthy curiosity. Bin Laden contracts are never awarded in cabinet meetings or through a public bidding process; they are negotiated directly with the royal house and its head chamberlain, Ali bin Mussalem. The bin Ladens, who dislike media exposure, often withdraw without warning from financial or commercial projects when their partners are too talkative. The bin Laden group and its subsidiaries never advertise in the press, and it is impossible for an analyst to gain advance knowledge of its strategy. One motivation for this secretive strategy is that some of the group's enterprises have served as intermediaries in official arms contracts between Riyadh and the Western powers.

The bin Laden clan carried out several major projects in the Saudi kingdom in the 1980s and 1990s: a $296 million contract for the construction of a ring road around Riyadh; the construction of housing for security forces in Jedda and Mecca; the construction of the reception hall for the royal *divan*, or palace, in Mecca; the enlargement of the Holy Places in Medina; and the construction and furnishing of one of the terminals at the Riyadh airport. The bin Ladens were even subcontractors for the construction of hangars during the Saudi–American Desert Shield operation at the time of the conflict with Iraq.

Strange as it might seem given Osama bin Laden's notoriety by then, in September 1998, the bin Laden family secured a new contract, for the construction of barracks housing 4,257 American soldiers stationed in the Gulf. This barracks, situated on a Saudi air force base in the desert some 170 kilometers from Riyadh, is a modern building, well designed from the point of view of security; the promoters of the project were well aware that the American expeditionary force had been badly damaged in 1996 by an attack against the al-Khobar Towers, which the Saudi government had provided to house the Americans. Two years later, the new housing for the American military (a large number of whom had been living since the attack in tent villages like the Bedouins of their host country) was constructed by the bin Ladens for $150 million, entirely paid by the Saudi government. The security services of the U.S. Central Command[9] went through the building with a fine-tooth comb before installing the airmen who provide support for the air force unit of the Prince Sultan base.

The projects awarded to the bin Laden group are no longer limited to the Saudi kingdom: in Lebanon, Yehia bin Laden is involved in the reconstruction of downtown Beirut devastated by the civil war; in London the group has a branch office, Binexport; in Geneva Sico, the Saudi Investment Company, is involved in many international deals. This company, established by the bin Ladens in 1980, is the flagship for the group's activities in Europe. It is headed by Yeslam bin Laden, and the board of directors is made up almost exclusively of members of the family clan, except for a Swiss citizen, Baudoin Dunant. This well-known lawyer from French-speaking Switzerland, who is on the boards of several dozen companies, came to public notice in 1983 when he agreed to represent the Swiss banker François Genoud, a controversial figure who had been a disciple of Hitler and sole heir of Goebbels's copyrights before becoming one of the financiers of the FLN during the Algerian War. The friendships of the bin Ladens sometimes seem surprising, but they are logical: François Genoud has always been pro-Arab.

Sico, as the parent company of the group's foreign interests, also has offices in London and in Curaçao in the Dutch Antilles. The latter outpost, established in 1984, manages among other things the relations of the bin Laden group with an American company, the Daniels Realty Corporation, a subsidiary of the Fluor Corporation, which, through the influence of the bin Ladens, was awarded many reconstruction contracts in Kuwait after the Gulf War. In France at the time, the bin Ladens were on the board of the Al-Saudi Bank, which was partially taken over by the Indosuez Bank, becoming the Banque Française pour l'Orient, before merging with the Méditerranée group of Rafiq Hariri, the Lebanese prime minister. The Al-Saudi Bank facilitated many arms deals in the Middle East beginning in the 1980s.

At present, the group, which remains secretive, still has extraordinary financial resources. The bin Ladens are said to use at least three planes to carry on their business: a King Air 90 Beechcraft registered in the United States belonging to the Saudi Investment Company S.A.; another plane of the same kind based in Zurich; and a Challenger III jet, owned by Bin Laden Aviation, registered in the Cayman Islands, the tax haven in the Antilles.

Once the name of Osama bin Laden began to spread through the Western press and intelligence reports, these planes were put under surveillance in various European airports. It turned out that the planes were often used for trips to France via the Cannes-Mandelieu airport. According to airport authorities, this point of entry would allow passengers on the planes to pass through less rigorous inspection than commercial passengers. Investigation revealed that the most frequent flight path for one of the two King Air planes was from Geneva to Cannes and back, and that Yeslam bin Laden often piloted the plane himself. In some years the intelligence services counted as many as two hundred round trips. The Challenger jet, on the other hand, seems to have been used almost exclusively for London-Geneva-Malaga-Lugano circuits. At least seven other twin-engine jets of the BAC III or Learjet[10] type used by the bin Laden group are said to have been registered in Switzerland for a time and subsequently to have changed registration and nation of ownership.

The frequency of these private flights also led European intelligence services to take an interest in representatives of the bin Laden family in France and Monaco, revealing that at least ten members of the clan regularly circulate among a residential neighborhood in Cannes, the rue Vernet, and the avenue Bosquet in Paris, the posh little town of Chatou in the Paris suburbs, and the boulevard de Suisse in Monaco. Various Western agents involved in this surveillance in Europe suspect that some members of the bin Laden family have not completely broken ties with Osama, particularly with respect to the management of his business affairs. According to some reports, Osama bin Laden has remained very close to his mother and to one of his brothers who have periodically urged him to give himself up to the Saudi government.

2 / From Riyadh to Peshawar

Before Osama bin Laden became a fugitive and a pariah, he was in the good graces of King Fahd. In 1980, already a wealthy businessman, bin Laden was a model Saudi subject who tried to serve his country as other members of his family had done earlier. Prince Turki al-Feisal, son of the late king and head of the Saudi intelligence services, had given him the task of organizing the missions of the "Afghan Arabs," hundreds of whom were then passing through Jedda on their way to Peshawar, Pakistan. These volunteers, called mujahedeen by the European press at the time, were streaming in from all Arab countries to support the fight of their fellow Muslims oppressed by the Soviets in Afghanistan. They were heroes in the Muslim world; their military training was under the direction of high-ranking Egyptian officers, who were often graduates of Western military academies, and funds were generously provided by several Arab countries and by the United States, which, according to official sources, supplied more than $285 million per year to the Afghan resistance. At the request of Turki al-Feisal, Osama bin Laden was the cornerstone of this recruitment network. But bin Laden was not merely obeying an order of the Saudi monarch; the idealistic and religious young man had made a choice genuinely based on his conscience and had decided to embrace the cause of the Afghan resistance.

Shortly after the Soviet army's invasion of Afghanistan in 1979, bin Laden gave up his air-conditioned palace and his lucrative commercial activities. The Afghan resistance was being organized in the mountains and drawing international sympathy. Sensitive to the "martyrdom of the Afghan brothers crushed by Moscow" constantly evoked in the Arab and

Western press, bin Laden joined this cause to demonstrate his courage and his faith, about which witnesses are unanimous. The liberation of Afghanistan became his personal jihad. He flew to Pakistan, and from there, like thousands of others, he entered Afghanistan clandestinely, bringing with him his four wives—two Saudis, a Palestinian from Syria, and a Philippine—and some fifteen children. He went first to Lahore and then moved closer to the border, to Peshawar, where he opened an office.

Peshawar, frontier post for the jihad, was an extraordinary city in the 1980s. One encountered the more-or-less official or more-or-less clandestine representatives of every agency that counted in the Islamic and Palestinian intelligence community, as well as agents from other countries worldwide. The situation was further complicated by the fact that the Soviet Union, in trouble on the ground in Afghanistan, had launched a process of terrorist destabilization in Pakistan, in large part because of Pakistani aid to the mujahedeen.

This subversive enterprise, in the tradition of KGB dirty tricks, was in the hands of commando groups of the WAD, the Afghan intelligence service. It was supported by the KGB, with its hundreds of technical advisers and enormous quantities of secret funds. In the context of the regional war being fought on its borders, Moscow had several goals. The first was to restrict Pakistani aid to the Afghan rebels and then to destabilize the country through violence in order to pave the way for its more long-term objectives: to bring Pakistan into the Soviet sphere of influence and give the Soviet Union access to the Gulf of Oman. In tandem with its subversive and terrorist activities, Moscow had also attempted in the 1970s and 1980s to establish a commercial presence in Pakistan, with an Aeroflot office, subsidiaries of its steel and oil industries, and a tractor factory. The Soviet presence had swelled considerably: in 1972, there were 56 Soviets in Pakistan; in 1980, their numbers had reached 1,374, even though no formal cooperation agreement justified these numbers. Anxiety about the burgeoning numbers led the Pakistani authorities to require the Soviets to reduce their diplomatic representation in Islamabad by half, a futile gesture, since among the hundred diplomats and embassy employees remaining, one-third still belonged to the KGB. The Soviets were thus able to continue their terrorist attacks in markets and other public places, primarily in Islamabad and Peshawar.

Throughout the 1980s, the invisible war that Soviet-dominated Kabul was waging against Pakistan was carried out through a campaign of deadly attacks. Directed by the KGB, the campaign was turned over to WAD agents infiltrated into the border regions and the refugee camps of Peshawar. Several hundred Afghan intelligence officers set up secret posts in Peshawar, Karachi, Lahore, Rawalpindi, and Islamabad. In order to establish better control over movements and alliances along the border, the KGB, with the help of the WAD, also reorganized the Afghan Ministry of Nationalities and Tribes. This amounted to redefining its mission according to the interests of the KGB: persuading the tribes to cease support for the mujahedeen and to help with sabotage actions in Pakistan on behalf of the WAD. To achieve this goal, the WAD received $200 million a year from Moscow. It is thus easy to understand that Afghanistan and Pakistan were already in the 1980s at the center of a regional powder keg.

Bin Laden had a precise mission in this chaotic Pakistan environment: to organize the infrastructure of the jihad against the Soviets in Afghanistan. But he soon discovered that he had to start virtually from scratch: he had expected to find the semblance of a revolutionary organization or a shadow army that was of modest size but was at least well organized and motivated. It was a great disappointment; neither in Pakistan nor in Afghanistan did the mujahedeen have any real organization. Amateurism ruled. Initially bin Laden decided to take charge of the logistics of the resistance in the Pakistani rear bases. He built schools, clinics, mosques, and shelters for refugee families. Soon thereafter, in Afghanistan, he constructed strategic tunnels in areas close to Soviet bases in order to give the mujahedeen fallback positions during battles. He also dug tunnels that made it possible for fighters to get close to the enemy without showing themselves. Osama bin Laden freely expended both his energy and the funds at his disposal, provided by wealthy Saudi donors. He became one of the pillars of the jihad.

In the early 1980s bin Laden turned to recruitment for the resistance, which was particularly afflicted with a lack of professionalism. He decided to concentrate his efforts on reorganizing the recruitment channels. In 1984, he made contact with the Palestinian Abdallah Azzam, a brilliant idealist close to Yasser Arafat, who had established the Office of Aid to the Mujahedeen in Peshawar. Up to 1990, tirelessly shuttling between Afghanistan and Saudi Arabia, Osama bin Laden was active on all fronts: recruiting fighters by the thousands and organizing their transport into the underground, establishing training camps, and supervising the building of fortifications and tunnels at the Pakistani border. He extended his commitment so far as to take up arms himself on some occasions. The legend around him has it that he often sat at the controls of his own construction equipment to build fortifications or bulldoze antitank trenches.

In the Urdu-language daily *Pakistan* on March 18, 1997, he contrasted his courage and personal involvement in events with supposed U.S. cravenness:

> During the jihad, the Russians attacked the region of Jaji. Tanks were attacking on the front and airplanes had also begun to drop bombs. I was stuck in a trench for several days. We could hear the enemy marching around us! Despite that situation, I fell asleep. . . . When I awoke, the enemy had disappeared. Perhaps they hadn't seen me. . . . Another time, a Scud missile exploded very close to me, but I was not wounded. Incidents like that have distanced me from the fear of death. But the Americans fear death. . . . They are like little mice. If it was possible to destroy Russia, the United States can also be decapitated.

According to several witnesses, Osama bin Laden was engaged in bloody hand-to-hand combat against soldiers of the Red Army in Jaji, near the Pakistani border, in 1986 and in Shaban in 1987.[1] He was reportedly slightly wounded, and he won all the early battles against the communist occupation forces, showing the rest of the world that the Red Army was not invincible. Soon after the 1989 Soviet retreat, bin Laden was involved in the Jalalabad airport battle together with a unit of Pakistani technical advisers; he was hit by shrapnel, thus earning his stripes as a mujahed, under fire, and not in a salon, a mosque in Geneva or London, or at the podium of the United Nations.

According to another less laudatory source, quoted by English writer Simon Reeve, Osama bin Laden conducted himself like a ridiculous madman during this battle; the mujahedeen were forced to shoot a dozen of bin Laden's men because of their incompetence in battle.[2] According to Reeve, in 1989 Osama bin Laden, gesticulating and yelling, urged some mujahedeen to lynch journalists from the BBC while they were filming Afghan guerrilla battles.

Around 1985, Osama bin Laden—who had taken the measure of the resistance and realized that the confrontation had a global dimension well beyond the conflict between occupiers and occupied and directly implicating the East and West blocs—began to establish contact with radical Islamist organizations in other countries in order to obtain support. He was in constant contact with Egyptian and Algerian Muslim fundamentalists, and he established his own organization, al-Qaeda (the Base), an Islamic movement largely supported by Egyptian militants, which engaged, among other things, in the recruitment and transport of fighters.

During the same period, Osama bin Laden fully committed to the resistance. He left the rear bases in Pakistan and permanently settled in the eastern part of Afghanistan, in the region of Nangarhar. He tried to get closer to the front lines fighting the Soviets, and he joined with the men of the Hezb-e-Islami (Islamic Party) movement of Gulbuddin Hekmatyar,[3] a rebel faction supported by the ISI, the Pakistani secret service.[4] According to Western sources, Osama bin Laden agreed at the time to assume the costs of operation for several of Hekmatyar's training camps, in particular in Khost. Nearly seven hundred Afghan Arabs are said to have received military training in these clandestine bases, along with several thousand Pakistanis, headed for subversive actions in Kashmir and later used for other clandestine missions in India.

These years at the heart of the resistance mark the origin of Osama bin Laden's reputation in the Arab world, where he is known and celebrated as a resolute fighter and only secondarily as a Saudi multimillionaire. In an interview with *Time*, one of his lieutenants, a Palestinian named Hamza Mohammed, described the extent of the admiration that bin Laden aroused at the time from other fighters of the jihad: "For us, he was a hero, because he was always in the forefront. He always managed to take someone else's place in the front lines. . . . He not only gave money to the cause, he gave the gift of himself. . . . He came here to live with Afghani peasants and Arab fighters. He cooked with them, ate with them, dug trenches like them. And that was the way of life and the style of bin Laden."[5]

During all these years of the Afghan holy war, Osama bin Laden, at the peak of his reputation, began to weave the web of contacts that he would be able to activate in the future. Meanwhile, Bin Laden Brothers for Contracting and Industry was prospering in Saudi Arabia under the direction of his brothers. In 1983, the group secured a contract for $3 billion for the restoration of the Holy Places of Medina and Mecca. The contract was awarded by the new king, Fahd. Osama bin Laden, whose image as a hero had helped assure that this contract would go to his family, is said to have received a commission of $30 million that was distributed to numbered accounts in Switzerland, Dubai, and Luxembourg.

On February 13, 1989, the last Soviet soldiers retreated and abandoned Afghanistan, although the communist regime of the new strongman in Kabul, Mohammad Najibullah, remained solidly established; the war remained far from over for the Afghani mujahedeen. However, in 1990, at the request of the Americans, the Saudis halted their subsidies and logistical aid to the Afghan Arabs, thus putting an end to Osama bin Laden's official mission.

Bin Laden had no intention of abandoning his idealistic aims in this way. Convinced as he was of the legitimacy of the battle of the Afghani resistance, he had already made substantial personal sacrifices; he refused to give up. He returned to Saudi Arabia, where he was welcomed as a hero by his compatriots. Before the king, his family, his advisers, the ulema, and the powers of the realm, he pleaded eloquently in the cause of his comrades in arms, but his partisan language neither charmed nor persuaded the authorities, who had already made the decision to withdraw from Afghanistan. It was a political decision, not open to question. Osama bin Laden apparently felt that he had lost ten years of his life and that he had been betrayed.

He mounted an opposition to the Saudi government, whose indifference to the cause of the Afghans he could not bring himself to accept; he began to speak openly, within his circle, of treason. Disillusioned, bin Laden also made secret alliances in Iran and Syria with opponents of the Saudi regime. The Wahhabi[6] monarchy, via the members and close associates of the bin Laden family, tried to reason with him. But bin Laden was inflexible; the battle of the Afghani mujahedeen had become his battle, and his commitment was now irreversible. There were also other, more profound and more political reasons beginning to obsess bin Laden. He no longer believed in the legitimacy of the royal family and no longer accepted its subservience to the United States. The suspension of aid to the mujahedeen was thus part of a larger motivation to oppose the regime.

The dissidence of Osama bin Laden had just begun. He would continue the battle of the jihad on his own initiative, in his own way, and with his own money. Thanks to the various companies in his personal group, distinct from that of his family, Osama bin Laden would continue as a free agent to arrange the transit of mujahedeen from the Egyptian organizations Islamic Jihad and Gamaa Islamiya to Pakistan, scorning the instructions of the Saudi royal family and American directives. (See appendix, document 3, which excerpts the interrogation by the Cairo police of Ahmed al-Sayed al-Najar, a major Egyptian Islamist leader.) To facilitate the movement of the fighters, Osama bin Laden secured false papers for them and gave them false employment agreements with his companies.

At that time, having already once disobeyed the king's orders, Osama bin Laden became more deeply involved in unconcealed dissidence. In his view, the Wahhabi regime had become corrupt and, even more serious, theologically deviant. Becoming more and more openly critical, perhaps convinced that his origins would protect him, this son of the privileged Mohammed bin Laden may have believed that he would benefit from a semblance of immunity. His status as a hero and his name did in fact protect him for a time, but the regime in Riyadh grew weary of his attacks and began to subject him to the same fate as other dissidents, victims of a repression whose severity usually depended on their rank.

Despite his antagonism toward the regime, at the outset of the Gulf War, bin Laden offered his government military and logistical aid. It was rejected, and bin Laden became even more bitter. He allowed his associates to have contacts with Baghdad. Osama bin Laden, who had decided to no longer serve the king and who had become a virulent opponent of the Wahhabi monarchy, had no alternative but exile. He had to leave Saudi Arabia. He found refuge on the other side of the Red Sea, in Sudan, where a 1989 military coup had installed a reportedly pious officer respectful of Islam, Omar Hassan al-Beshir.

3 / Exile in Sudan

Osama bin Laden's departure for Sudan in 1991 was only the beginning of a long period of wandering. In Khartoum, the capital of an African country but one that was Arab and Arabic-speaking, Osama bin Laden thought that he could live according to his habits and his convictions, and he believed that he had found a congenial environment. Sudan was one of the few countries that had supported Iraq during the Gulf War, siding against the Saudi and Kuwaiti monarchies and guaranteeing both an enduring hostility on the part of the Americans and rather ambivalent relations with Riyadh. These were positions that bin Laden found agreeable. Moreover, he had visited Sudan in 1983 and had been impressed by the opportunities it afforded for investment and development in agriculture. Sudan would be a safe haven for him, but he also intended to do business there.

In the early months of his Sudanese exile, Osama bin Laden was housed in a disused barracks in a neighborhood of Khartoum North, on the banks of the Nile. He then moved into his own house in the Riyadh residential neighborhood of the Sudanese capital, on the other side of the airport, a neighborhood inhabited by businessmen and influential political figures such as Sheikh Hassan al-Turabi, the instigator of the 1989 coup. The bourgeois residences of the Riyadh district are imposing and often luxurious, with as many as five stories, adorned with hanging gardens and surrounded by high walls. Every house is patrolled at night by a *gaffir*, or guard, although there is little crime in Khartoum, and Osama bin Laden's guard was particularly vigilant. Bin Laden had both ends of his street blocked off and stationed his private militia of former fighters in Afghanistan to inspect vehicles.

Khartoum was at the time full of spies. From Egypt, Israel, the United States, and Great Britain, all these more or less secret agents tried to track the movements of Islamist extremists who had been granted asylum in the country while also keeping an eye on one another. The country had a bad reputation: according to several Western reports, the government provided space for training camps in the desert not far from Khartoum for guerrillas from Algeria, Tunisia, Egypt, Lebanon, and other countries.

American satellite photos showed military camps in the desert between the capital and the towns of Wad Madani and Atbarah,[1] but no one really knew whether they were the official establishments of the Popular Defense Forces (PDF, a sort of volunteer national guard) or camps for the Palestinian Hamas, the Algerian Armed Islamic Group (GIA), the Egyptian Islamists, or the Lebanese Hezbollah.[2] In the absence of contrary evidence, the terrorist hypothesis finally prevailed, and Sudan, which reacted sluggishly to the accusations, developed a sinister reputation.

In Sudan, Osama bin Laden, accompanied by a small troop of loyal Afghan Arabs to protect him and assist him in business, gradually reconstructed his familial, social, and professional environment. He opened an account in the al-Shamall Islamic Bank, in which, according to several sources, he deposited $50 million, helping to recapitalize the establishment. He set up a battery of companies: the Wadi al-Aquiq Company specializing in import-export; the Taba Investment Company, which marketed agricultural products such as gum arabic,[3] sesame, corn, and sunflowers; al-Themar al-Mubarak, an investment company; and al-Hijrah Construction and Development, which focused on Osama bin Laden's principal specialty, public works. In Sudan, as in Saudi Arabia, bin Laden did what his father had taught him to do: he made deals. According to Western secret services, these companies were front organizations used for buying arms and supplying them to Islamist terrorist movements throughout the world and to provide cover for the frequent travels of the members of the al-Qaeda organization bin Laden had established in Pakistan.

Osama bin Laden lived in fairly luxurious exile in Sudan for five years, near the historic city of Omdurman and on a farm to the south of the capital. To those who knew him in Khartoum, he appeared to be a peaceable, friendly businessman primarily concerned with his companies and his family. He mixed little with the Sudanese and had little social life, unlike another fugitive settled nearby at the same time, on the other side of the airport runways in a house on Africa Road, the Venezuelan known as Carlos. Carlos had not adopted a discreet posture; he openly flaunted his mistresses and made a spectacle of himself at the Armenian Club, where he sometimes got so drunk that he would fire his gun into the air.[4]

Osama bin Laden, in contrast, neither bothered nor shocked anyone. The Sudanese were used to seeing many immigrants settle in Khartoum and then move on when their fortunes improved. Sudan at the time was an open country that did not require an entry visa for citizens of Arab countries. Bin Laden was at home in Khartoum, and nothing differentiated him from a Sudanese other than the heavy security surrounding him, which made some of his neighbors think that he was a Saudi prince who had come to the aid of Sudan.

Sudan was turbulent in the early 1990s; the U.S. State Department had put it on the list of countries sponsoring international terrorism. One figure at that time occupied a central place in the public life of the country: Sheikh Hassan al-Turabi, leader of the INF, the Islamic National Front, who had just supported the rise to power of an openly Islamic junta and was considered one of the closest advisers of the new president, Omar Hassan al-Beshir. Western analysts viewed Sheikh al-Turabi as the brains behind the coup d'état, which they believed he had organized and sponsored himself, while al-Beshir merely followed his orders, in keeping with the Sudanese proclivity for government coups, violent or not.[5] Osama bin Laden and this clever, eloquent, and intelligent man, who was also his neighbor, established close relations fostered by a common vision of a universal and semiutopian Islam without borders.

Al-Turabi was more than a politician; he was an icon admired or feared by all. He had always attempted to attach the spiritual dimension of Islam to a national, international, or even internationalist political dimension that was inherently appealing to the idealist in bin Laden. In black Africa, certain Muslims had nicknamed this small, frail, always smiling multilingual Sudanese the "black pope." The distinctive career of Sheikh al-Turabi provides some explanation for his importance in the international Islamist galaxy in the 1990s and some justification for the fascination he exercised on the exiled bin Laden, far from the politics of his country and in search of a mentor or an accomplice with whom to share his ambitions for a rebirth of Islam. No doubt over a glass of ***karkadeh,***[6] the two men talked of such a reformation, as al-Turabi had done when he frequented the Parisian intellectuals of the boulevard Saint-Germain as a student at the Sorbonne.

Sheikh Hassan al-Turabi was born in 1932 in Kassala, a city on the border between Sudan and Eritrea. His childhood was spent in the shadow of religious teachings inherited from an ancestor who had proclaimed himself mahdi,[7] or spiritual guide, in the seventeenth century and who had attracted disciples from all corners of the kingdom of Sennar, a province in the east of the country. Al-Turabi's career was a methodical ascent toward both political power and religious authority. A graduate of the University of Khartoum in the 1960s, he pursued studies in London and Paris, acquiring a polished command of French that often surprised journalists. He had been eager to absorb Western culture, probably the better to oppose it thereafter.

In October 1964 violent student demonstrations and a general strike brought about the fall of the regime of General Ibrahim Abbud that had governed Sudan since 1958. It was then that al-Turabi entered politics. Already in contact with the Egyptian Muslim Brotherhood, he entered into relations with the Islamist elite of Sudan and became the general secretary of a small party that he founded, the Front of the Islamic Charter. In 1969, he was jailed on orders of President Gaffar Nimeiry. He spent seven years behind bars amid an atmosphere of political purges directed principally against Islamists and was then named attorney general by the same President Nimeiry. Al-Turabi called for the application of sharia.[8] The wind had shifted, and Nimeiry now needed religious cover. In April 1985 Nimeiry was ousted while on an official visit to the United States. Sadik al-Mahdi seized power. (Al-Turabi had married al-Mahdi's sister a few years earlier.)

In this context of coups d'état and anarchy, Hassan al-Turabi resumed his ascent to power by relying on Islam and shrewdly establishing opportunistic alliances with diverse forces. The political party that he had founded, which became the National Islamic Front in 1985, began its march to power; it was to become the largest party in Sudan. Without breaking ties with the Muslim Brotherhood, al-Turabi added to his Islamism some Sudanese components of his own devising, such as references to the impoverished popular masses and to the conflict between the north and the south of the country. His anticapitalist Islamism, which was nevertheless not Marxist, became an explosive factor in the political arena. Al-Turabi succeeded where Nimeiry had failed; with the Islamist movement, he helped to break the influence of the white, Greek, and Armenian oligarchy that controlled a large part of the country's economic life, though he spent more time in Cairo or on the Côte d'Azur than in Khartoum.

In 1989, Sudan remained torn by internal political conflict and by a civil war in which southern rebel forces opposed the centralizing authority of Khartoum.[9] On June 30, General Omar Hassan al-Beshir, backed by al-Turabi's party, seized power. A few months later, he set up a government with a strong Islamist slant. Al-Turabi, who had spent most of his life in clandestine combat against colonialism, communism, atheism, and Nasserism, was projected into prominence on the Sudanese public stage. Broadly supported by the population and by the Islamists, General al-Beshir's government attempted to rebuild the enormous country that anarchic democracy, a costly civil war, and foreign intervention had led into chaos.

Having reached the top, more influential than ever, in order not to hinder the new leader of the country, Hassan al-Turabi stepped away from day-to-day politics and recast himself as an ideologue. His encounter with Osama bin Laden was decisive: the Saudi provided him with the financial means to realize his ambitions and underwrite support for his broad program of pan-Islamism.

In April 1991, in the aftermath of the Gulf War, along with about fifty Islamist movements in Africa and Asia, al-Turabi founded the PAIC, the Popular Arab and Islamic Conference (see appendix, document 4). Al-Turabi intended to crystallize discontent in the Arab world by bringing together under a single banner hard-line Islamic militants and nationalists. He shrewdly set forth a vague and confusing political and religious platform casting a wide net: the Algerian FIS (Islamic Salvation Front), the increasingly well-known Taliban, Philippine nationalists, French of North African origin in the Paris suburbs, and Palestinian movements—all saw themselves in it and participated in the work of the first meeting in Sudan. Al-Turabi molded his identity after Nehru, Tito, and Khomeini; he sought another path for political Islam, which he would eventually find.

This organization, which received a good deal of media attention, was very soon identified by the West as an Islamist international organization, and some even saw it as a terrorist international organization, at the service of the most extremist of the Islamic movements. Al-Turabi emerged as the prophet of a total Islamization. The Western press, which had just begun to notice him, attributed to him intelligence, charm, eloquence, and limitless power, including power as the hidden ruler of Sudan and as the instigator of all Islamic rebellions on the planet.

All the same, Hassan al-Turabi was still at the time welcome in most Western capitals. In 1992, he was the guest of the Royal Institute of International Affairs and the Royal Society of Arts in London, not to mention a subsequent trip to the United States, where he was officially received in Washington.

For several years, up to 1995, with the financial assistance of Osama bin Laden, who spent prodigally for his new associate, al-Turabi was able to organize a conference in Khartoum bringing together Islamist organizations and leaders from around the world.[10] Generously welcomed by the PAIC, itself sponsored by Osama bin Laden, delegates and journalists from around the world were invited by the hundreds to the Hotel Meridian, the Grand Hotel, and the Hilton of Khartoum. For a week, the radical Islamists welcomed by Sheikh al-Turabi transformed the Sudanese capital into the headquarters of global Islamic fundamentalism. From the podium of Friendship Hall in Khartoum, a conference center built by the Chinese on the banks of the Nile, one could hear public speeches from such controversial leaders as the American Muslim extremist Louis Farrakhan, fallen leaders of the FIS such as Anwar Haddam, Georges Habbash of the Popular Front for the Liberation of Palestine (one of the historic leaders of the PLO, a Christian), and representatives of the emerging Afghan Taliban. Al-Turabi could have been seen haranguing young male and female militants armed with Kalashnikovs or receiving his foreign guests on a boat cruising on the Blue Nile, in a decidedly touristy atmosphere, accompanied by a Sudanese orchestra.

Despite Osama bin Laden's financial aid, Hassan al-Turabi's international conference never managed to bring the Islamic organizations together into a single disciplined Islamist international organization speaking with one voice. Bin Laden eventually left Sudan, where he had become persona non grata (his presence caused concern to the Khartoum authorities, who were subject to pressure and threats from abroad), and the utopian and at one point compelling vision of al-Turabi no longer enjoys currency. The ambitious pan-Islamic program has become a chimera. Excluded from public life by his own party and by the Sudanese government, al-Turabi lost his position as president of parliament. Sudanese society was swiftly modernizing and refused the constraints of a rigid Islam like that of the Taliban.

Hassan al-Turabi had already become a historical figure for the younger generations. A respected man, but a man from the past, marked by the failure of the PAIC, al-Turabi founded a new party on June 27, 2000, but for many Sudanese, this was his swan song, and the "black pope" was condemned to become a wise man politely listened to. Osama bin Laden's investment had not produced the anticipated results. And on February 23, 2001, al-Turabi was again thrown into jail by his government, accused of having tried to establish an alliance with the armed rebels fighting for independence of the south, who are not even Muslims.

During his time in Sudan, Osama bin Laden also tried to develop his al-Qaeda organization, the movement that he had established in Pakistan as a complement and alternative to the mujahedeen movement of the Palestinian Abdallah Azzam. The latter had been opposed to the establishment of another recruiting agency, but bin Laden had insisted. Supported by the Egyptian Ayman al-Zawahiri,[11] he was intent on having a distinct organization under his control. Al-Qaeda began to play a significant role only after the death of Azzam,[12] and even then, only after the Soviet withdrawal from Afghanistan. According to experts in Islamic law, al-Qaeda was not established following the rules of sharia; a council should have been set up, and it should have chosen an emir. Apparently, the founders of al-Qaeda paid no attention to these rules, making the organization a shadowy or even illegal structure from the point of view of Islamic law.

The name of this mysterious movement appears in hundreds of American reports, including the files of the New York grand jury that examined the charges against Osama bin Laden.[13] For the American police and the U.S. Justice Department, the simple fact of contact with al-Qaeda justifies an arrest and constitutes an aggravating factor in the event of other charges. This was the case for Wadih al-Haj, an American citizen implicated in the attack in Nairobi, and for another associate of Osama bin Laden, the Sudanese Mandouh Mahmoud Salem, arrested in Friesling, Germany, on September 16, 1998, accused by the U.S. Justice Department of having organized arms shipments on behalf of al-Qaeda and of having been its treasurer.[14]

According to the United States, al-Qaeda and its members have had no purpose since 1990 other than mounting anti-American operations, freely using Osama bin Laden's financial resources in several countries where he has or has had bases: Sudan, Lebanon, and Afghanistan.

Because of his sinister image, the presence of Osama bin Laden in Sudan cost the country very dearly, even after he moved to Afghanistan. On August 20, 1998, when President Bill Clinton ordered that Tomahawk missiles destroy a factory in the heart of Khartoum North, he was convinced on the basis of intelligence available to him that he was ordering the destruction of one of bin Laden's strategic establishments in Sudan. The neighboring residences were not hit in the raid. The strike was "surgical," to use the military term, and the damage was strictly contained within the walls surrounding the factory that had been set up in a residential neighborhood of the capital. On the same day, other missiles were fired on bin Laden's headquarters in Khost, Afghanistan, in reprisal for the anti-American attacks in Nairobi and Dar es Salaam (see appendix, document 5). The reason invoked to justify the raid on Khartoum was that the al-Shifa factory was producing VX nerve gas used in chemical weapons.

No journalist really accepted Washington's hypothesis.[15] The prestigious English magazine covering military affairs, *Jane's International Defence Review,* spoke of a "failure of American intelligence." The U.S. Department of the Treasury finally had to release the $24 million that had been frozen in accounts opened by the real owner of the factory, the Sudanese businessman Salah Idriss. Beyond the material damage, the shadow of Osama bin Laden in Khartoum provoked a break in diplomatic relations between the two countries and fostered a conflict no longer really justified by the regional political context.

On the other hand, Osama bin Laden's friendly relations with Hassan al-Turabi helped him to secure several public contracts and ultimately led to his participation in building many highways and large-scale public works, such as the Port Sudan airport and the road from Shandi to Port Sudan, covering twelve hundred kilometers, for which the Sudanese government is said to have paid bin Laden in goods: sesame seeds, sunflowers, and gum arabic that he resold in Middle Eastern markets. According to several Saudi sources and an article in the July 31, 1994, issue of the Cairo newspaper *Al-Wafd*, this concession for Sudanese agricultural products was granted for ten years, but there is nothing to indicate that bin Laden and the Sudanese have continued to apply them, even though these contract terms have been acknowledged.

Osama bin Laden's presence in Sudan up to 1995 and particularly his friendship with the subversive Sheikh al-Turabi exasperated the Americans to the point that Washington pressured Riyadh to take action against him. Finally, Riyadh issued an arrest warrant for bin Laden. The Saudi authorities charged him with supporting fundamentalist groups involved in terrorist actions in Algeria and Egypt and also with having ties to a religious opposition that had tried to establish an independent human rights organization in Saudi Arabia in early May 1996. It was said at the time that the arrest warrant was a formality to appease the Americans and that it would not really affect existing relations between the royal family and the bin Laden clan. There is no doubt that Osama alone was the black sheep of the family; the bin Laden group remained untouchable in Riyadh.

In February 1994 the Saudis took the exceptional step of depriving Osama bin Laden of Saudi citizenship. Now a stateless multimillionaire, Osama bin Laden had nothing to lose and unreservedly played the role of opposition force in exile. He wanted to undermine the monarchy, and to this end he patiently cultivated a network of international friendships within the Islamist galaxy. From Khartoum, Osama bin Laden maintained steady relations with Sheikh Omar Abdul Rahman of the Egyptian Gamaa Islamiya; with his Egyptian friend Ayman al-Zawahiri of Islamic Jihad; and with many members of the Saudi opposition in exile in the Middle East and in London. He shrewdly established the foundation for what would become the Bin Laden Brotherhood, an informal transnational organization that he would later put at the service of the legendary Islamic Legion that he had helped to set up during his time in Afghanistan.

In May 1996, Saudi and Western pressure on the Khartoum government became too intense, and Osama bin Laden, who had heard rumors that he was to be expelled from Sudan, or even extradited to Saudi Arabia, decided to leave the country as quickly as possible. According to the *Lettre de l'Océan Indien,* a usually very well-informed French publication, Osama bin Laden was told of the negotiations over his fate by Isam al-Turabi, the youngest son of the leader of the National Islamic Front. It appears that Isam al-Turabi had had business dealings with Osama bin Laden and that he warned him before an extradition agreement had been reached. A few months later, Saudi sources in London confirmed that bargaining had indeed taken place. According to them, soon after Osama bin Laden left, the Saudi authorities expelled representatives of the southern Sudanese rebel John Garang from the kingdom and stopped supplying arms to his movement, the Sudanese People's Liberation Army (SPLA). For his part, in an interview of March 18, 1997, with Hamid Mir of the Urdu-language daily *Pakistan,* Osama bin Laden stated diplomatically: "After our holy war in Somalia, the United States asked Sudan to deport me. Sudan was promised that economic aid would resume. So I returned to Afghanistan, but assistance to Sudan was not restored."

Bin Laden, who had often wondered where he would be able to live if he were driven out of Sudan, and who had rejected the idea of settling in a Western country (the British embassy in Khartoum had in any case informed him at the time that he was persona non grata on British territory), embarked for Afghanistan on board a Hercules C-130 cargo plane, specially outfitted for him, his wives, his children, and nearly 150 associates. Six hours later, he landed in Jalalabad. He was at home in an Afghanistan where he had already shed blood and where he would be welcomed as a brother.

4 / Among the Taliban

Osama bin Laden left Sudan in May 1996, almost two years after the terrorist Carlos was tracked down there by General Philippe Rondot of the French intelligence service and handed over to France.

In the months preceding the deportation of Carlos, Khartoum had demonstrated its good will in the fight against terrorism. Osama bin Laden had become as troublesome as Carlos, if not more so, and he was subjected to increasing harassment; he was finally driven to leave the country with his guard and his entourage, which at the time included elements of the GIA. The most inflammatory among them even delivered a fatwa sentencing Sheikh Hassan al-Turabi to death for having given in to Western pressure to deport their leader.

A few months after leaving the country, bin Laden declared that he had no intention of returning to Sudan, a country that had, according to him, "sold the Afghan Arabs for a pittance." He also asserted[1] that he had escaped two assassination attempts, in Omdurman and at his Riyadh house in Khartoum.[2] The agreement with al-Turabi was definitely at an end. Bin Laden felt betrayed by the realpolitik adopted by Khartoum partly in order to escape from diplomatic isolation.

Immediately after arriving in Jalalabad, bin Laden moved to an area not far from the Pakistani border, where he stayed for some time. According to several sources in Asia and the Middle East, he settled in a region of Afghanistan with a majority Shii[3] population who might be able to help him flee to Iran in case of danger. This was well before the Taliban made their entry into Kabul in September 1996. In the Saudis' view, Osama bin Laden, who was immediately granted unconditional asylum in Afghanistan, was under the protection only of the Shii Hazara clan, who were indifferent to the demands of the United States. According to other observers, ethnic groups such as the Uzbeks of General Abdul Rashid Dostum or the Tajiks of Commander Ahmed Shah Massoud, potential American allies, would have agreed without hesitation to turn him over.

Taking advantage of the anarchy reigning in Afghanistan, Osama bin Laden disappeared, escaping from both the Americans and the Saudis. According to American intelligence, in the course of his travels between Iran and Afghanistan at the time, he set up a drug-trafficking network with Afghan veterans of Gulbuddin Hekmatyar's Hezb-e-Islami in order to restore his organization's finances, because his hurried departure from Khartoum had cost him a great deal.

A few months after he settled in Afghanistan, a new element began to play a role in bin Laden's favor; the country, torn by civil war, witnessed the emergence of a new political force, the Taliban. These soldiers of Islam, calling themselves students of theology or soldier-monks, first appeared in the Islamist galaxy in the summer of 1994. They are Sunni Muslims, influenced by the Deobandi school of thought, which originated in Deoband, near Delhi, in 1867, with the establishment of an Islamic theological school. A century after the founding of the first Deobandi school, there were nine thousand such schools in south Asia, and the influence of that philosophy had spread far and wide. These *madrasas*, or religious schools, originally had a dual focus in India under the British Raj: to inculcate in Muslims an Islamic education as opposed to a secular one and to oppose British rule. After 1947, at the time of India's independence and partition, when the Muslim areas of colonial India were established as the separate state of Pakistan, the centers of Deobandi learning shifted to the Pakistani cities of Karachi, Lahore, and Peshawar. Deobandi philosophy stresses *taqlid*, or acceptance of old interpretations, rather than reinterpretation of religion according to the times.

Afghans were part of a steady stream of scholars traveling to Deoband, and later to Pakistani madrasas, to receive the teachings of the Deobandi school. The Taliban were heirs to that tradition. With time, and as understood by the Taliban, it has been characterized by increasing orthodoxy, a restrictive view of the role of women, and opposition to minority sects, including Shiism, the state religion of Iran. Until the Taliban came to the forefront of the Afghan political scene, it was the Islamists, generally products of a state education, who combated the forces of secularism and communism. The Taliban, in contrast, were products of the traditional madrasa education. The Taliban movement was swiftly characterized by great openness to the various ethnic groups in the country; indeed, it included representatives of the Pashtuns, the Tajiks, the Uzbeks, the Baluchis, and the Hazaras.

According to some Western analysts, the Taliban movement was yet another manipulation of the omnipresent Pakistani military intelligence services, the ISI. They claim that the Taliban movement arose from the conflict between the ISI and the Pakistani minister of the interior during President Benazir Bhutto's second term.[4] Regardless of its origins, whether it was set up by military intelligence or emerged from spontaneous popular demand, the Taliban movement changed the face of Afghanistan in less than four years. Osama bin Laden established fairly good relations with it, except that his anti-Saudi declarations embarrassed the Taliban, who received significant aid from Riyadh. He was thus granted the status of refugee, with the accompanying requirement to remain discreet.

According to the most recent estimates, the Taliban at their peak numbered at least sixty thousand. The core of the organization was made up of Muslim students who began attending madrasas in Pakistan, a large number of which were financed by Saudi Arabia. Between 1989 and 1991 these schools, which had become centers of reflection or sects in the Islamic sense, drew several thousand mujahedeen who were disappointed by the demobilization of the resistance in Afghanistan. In 1995 there were 1,686 of these establishments in the Punjab region of Pakistan, and by 1997 their number had reached 2,500. More than 200,000 students have been taught in these institutions. The spread of the madrasas from Pakistan to Afghanistan was fostered by the dissolution of Afghan society and by the economic crisis. Youths who would otherwise be destitute could indeed find food and shelter in the madrasas, not to mention a political line that was simplistic but attractive, which described them as the natural and legitimate leaders of the country and justified their taking up arms to seize what was rightfully theirs in the name of divine law.

For the Indian authorities, the existence of these institutions in neighboring countries, Pakistan and Nepal among others, became a constant threat. Some Koranic schools are said to be in reality covers for terrorist activities aimed at Kashmir. Nepal, whose southern border is only a few hundred kilometers north of Delhi, is said to harbor 66 madrasas financed and controlled by Islamic nongovernmental organizations (NGOs) openly preaching an anti-Indian fundamentalist Islam. The border between India and Nepal, open since the 1950 peace and friendship treaty between the two countries, now appears to have become a weak point in Indian security. The involvement of madrasas in regional destabilization, particularly in the border regions of the Indian states of Bihar and Uttar Pradesh, was revealed through the arrest of an illegal immigrant in Bombay in June 1999. Indian investigators learned from questioning him that one of the schools had been used to hide AK-47 assault rifles, thus confirming that the networks of religious schools sometimes fulfilled a dual purpose.

Enjoying unconditional Pakistani support, the puritanical religious movement of the Taliban, which had adopted the aim of ridding Afghanistan of its corrupt mujahedeen and converting or eliminating heretics, had swiftly developed into a genuine militia. In 1996, it had several hundred tanks and a squadron of Soviet Mig jet fighters, for which the Taliban required the services of mercenary pilots, veterans of the communist regime of Mohammad Najibullah.

During their rise to power, the Taliban demonstrated persuasive abilities, and influential leaders such as Fazlur Rahman, head of the Jamaat-i-Ulema-Islam in Baluchistan, lent support to several groups of "students" who later received military training from the Frontier Constabulary Corps and Pakistani reconnaissance units in camps in Baluchistan close to the Afghan border.

The various Taliban seminaries scattered over Pakistani territory were able to house several thousand students, as for example, the Jamaat-i-Ulema-Islam school in New Town, near Karachi, which had more than eight thousand students. According to several sources, it was precisely in this nursery of new Islamic thought in New Town that the spiritual leader of the Taliban, Mullah Mohammed Omar, was a student. There too, in the early 1980s, Osama bin Laden financed the acquisition of the mosque of Binnori, as well as a house for the then unknown imam of that holy site, the same Mullah Omar.

Mullah Omar was a Pashtun veteran. He commanded a mujahedeen unit, and his record is that of a heroic soldier. He was wounded several times during the ten years of the war of liberation, and his associates say that a piece of shrapnel blinded him in one eye during a battle with the

Soviets. Knowing that his eye was lost and that he risked infection, they say that Omar ripped the eye from its socket and then wiped his bloody hand on the wall of a mosque in Singesar, fifty kilometers west of Kandahar; the bloody trace has been piously preserved as a relic.

Mullah Omar received a revelation of his religious mission in a vision in 1994. After he had withdrawn to the same little village of Singesar to devote himself to the study of the Koran and to keep his distance from the chaos enveloping his country, the prophet Muhammad appeared to him in a dream and ordered him to put an end to the reign of terror imposed by a local warlord, a corrupt rapist and thief. With fifty veterans who had fought under his command, Mullah Omar, it is claimed, eliminated the tyrant, confiscated his possessions, and redistributed them to the people. According to a more prosaic version, his neighbors informed him while he was at prayer that two girls had been abducted, had their heads shaved, and been raped by some mujahedeen at a checkpoint. In retaliation, Mullah Omar took command of a small group of veterans and attacked the band of outlaws with a few old Kalashnikovs and then hung their leader from the gun on a Soviet tank.

Out of legend or reality, the Taliban movement had come into being. Within a few weeks, hundreds of idle mujahedeen joined the militia, taken with this mountain Robin Hood brandishing the flag of Islam and unafraid of action. In less than three years, the man who was now called the Emir Ul-Mumineen, commander of the faithful, managed to gain control over twenty of the thirty-two provinces of Afghanistan.

Bolstered by a simple ideology, an iron discipline, and the rigorous moral values imposed by its leader, the rapid rise of the Taliban movement began in 1995 with the capture of the town of Doorahi, near Kandahar. It seems that at the time the Taliban had taken on the mission of controlling the border in order to block the entry of prohibited goods into Afghanistan. Before the march on Kabul, the second stage was the capture of the town of Spin Boldak. Encouraged by their success, the Taliban, who then numbered only a little more than two thousand, began to recruit, and six months later they were already thirty thousand strong. They were not short of weapons. Indeed, Pakistani intelligence services, assisted by American spy satellite photographs, had given them the precise locations of the caches where the retreating Soviets had abandoned their arsenals. The Taliban thus had access to tens of thousands of weapons and the ammunition stored in nearly four hundred trucks hidden in caves near the Pakistani border.

However, as the Taliban advanced inexorably toward the capital, they fought few battles, and a dozen provinces fell without opposition. Coming on the heels of these surrenders, the capture of Kabul in September 1996 was also not a major military event.

The method of encouraging desertions in the ranks of the enemy swiftly became a strategy for the Taliban, who could thereby defeat a weakened opponent without really exposing themselves in combat, at which they were perhaps not very skilled. By means of shrewd political and religious conditioning, the Taliban managed to persuade tribal warriors to rally to their movement. Numerous desertions from the ranks of the Pashtun militia fighting with Massoud in defense of the capital, as well as his isolation following the loss of the supply line from Jalalabad, drove the Tajik militia to abandon Kabul, thus turning over the city to an army of amateurs and arrogant theoreticians, who were pompous, semiliterate, and full of a sense of their own power.

In February 1997 the Taliban were in the Ghorband Valley, bordering the Panshir Valley, Massoud's stronghold. There too, minor warlords went over to the other side without fighting, often with their weapons. And there too, the Taliban advanced, more often than not entering open towns.

In the zones under their control, the Taliban immediately imposed sharia in its strictest form, which is also the most questionable interpretation from a Western perspective, with punishments that included stoning, flagellation, and amputations. Western technical progress was outlawed, and bearded madrasa students built public bonfires of video cassettes, VCRs, and televisions. Cassettes of Western music, confiscated from trucks or in public places, were crushed underfoot. Pleasure was prohibited in almost every form; even children no longer had the right to fly kites in the sky over Kabul. More seriously, capital punishment was applied without restraint, and Afghan women, swathed in burqas, with mesh covering their eyes, were reduced to the role of slaves or breeders, denied the right to study or to go out unaccompanied by husbands or brothers. The men, required to grow beards at least a hand-width long, were forced at gunpoint to go to the mosque five times a day. Order very soon reigned in the Afghanistan of the Taliban, an order founded on terror and informers.

But there was unquestionably a double standard in this rigid order claiming to be guided by integrity and justice. The religious militia, leather whips in their hands, tirelessly patrolled the streets and bazaars in pursuit of violators of moral rigor, while the stalls of opium dealers stood openly next to those of truck farmers. Every day in the Kabul stadium, before a silent, petrified crowd, executioners "cleanly" cut off the hands or feet of petty pickpockets and then displayed them on television, but at the same time the big shots of the heroin trade, protected by the powerful Taliban leaders, pocketed their profits, even though the business was officially condemned by the regime, and rode their all-terrain vehicles, imported at huge expense, down miserable streets that had become open sewers. The double message fostered the corruption and venality of the masters of Afghanistan, hypocritically unfurling over the desert the white flag of purity.

The neighboring countries were the first to react to the new Afghan order, which threatened to spread. When the Taliban reached the borders of Uzbekistan, President Islam Karimov expressed his fear of seeing the Taliban expand along the borders of central Asia. He called on the U.N. Security Council to observe the developing situation.

In a second stage, international opinion also mobilized against the Taliban, including in the United States, which no longer saw them as anticommunist fighters; times had changed. But paradoxically, these bearded men, whom the press called obscurantist extremists, swiftly adapted to the new constraints that went along with the power that they had just shrewdly acquired. Perhaps under pressure from their sponsors in the ISI, the Taliban leaders learned how to be accommodating and finally allowed journalists to photograph some of their fighters. They agreed to explain their vision of the status of women, then slightly relaxed the constraints on them, and publicly admitted that Afghanistan was a multiethnic country.[5] They explained that sharia had had positive effects on criminality; it is indeed difficult to deny that while they were in power, highway robbers no longer held travelers for ransom and crimes of violence became infrequent. Finally, in an ultimate effort of persuasion or an expression of compromise, the Taliban rejected the temptation of isolationism. On the contrary, they declared themselves open to the rest of the world, an attitude that troubled their detractors and demonstrated their acute sense of realpolitik. And yet, as the twenty-first century began, the Taliban regime was recognized by only three countries: Pakistan, Saudi Arabia, and the United Arab Emirates.

In this Afghanistan that had gone from one disaster to another in the course of twenty-odd years, scarcely emerging from feudalism before it fell into obscurantism after passing through communist tyranny, Osama bin Laden organized his life, or his survival, as a nomad. From his numerous and carefully camouflaged hiding places, he continued even more assiduously to lead the Bin Laden Brotherhood and to carry on his anti-American campaign. He and his supporters prepared a plan for fighting against American presence in the Gulf with large-scale actions against American armed forces stationed in Saudi Arabia.

Soon after his arrival in May 1996, according to reports published by the newspaper *Al-Watan al-Arabi* (Arab Nation) on July 19, 1996, on the basis of testimony from an anonymous participant, Osama bin Laden was already on the front lines of the jihad. At a meeting held in a place so distant from anything in the desert mountains that it was impossible to be sure whether it was in Afghanistan or Pakistan, although it was near an Afghan Arab training camp, the major Islamic fundamentalist leaders of the world came together. At twilight in front of an enormous chief's tent, lit by electricity from a generator, a fleet of luxurious all-terrain vehicles efficiently deposited visitors wearing turbans or military fatigues. Lookout posts could be glimpsed on surrounding promontories. Inside, seated on cushions or carpets, were patiently waiting the current leaders of terrorist warfare: Osama bin Laden's friend, Dr. Ayman al-Zawahiri, militant Islamists from London, Teheran, and Beirut, Algerians from FIS, a repre-sentative from Gulbuddin Hekmatyar, Egyptians, and militants from Hez-bollah. They were all there, extremist fundamentalists from every organization and of every tendency. They all calmly discussed the need for a united Islamic front to "counter American and Israeli arrogance." At the entry of Osama bin Laden, accompanied by the Afghan Abdul Rasul Sayyaf, everyone fell into a respectful silence. But the discussion resumed with vigor until morning, while bin Laden mechanically scratched his beard, silent, allowing Sayyaf to present his strategy.

During a second meeting the next night, the participants adopted an unambiguous resolution, "to oppose at any cost foreign forces stationed on Muslim land." The participants also decided to set up several committees for planning, finances, military actions, and mobilization.

Through the intermediary of his network in Europe and on Internet sites that he indirectly subsidized, bin Laden tailored his propaganda, letting it be known that he was not responsible for attacks in Saudi Arabia, but he was nevertheless pleased by them. According to him, the attacks were only warnings presented by pious Muslims to inform the Americans that they should withdraw in order to avoid a conflict between the Islamic legions and the American forces.

On August 23, 1996 (year 1417 of the Hegira), a document signed by Osama bin Laden that the Americans called a declaration of war, circulated throughout the Muslim world, transmitted by the most militant imams, the media of the Arab world, and numerous Internet sites. This twenty-page appeal, entitled "Against the Americans Occupying the Holy Places: To Drive the Infidels from the Arabian Peninsula," was directed as much against the Saudi regime as against the American government. The following excerpt indicates its tone:

> It should not be concealed from you that the people of Islam have suffered from aggression, iniquity, and injustice imposed on it by the alliance of Zionists and crusaders [Christians] and their collaborators; to the point that Muslim blood has been sold cheaply and Muslim property has become spoils for the enemy. Their blood should be spattered in Palestine and Iraq. The horrible images of the massacre of Cana in Lebanon are still fresh in our memories. As are the massacres in Tajikistan, Burma, Kashmir, Assam, the Philippines, Ogaden, Somalia, Eritrea, Chechnya, and Bosnia-Herzegovina. These massacres freeze the blood and shock the conscience.[6]

Osama bin Laden was also attempting to shock the conscience of his disciples and the undecided. By means of a shrewd manipulation, he attempted to present Muslims as the universal victims of an international coalition.

> We, my group and I, have suffered from these injustices. We have been prevented from addressing Muslims. We have been hounded in Pakistan, Sudan, and Afghanistan, which explains my long absence. By the grace of Allah, we now have a secure base in the high mountains of the Hindu Kush, in Khorassan, where—thanks be to Allah—the largest infidel army in the world [the Soviet Union] was destroyed. And the myth of the superpower was swept away while the mujahedeen chanted *Allahou Akhbar*. From these same mountains, we

> are now working to put an end to the injustice that has been imposed on the Muslim community by the alliance of the crusaders and the Zionists, particularly after the occupation of the blessed land around Jerusalem, after the occupation of the road taken by the Prophet (may Allah bless and praise him), and of the land of the two Holy Places. We ask Allah to grant us the victory. He is our Benefactor and the All Powerful One.

Bin Laden concluded unambiguously: "In these circumstances, driving the enemy out of the country is one of our primary duties."

Illustrating his argument with references to the history of the Muslim world and to its many heroes who had already shed their blood in fighting against the infidels, Osama bin Laden directly addressed the Americans:

> The young men you call cowards are competing with one another to fight you and kill you. Listen to what one of them says: "The army of crusaders turned to dust when we had al-Khobar blown up by the brave young men of Islam who do not fear danger." For more than ten years, these young men shouldered arms in Afghanistan, and they made a vow to Allah that as long as they live they will continue to bear arms against you until—by the will of Allah—you are driven out, beaten, and humiliated.

In the same document, seen by the militants of the Bin Laden Brotherhood as a model declaration of war, bin Laden called on Muslims to remain united and not to start a civil war in Saudi Arabia or elsewhere in the Arab world. He called on them not to choose the wrong enemy, not to endanger the oil infrastructure of the peninsula, essential for the development of the Arab world, but instead to carry on economic warfare against American interests by asking women to boycott products made in the United States.

Transmitting these nonstop attacks on America and Saudi Arabia and provoking in return condemnation from the West as a whole, bin Laden's satellite telephone was operating in such high gear that his "protectors" warned him of the risk of being traced. American military surveillance systems could locate him to within a few feet by tracing his telephone signals and could easily fire a missile at his hiding place. This is what finally happened on August 20, 1998, with the bombing of one of Osama bin Laden's camps in the Khost region. The Tomahawk missiles missed their principal target, and essentially caused only material damage. The next day, the voice of Osama bin Laden rang out on a radio station and on his satellite telephone: "Thanks be to God, I am alive."

Following this attack on one of his bases, and on the advice of supporters in the Pakistani intelligence service, Osama bin Laden thereafter used a more "ecological" method of communication, consisting of attaching radio transmitters to domesticated falcons. With an antenna thirty-four centimeters long, the birds, normally trained as hunters, also became messengers able to transmit radio messages to Osama bin Laden's agents on the ground. The capture of one of these birds made the method known.

According to the Americans, the August 20 raid was not intended to assassinate Osama bin Laden but to inflict material damage on the terrorists. This is a delicate point in the United States, where executive order 12333 prohibits a government employee from involvement in an assassination or even in an assassination plot. The Americans thus disclaimed any intent to eliminate Osama bin Laden. According to intelligence services, the Khost target was known to be a training and housing complex designed for organizing attacks against the United States. According to several reports from deserters from the Bin Laden Brotherhood at the time, the personnel on the base had significantly grown, indicating an increase in force that could be justified only by plans for terrorist actions. In short, the United States had no regrets, and Secretary of Defense William S. Cohen told the press on August 23: "There could be more strikes."

After the raid, the American government also informed humanitarian aid agencies that it would be unwise to resume their activities in Afghanistan. The warning was unambiguous:

> Washington warns foreigners planning to go to Afghanistan that, according to available information, Osama bin Laden is still in Afghanistan and that he is active there. From Washington's point of view, this could endanger the lives of those foreigners who wish to resume their work in Afghanistan. Washington reserves the right to strike any location in Afghanistan that might be concealing terrorists. Washington warns the United Nations and foreigners wishing to return to Afghanistan that it will not be possible to give them advance warning to withdraw.

At the time, Osama bin Laden was seen on several occasions in the car of the "emir of the faithful," Mullah Mohammed Omar, who was no longer a mere religious leader, but had become the chief figure in the Afghan regime. It was said that Osama bin Laden had left his Jalalabad residence to settle finally in Kandahar simply as an expression of his wish to be near a spiritual guide who was precious to him. According to other reports, he had in reality made an agreement with the Taliban, purchasing his protection for $50 million. He then began dividing his time between Kandahar and secret residences in Kharassan and Zara al-Handakush. According to Milton Bearden, former CIA station chief in Afghanistan, Osama bin Laden is a chameleon who adapts to his environment; he can hide in a mountain cave and become as hard to find as a needle in a haystack, or live, as he did in Kornaha, southwest of the camp struck by American missiles, in a house with three-yard-thick clay and straw walls, but with a luxurious interior that would not be out of place in Beverly Hills.

In March 1997 bin Laden had settled near Jalalabad. His base was called Najm al Jihad, Star of the Holy War. He also had a hideout set up in a cave near Jalalabad, three rudimentary rooms guarded by several hundred men, including a group of Algerian fundamentalists trained in chemical warfare techniques and making up part of his personal bodyguard.[7] This cave, from which a tunnel led to a road running deep through a ravine, was an impregnable hiding place, bare of comfort but nonetheless equipped with portable computers and a satellite telephone, not to mention a fine library of Islamic works of which the fugitive was particularly proud.

Mullah Omar and Osama bin Laden were very close. A hot line recently still connected the two fundamentalist leaders; Osama bin Laden answered at 925 12 53 06. Bin Laden was always generous to the cleric: he bought a house in Kandahar for him, his three wives, and his four children. But he also supported him politically by financing several projects that put the Taliban in a good light, including the construction of an irrigation canal in the province of Helmand and the provision of electricity and water for Kandahar. In exchange, Osama bin Laden was always free to travel among his various residences: the camp in Rishkor, eighteen kilometers south of Kabul, the camp in Khost, and a house near the Intercontinental Hotel in Kabul.

Bin Laden also maintained friendly relations with other religious organizations in the region who had representatives in Kabul or Jalalabad. He was in close contact with the Pakistani fundamentalist organization al-Badr and with the militants of Tabligh (an Indian-Pakistani Islamic proselytizing association), both of which he generously financed. For bin Laden, the Tablighi were a significant asset, because they had two religious establishments located not far from Baku, the capital of Azerbaijan. One was headed by a Somali, with the assistance of two Yemenis and a Saudi, and the other was entirely led by Yemenis. These two centers trained preachers called to work in Chechnya and Daghestan, two regions of southern Russia with large Muslim majorities challenging the Moscow government, in which Osama bin Laden had begun to get involved. (The leadership of the Caucasian mujahedeen, however, continued to deny any association with bin Laden; see appendix, document 8.) These Tabligh institutions also served as liaison offices for other Islamist organizations, particularly for those helping to send mujahedeen to fight in the jihad alongside the Chechens.

Osama bin Laden thus remained politically very active in exile. On February 23, 1998, according to Arab sources, he organized a meeting in Pakistan near the Afghan border. In the course of this conclave, the delegates, which included the Egyptians Rifai Ahmed Taha and Amin Dawari and the Pakistani Fazal ul-Rahman, leader of the al-Ansar movement, created a world front for the jihad, with the United States as the principal adversary, but also with a special mention for France, accused of persecuting Islamists both at home and in Algeria. (See document 9, claiming credit for the attack at the Saint-Michel metro station in Paris, and document 19.)

In his communiqués and diatribes distributed from Afghanistan, Osama bin Laden also admitted to his involvement in Somalia, where he claimed to have sent 250 mujahedeen in the jihad against the Americans. He accused France of supporting the junta in power in Algeria and of persecuting the four million Muslims living on its territory because they refused to abjure their Islamic identity. These statements, published in the Pakistani newspaper *The Muslim*, and picked up by the various outposts of the bin Laden network in Europe, contained all the ingredients needed to inflame susceptible adherents in mosques around the world, including those in the economically depressed suburbs of French cities. Bin Laden also declared his support for the Taliban and emphatically advocated their alliance with the Iranians, who were in his view the only true Muslims in the world, true Islamists who, moreover, shared the common enemy, the Americans.[8]

The Taliban regime returned the favor. On November 20, 1998, a Taliban spokesman, Abdel Hai Mutmaen, stated that Osama bin Laden had been "found innocent of all the accusations of terrorism uttered by the United States and that he was therefore welcome in Afghanistan." Mutmaen emphasized that the Afghan Supreme Court would consider none of the charges concerning the attacks against the American embassies in Dar es Salaam and Nairobi, because it had set a deadline for the presentation of conclusive evidence, and that evidence had never come before it. Mutmaen concluded, however, by saying: "He may live in Afghanistan as a Muslim guest, but he will continue to be barred from political and military activity."

The Americans saw these official declarations as a smokescreen. In fact, some months earlier, in February 1998, Osama bin Laden had openly established the IIF, the International Islamic Front, with the mission of fighting Christians and Jews. According to several Western sources, Pakistani militants were closely associated with this new organization through an association that was particularly active in Kashmir, known as Harkat ul-Ansar. At the time, bin Laden associates Abdelaziz al-Masir, Abu Haser, and Abu Ibrahim were also using Indian territory as a secret meeting place, particularly the Kashmiri city of Amritsar, from which fundamentalist leaders traveled to meet bin Laden. This use of Indian territory demonstrates the continuous involvement of bin Laden in Kashmiri affairs, and there are even reports that he was implicated in the Pakistani raid in the Indian province of Kargil.[9] His participation in this operation was supposedly planned at a secret meeting in Peshawar in December 1998, at the invitation of the authorities of the North-West Frontier Province of Pakistan.

It is clear that Osama bin Laden was in his element in that chaotic region of the world, which harbored extremists of all stripes. A mere enumeration of the military and paramilitary establishments in the region is enough to explain why the majority of international experts called it a powder keg. The presence of many training centers in Afghanistan, and also in Pakistan, was greatly facilitated by the porousness of the border. Camps harboring militants involved in the Kashmiri conflict were distributed along the border, in the Afghan provinces of Nangarhar, Pakhtia, Logar, and Kunar. Most of these sites had been under the control of Gulbuddin Hekmatyar before falling into the hands of the Taliban. According to available information, the camps in these four provinces welcomed recruits from Pakistan and Kashmir, as well as mujahedeen from Algeria, Tunisia, Saudi Arabia, Iraq, Egypt, Jordan, and Palestine. The province of Pakhtia, in the region of Khost, contained two of the most important training centers, al-Badr 1 and 2, a complex covering about twenty square kilometers. It was surrounded by barbed wire and equipped with watchtowers. Constant training of more than 350 fighters supposedly went on at these bases, particularly of Pakistanis subsequently sent to Kashmir and Arabs sent on guerrilla operations in Chechnya and Bosnia. The instructors trained recruits in the classic techniques of low-intensity combat: the manufacture of homemade bombs and the handling of automatic weapons and missile launchers. Other camps on the border, Omar, al-Khuldan, and Faruk, were supposedly used chiefly by mercenaries on the way to Chechnya. The Abu Bakr camp near Khost was specially devoted to mine laying, high-level training provided by Egyptian advisers from Ayman al-Zawahiri's Islamic Jihad.

A list of these Afghan camps would be long, because some of them were simple tent villages that change location according to several considerations, weather conditions, or security—bin Laden's Khost base, for example, which was hit in an early American raid. Some camps originally set up in the Peshawar region were moved to the Afghan mountains. It seems that the major establishments before the fall of the Taliban regime were the camps in Jali, Spin Shaga, and Shapuli in the province of Pakhtia. There were four major camps in the province of Nangarhar: Teraki Tangi, Mauzaffarabad, Dehbala, and Nazian Shinwar, training chiefly Kashmiris. In the same province, the Jalalabad camp specialized in the training of Arab militants to be sent on terrorist missions to Western countries. A final camp, Darunta, headed by an Egyptian going by the name of Abu Abdallah, devoted each session to the training of three hundred mercenaries from the Philippines, Malaysia, Turkey, and Egypt, most of whom were sent to fight with the Islamic Legion in Bosnia, Chechnya, and Azerbaijan. An Algerian explosives specialist, whose name is unknown but who is close to the AIS (Armee islamique du salut), has been training future terrorists there since 1996.[10]

The province of Kabul also had its own camps, run by the Taliban less than fifteen kilometers from the capital. An office for the support of the mujahedeen, a branch of the celebrated Peshawar office of the Palestinian Azzam, was opened in Kabul and headed by an Egyptian, Abu Mohsen. Beginning in 1996, the office was run by an Algerian, Bujemah Bunua Anas, close to the Islamic Salvation Front (FIS) and Azzam's son-in-law. He was deported from France in 1992 and is now said to hold an Afghan diplomatic passport.

The other Afghan provinces of Logar, Kunar, Badakhshan, Kunduz, and Takhar contained at least thirty camps, most of them under Taliban control.

Western intelligence services and testimony from Islamist fighters confirmed that there were also many camps on the Pakistani side, sometimes under the cover of madrasas. These training centers, largely supported by the ISI, but also financed by naïve nongovernmental organizations sometimes totally unaware of their military activities, are chiefly located in the North-West Frontier Province. The best known and most active of these establishments were supposedly the camps of al-Sada, north of Peshawar, headed by an Egyptian, Abu Hashim, nicknamed Suheib. Other camps were said to be located in the Khyber Pass region or in the region of Bajaur. It also seems that when Osama bin Laden set up al-Qaeda, it opened its first training center near Peshawar. But it is probable that bin Laden transferred all his activities to Afghanistan, although he maintained many networks in the Pakistani army and intelligence services.

Osama bin Laden always managed in one way or another to receive his guests and to move around, even to leave Afghan territory, but he remained impossible to capture. "Revelations," which probably amount to disinformation, asserted that an American commando group infiltrated into Afghanistan from Peshawar in April 1998 in order to eliminate bin Laden in Kandahar. This plot, according to bin Laden's associates, was "very fortunately foiled by former agents of the Khad," the Afghan secret service now under Taliban control. This rumor of an attempted American raid, carefully orchestrated, spread through several Internet sites no doubt financed and sponsored by Osama bin Laden himself. In his mountain fortress, the rebel polished his image as a martyr.

In February 1999 his companion in the jihad, al-Zawahiri, assembled the operational members of various groups close to bin Laden in the Jalalabad camp following the arrest of many Islamists, particularly in Egypt. In the same month, bin Laden disappeared from view. It was said that he had set up another secret base in Fahimhaddah, near Jalalabad, and that he and his entourage had left Kandahar in February, probably without his family. His impressive armored convoy had passed through Nimroz, Farahand, Bola Bluk Uruzgan, and Baghlan, before disappearing in the mountains. Osama bin Laden had now really gone underground, and the Taliban spokesman Mullah Abdel Hai Mutmaen acknowledged on June 21, 1999, that, although Osama bin Laden was still in Afghanistan, his movements were not known to the authorities. It is now certain that he had built, somewhere in the remote Afghan mountains, a hidden and heavily armed fortress, even though he did not live there. It has often been noted that he traveled in convoys protected by Stingers and that several identical Viper armored vehicles would be sent in different directions before each of his movements.

Osama bin Laden's movements were sometimes restricted by political and diplomatic considerations that he no doubt wished he could ignore. In November 1998, when he was invited to an Islamic conference in Pakistan, he was informed by Islamabad that his presence in Pakistan was incompatible with the forthcoming visit of Prime Minister Nawaz Sharif to Washington. Osama bin Laden had to be satisfied with sending a message of solidarity to the participants from his mountain fortress.

Whether or not Osama bin Laden had disappeared without a trace, for the American government and the U.N. Security Council, the guiltiest party involved was the independent and uncontrollable Taliban, who had too long provided asylum for the Saudi. On July 6, 1999, President Clinton imposed economic sanctions on Afghanistan. As in every one of their statements about bin Laden, the Taliban answered with an evasion: "Osama bin Laden is in Afghanistan, but we do not know where."

The Taliban resistance to surrendering bin Laden gave rise to much speculation. According to some, Osama bin Laden was in reality the true leader of the Taliban, and he had confirmed it by offering his daughter in marriage to Mullah Omar. According to others, he had simply paid a high price for his security and was financing the secret drug laboratories that had been set up in Afghanistan.

5 / The Islamic Legion

In less than ten years, Osama bin Laden became one of the essential agents of the international Islamic struggle, in large part because of his unreserved commitment to what some analysts have come to call the "Islamic Legion": an army that is seen as a secret army, with no real legal status, still less a centralized command, and with no unified system of financing like that of Hezbollah, for example, but having nonetheless an international presence. It was in this Islamic Legion, with no real command structure, but with a real presence on the ground, that Osama bin Laden had his first combat experience. A better understanding of how and why this Islamic Legion came into being will make it easier to grasp Osama bin Laden's personality and to see how he helped in its growth.

On December 27, 1979, the Soviets invaded Afghanistan, to the astonishment of the Western world, which had not witnessed such a direct confrontation since the Bay of Pigs affair in Cuba nearly twenty years earlier. Public opinion was troubled and shocked, but no one had yet realized that Moscow had unawares just given the Muslim world a great cause that would occupy its attention for several decades. The entry of the Red Army into Kabul gave the signal for a major international campaign of recruitment of mujahedeen, all united in brotherhood by the holy war against the atheist oppressor. As a direct consequence of the formation of the "Islamic International Brigades," the Soviets were finally defeated and the Red Army withdrew from Afghanistan, leaving behind a new Afghan communist regime and the conditions for another form of chaos and domination, as inauspicious for the development of freedom as the Soviet occupation itself.

From 1980 to 1990 these volunteers from the Muslim world, trained in

Pakistan by the best Western instructors (in the name of anticommunism), were the spearhead of the guerrilla war against the Red Army. There they earned the name of Afghan Arabs or "Afghans," a name that is still respected today throughout the Muslim world, including North Africa, and especially Algeria, but also in Paris and the economically depressed suburbs of France. At the time, the Soviet invasion was deemed unacceptable, and the mujahedeen were universally called the resistance or "freedom fighters." No one would have dreamed of putting the subjection of the Afghan people on the credit side of the "overall positive balance sheet of socialism," as the French Communist Party claimed.

But history reversed itself, and the Afghan Arabs came to be seen by the West, especially by the United States, as the most ungrateful of renegades. It was out of the question for the American government to forgive them for having become "terrorists" after having shared the same Soviet enemy for ten years. American supporters of the Afghan resistance of the 1980s, sitting in their cozy offices on the Potomac, far from antipersonnel mines and the call of the muezzin, now had the impression that their former allies were deliberately insulting the United States. Their bitterness is both comprehensible and justified. And yet, since 1980, the saga of the mujahedeen of Afghanistan had been made of nothing but surprises, betrayals, and reversals.

It would have been difficult in 1980 to predict that the Sunnis, who provided the bulk of the Arab forces mobilized against the Soviet army and shared the aversion of most Western countries for Moscow, so much so that they were seen as "good Muslims," would be able to change sides and finally join in a jihad against the West. In reality, many Afghan Arab fighters were loyal only to themselves, and the pill was all the more difficult for the United States to swallow because Washington had spent freely to support them. Were these mujahedeen, whom America criticized for their short memory and political inconsistency, idealists or opportunists? They were no doubt a blend of the two, but the ideal often won out as the situation became more radicalized.

Most Muslims who joined the Afghans against the Red Army were sincere. Many paid for their courageous commitment with their lives. But a few hundred, or perhaps a few thousand, joined up only to escape from the security services of their own countries, which were only awaiting an opportunity to arrest them for terrorism. However well founded such accusations may have been, it was tacitly agreed in most Muslim countries at the time that joining the jihad against the Soviets would wash away past indiscretions or even subversive activities. A mujahed would secure amnesty and sometimes glory for his family if he fell on the field of battle. The irony of history is that it was precisely these same fighters, most often with terrorist weapons, who were leading the battle against the West from Afghanistan or Pakistan in the last months of 2001.

Unlike the Palestinian organizations of the 1970s and 1980s, the Afghan Arabs were not supported by any government, and the only thing they had in common was their past: training camps in Pakistan and Afghanistan, a shared ideology, and the feeling of being brothers in arms who had gone through the worst ordeals together. To understand the fate and the trajectory of these Afghan Arabs, we have to go back to 1978, when the Afghan people were organizing to resist the invasion.

In January 1979, after difficult negotiations among rival factions, the oppressed Afghan people established the Islamic Resistance Alliance. In February 1979 the rest of the world mobilized, but only after the kidnapping and assassination of the American ambassador in Kabul. President Carter imposed economic sanctions on the Soviet Union and began supplying unrestricted aid to the Afghan resistance. In 1981 the resistance was reinforced, at the instigation of the new American president, Ronald Reagan, who coordinated with Pakistan and Saudi Arabia an international alliance designed to arm the mujahedeen effectively but secretly. Pakistan then became the sanctuary for the resistance against Moscow, and the United States was openly supporting a jihad. The director of the CIA, William Casey, was charged with organizing assistance to Afghan Islamic fighters.

From 1983 the principal nations involved in military and financial support for the Afghan resistance were Saudi Arabia, the United States, and Pakistan, but many other governments, such as Morocco, Egypt, Jordan, Oman, and Turkey, also helped, more occasionally but just as generously, to aid the Afghan people. The Afghan cause garnered unanimous support; according to some reports that have now been confirmed, Israel was also involved on the ground in Afghanistan alongside hard-line Islamists, in circumstances in which the American services did not want their military advisers directly involved.[1] But in February 1989 Ronald Reagan and Soviet leader Mikhail Gorbachev reached an agreement on the withdrawal of Soviet troops, marking the end of American aid to the resistance fighters.

During the 1980s, nearly 40 percent of Western military aid went to the Hezb-e-Islami rebel movement of the fundamentalist Islamic leader Gulbuddin Hekmatyar, living in exile in a little house in the university neighborhood of Peshawar. When I met Hekmatyar in 1988 in his residence, under tight security conditions, the religious leader was still uncertain about political matters but was surrounded by Pakistanis from the ISI, who were competent and well organized. Hekmatyar was not yet fully aware of the consequences of the Islamic uprising that he had provoked nor of the role that the Islamists would be able to play in Afghanistan, but his Pakistani supporters already had a precise vision of the new Afghanistan.

Hekmatyar had not yet reached his full stature, and the Pakistani secret services were urging him on, but not to the extent of being able to manipulate him. Intelligent, calculating, and shrewd enough to accept the assistance of Islamabad, although not losing his identity in selling himself to the Pakistani military, Hekmatyar was then leading from Peshawar a solid network of mujahedeen and mullahs that would finally cover all Afghanistan, thanks to subsidies from abroad. This was aid to which Hekmatyar could almost lay a legitimate historic claim; he belonged to an important ethnic group, the Kharuti clan of the Pashtun tribe. This tribal component was a reality of Afghan feudal society that the sponsors of the resistance had to take into account. Other organizations, such as the National Islamic Front, Qadissiya,[2] and the National Salvation Front of Afghanistan also received external financing in the name of the anticommunist crusade, but they could not compete with Hekmatyar's movement.

The assistance offered to the Afghan resistance ranged from supplying costly Stinger missiles, delivered directly from the United States or through Saudi Arabia, to the setting up of commando training centers. Some dangerous missions on the other side of the border, in Soviet Tajikistan and elsewhere, were carried out by joint Afghan-American teams. On the ground, the ISI really directed operations, handled logistics, and supervised the training of resistance fighters.

A few years later, with the withdrawal of the Soviets, these thousands of fighters to whom nothing had been refused and who had received exceptional military training, had become "Afghans" and had not laid down their weapons. For them, the jihad continued, first against the Kabul government, which was still communist and still oppressive. Others had returned to their own countries where, armed with their experience, they began fighting against established governments in order to encourage an Islamist uprising, as in Algeria, Tunisia, and Morocco (see appendix, document 11). Others moved to Europe where they became mercenaries in Bosnia or terrorist bombers in France.

The Islamic Legion is not a myth. There is no memorial on which you can read the names of the soldiers fallen in the Afghan mountains, nor is there any roster bearing the identification numbers of these shadow warriors, but the number of "Afghans" of various origins who went to Pakistan reached several thousand, perhaps several tens of thousands, within a few months. In the years following the Soviet invasion, the Pakistani consulate in Algiers issued 2,800 visas to young Algerians going to fight the Red Army, while many others, who were not counted, went through Jordan or Iran. According to one of General Massoud's officers, interviewed in January 1997, Algerian fighters unquestionably entered Afghanistan through the many humanitarian organizations operating in Pakistan, going particularly to three camps where a special unit was trained, the "Algerian Koran Brigade." Losses among the Algerians in the Islamic Legion were particularly heavy, but a reasonable estimate is that three thousand "Afghan Algerians" are still alive and have become hardened veterans. A small part of the Algerian contingent stayed behind in Afghanistan, and remained loyal to Massoud, one of its first leaders.[3] More than half these "Afghans" returned to Algeria. Some of them continued to recruit for the Pakistani training camps; others joined the GIA underground after the cancellation of elections in 1992. According to Algerian intelligence services, nearly one thousand veterans came to Algeria in several waves up to the spring of 1994, contributing to the explosions of violence there that have caused at least sixty thousand deaths since 1992.

The Afghan veterans can be found in almost all theaters of operation of so-called low-intensity conflicts; they are in Azerbaijan, Bangladesh, Burma, Malaysia, Chechnya, western China, Egypt, India, Algeria, Morocco, Uzbekistan, the Philippines, Tajikistan, Tunisia, and Yemen. This is not to mention the sleeper cells established particularly in France and the United States, and in London, ironically known among certain Islamists as the principal Arab city in Europe.[4] *Jane's International Defence Weekly* estimated that the "Afghans" numbered 14,000: 5,000 Saudis, 3,000 Yemenis, 2,000 Egyptians, 2,800 Algerians, 400 Tunisians, 370 Iraqis, 200 Libyans, and a handful of Jordanians.

This "holy alliance" between Islamic Legionnaires and the Afghan people, which lasted for twenty years, was not the result of a random impulse. It began in 1980, on the initiative of Abdallah Azzam, a Palestinian who is no longer alive. A sympathizer of the Jordanian Muslim Brotherhood, who had rallied to Islamism in the 1970s, he came to Peshawar in 1980, where he established the Maktab ul-Khedamat Mujahedeen, the Office of Services for the Mujahedeen. This agency used Saudi funds to recruit mujahedeen. For months, Abdallah Azzam traveled throughout the Arab world in order to establish an "Islamic Support Legion" inspired by a mystic ideal then lacking among the Afghan resistance, which was made up of excellent fighters still shackled by a feudal system.

In 1995, following an attack on the Egyptian embassy in Islamabad, the Office of Services for the Mujahedeen was shut down by the Pakistani authorities. But the recruitment and military training circuit, perfected during the Soviet occupation of Afghanistan, was never dismantled, neither at the end of the war nor after the office was officially closed. In particular, it welcomed several leaders of the FIS (the Algerian Islamic Salvation Front) deported from France in August 1992 and in 1993, including Kamar Eddin Kherban, a former Algerian air force officer and member of the Instance exécutive du Front islamique du salut à l'étranger (IEFE), the foreign executive organization of the FIS.[5] Well before Kherban joined up, another member of the IEFE, Bujemah Bunua, alias Abu Anas, had married the daughter of the organization's founder and had taken over its leadership on the death of his father-in-law. Abdallah Azzam, founder of the first battalion of Arab mujahedeen, was killed by a car bomb in Peshawar in the fall of 1989, while on the way to the mosque with his son.[6] This suggests the key role played by Peshawar and the Office of Services for the Mujahedeen in the training of "legionnaires" for Afghanistan. According to some French counterespionage experts, it was very likely that the idea of establishing the Algerian GIA arose in the early 1990s in Peshawar, which had become a nest of Islamist militants.

In 1994, only a few months before the attacks in Paris, the Pakistani recruitment networks were operating in high gear.[7] The services of the French embassy in Islamabad had on several occasions drawn the attention of the director general of the Police International Technical Cooperation Service (SCTIP) in Paris to several French citizens who had come for courses "of terrorist training in Pakistan or the surrounding region," probably in Afghanistan. At the time, the trainees were welcomed by a guide answering to the pseudonym of Aissa, Abu Quassim, or simply "the Afghan." The recruitment network's correspondent in Islamabad had a portable telephone whose number was found in the address book of Maaloui Monahim Ben Amar, an "Afghan" arrested in Perpignan on July 24, 1994. Recruitment was not confined to the dangerous suburbs of Paris, Lille, and Lyon, but covered all of France.

Several former militants of the FIS have revealed that commando training in Afghanistan took place over long periods, between ten weeks and eighteen months, in at least four camps, located in Charyasab (for a time the headquarters of Hekmatyar), Kunjak, Jaji, and in the province of Pakhtia, near the Pakistani border. Recruits learned the use of assault weapons, Soviet AK-47s, Czech Scorpio machine pistols, and American missile launchers such as the RPG-7 (rocket-propelled grenade). Evidence indicates that Algerian and European trainees were very quickly enlisted for actual sorties in the Afghan guerrilla war, which led to heavy losses in their ranks. Sometimes, but less frequently because of the cost of the missiles, commando groups were instructed in the use of Stingers, very few of which had been used, much less returned after the anti-Soviet war, much to the distress of the Americans, who were afraid that their own weapons would one day be turned on American targets.

Psychological training of recruits was essential; it was based on long self-criticism sessions after missions, and religious training (see appendix, document 12) held a very important place, particularly at funerals of fighters killed in combat. According to witnesses, burials were interminable ceremonies full of religious discourse and readings of the Suras, or Koranic verses.

For several years, the legionnaires took advantage of the sympathies of the Pakistani secret services to enter Afghanistan from Pakistan. But, beginning in 1994, the ISI stopped openly facilitating the transfer of trainees, and Islamic charitable organizations, such as the IIRO (International Islamic Relief Organization) and the al-Kifah Refugee Center took over, becoming nothing but smuggling organizations in humanitarian disguise, making it possible for Islamist militants to travel from Marseille to Peshawar, through Dakar or Djibouti, on the pretext of more or less charitable missions. Some of these organizations (see appendix, document 13), established in Peshawar and accredited by the U.N. High Commission for Refugees (UNHCR), are known even today for their unconditional support for the jihad.

In November 1995, for example, a young Muslim whose first name was Muldi gave evidence to the Direction de la surveillance du territoire (DST), describing how recruitment could become hijacking, or even kidnapping. This young man with a degree in mathematics, had gone to Afghanistan via Algiers in the early 1990s in order to be a teacher. His trip had been organized by the Tabligh.

The Jamaat al-Tabligh is a movement for the propagation of Islam, of Pakistani origin, established in 1927 by the cleric Mawlana Mohammed Ilyas. This fundamentalist organization is in favor of unrestricted application of sharia. The Tabligh headquarters is located in Pakistan, with a European office in Dewsbury, a suburb of Leeds. The Tabligh opened an office in France in September 1972 under the name Faith and Practice; its official location is in Clichy, but the informal headquarters is at the Omar mosque on rue Jean-Pierre Timbaud in the eleventh arrondissement of Paris. The organization controls numerous mosques in northern France and in the Paris region, probably more than one hundred. Proselytizers for the Tabligh go in search of the faithful; these itinerant preachers call for support of bin Laden. In groups of three, four, or five, led by an emir, they preach in the street, in markets, and even in the homes of the undecided. Hospitals and prisons are a secondary target where they have recruited very successfully. In 1993, a tour of France by eight Tabligh dignitaries from Pakistan gave the French Ministry of the Interior some indication of the strength of the organization, which has prospered to the point that it has several provincial centers, in Saint-Sabel, Auvergne, Meyzieu, Vaux-en-Velin, and Lyon.

Muldi was probably unaware of the nature of the powerful militant and religious machinery that had organized his stay in Pakistan. In Peshawar, he did in fact teach classes in a Koranic school and was housed in a villa known as the "house of the French," but he was very soon recruited for commando training. Having begun as a teacher, Muldi ended up spending several weeks in the mountains under the orders of Afghan veterans learning guerrilla techniques for which he had not volunteered. The young French citizens of Maghrebi origin who were sentenced in Fez in January 1995 for their participation in attacks in Marrakech in the summer of 1994 had also followed a training program in Afghanistan in 1992.

This Pakistani network had become of such concern that, by October 12, 1995, Judge Jean-Louis Bruguière had requested that the DST pay closer attention to all French citizens returning from Pakistan, where they had gone officially to study the Koran (see appendix, document 14; the border police were concerned as early as May 1993). Among the few dozen witnesses interrogated by the DST, almost all had the same profile. Natives of France or North Africa, they were all unemployed, all came from economically depressed suburbs, and were in conflict with contemporary society. Almost all admitted without too much persuasion that they had taken military training "somewhere in Afghanistan or Pakistan, in the mountains." But they didn't really know where. Most of these sham students had another point in common; as if by accident, they lost their passports shortly before their return, and the Islamabad consulate had to issue papers allowing them to return to France. Their passports provided material for the organization's counterfeiters. Once back in France, some of these trainees became low-level shadow warriors in the ranks of an organization, but others became leaders or recruiters. One of these Afghan Arabs, Abdelkader Hemmali, was arrested in December 1994 while actively engaged in setting up his own network shortly after his return to France. In November 1998, Ben Abdelkader, another French citizen of North African origin, was sentenced to twenty years in prison in Albania for the murder of an Albanian student. In the course of the trial, he admitted that he had worked for the Bin Laden Brotherhood, which had recruited him as a combatant when he had been in Albania the previous April. Representatives of the organization had at the time promised him funds to fight in Kosovo.

According to a confidential report of the French organization UCLAT (Unit for Coordination of the Antiterrorist Struggle), dated December 27, 1996, while recruitment has relied largely on the vulnerability of the young men approached, the profile of the recruiter is even more important. Indeed, as Irène Stoler, the head of the antiterrorist section of the Paris prosecutor's office, has pointed out, military training is always associated with psychological conditioning based on hatred of the West and the rejection of so-called materialist values. Islamist terrorists use recruiting agents who, in addition to their knowledge of Islam, their appreciable financial resources (at least in the view of their penniless young recruits), and their direct contacts with leaders of organizations such as the GIA, also enjoy a notoriety acquired in theaters of military operations considered prestigious, particularly Bosnia and Afghanistan (see appendix, document 13). It is thus easier for them to inspire the young candidates for the jihad eager to come to blows with Western society.

By February 1995 European police forces had infiltrated or dismantled enough networks in France, Tunisia, and Morocco to have a more precise idea of the modus operandi of the recruiters and the nature of their networks. The most active training camps at the time were those in Baktia and Schehar Siab in Afghanistan. Reports at the time indicated the existence of training with extremely sophisticated explosives, such as the celebrated C4, which has been used by most of the major terrorist organizations in the course of the last decade. There were also camps hidden in Pakistan that were reserved for training in the preparation of car bombs. Intercepts by British and other secret services recorded exchanges between Islamists in France and Great Britain with trainees in Pakistani camps headed by a certain Abu Kassem. These taps revealed that in 1995 Kassem was trying to recruit in the Islamic communities of Europe, chiefly in France, Great Britain, and Germany, in order to train young men ideologically for suicide missions in Europe.

Recruitment intensified shortly before the 1995 Paris attacks. Other Islamist radicals were in the process of raising a kind of legion for Bosnia. These volunteers would end up bolstering the ranks of trainees in Afghanistan. Most of those later sent to fight in Bosnia belonged to a unit called the "phalanx of the faithful." Some of these future martyrs were also directed toward the Islamic Jihad movement in Palestine. The head of that organization, Fathi Chakak, had announced in late 1994 that he intended to organize suicide commando groups with one hundred volunteers to conduct operations against Israeli forces, but also against anyone fighting Islam in Europe and Algeria. This number of one hundred fighters willing to commit suicide for the jihad may seem exaggerated, but the truth is even more frightening.

According to a survivor from one of the camps, candidates eagerly lined up at a base in Lebanon where he had been trained to become a walking bomb. Accompanied from beginning to end of their training by an imam charged with motivating them spiritually, the apprentice suicides ended up begging their teachers to send them on a mission, so great was their impatience to enter paradise, or their nervous tension and desire to put an end to that internal pressure. These commandos received rudimentary military training and their living conditions were monastic up to the day of their mission. The Islamic Jihad in Palestine, which had its offices in Iran, was then receiving financial support of more than $200,000 a month to purchase weapons and explosives and to cover the costs of training the suicide bombers.

According to the newspaper *Al-Watan al-Arabi* of June 7, 1997, a similar camp was located on the Pakistani-Afghan border. Five thousand sacrificial volunteers from around the world between the ages of sixteen and twenty-five were in training for a final and definitive participation in the jihad (see appendix, document 16). The camp was led by a Pakistani nicknamed al-Archad (the best guided).

Other recruitment circuits relied on Hamas in Palestine.[8] We also know that several guerrilla fighters in the Blida region of Algeria were trained by Yehia Ayache, better known as "the engineer," the man who was then training future human bombs in Hamas camps. In September 2000 and January 2001, bin Laden sent emissaries to Hamas after the outbreak of the new Intifada. Other, even more numerous recruits, who had joined the ranks of the GIA or the AIS, were trained in camps of Hezbollah-Palestine. The militants of that organization received military training in Hezbollah camps in Lebanon or camps of the Popular Front for the Liberation of Palestine–General Command (PFLP-GC) of Ahmed Jibril, a formidable Palestinian militant converted to Islamism and possessing bases in Lebanon, Iran, northern Europe, and even in Germany, according to the Bundeskriminalamt (BKA), the German counterespionage service.

Almost all the Islamists who played an important role in the 1995 Paris attacks had a common denominator, although their social origins were very different; they too had either been trained in Pakistan or Afghanistan or had been pivotal elements in the recruitment networks for Islamist terrorists. This was true for Abu Fares, alias Rashid Ramda, editor-in chief of *Al-Ansar*[9] in London, also known to have financed the perpetrators of the attack on the Saint-Michel metro station on July 25, 1995. Ramda himself went to Pakistan and was also an organizer of training sessions in Afghanistan for the Islamists of England.

It has been reported that it was also in these camps that training was given to Adam Adel Ali, alias Adam Khan Baluch, alias Dr. Adel Sabah, better known by another of his forty aliases, Ramzi Yussef, orchestrator of the 1993 attack on the World Trade Center. Originally named Abdel Basit Mahmoud Abdulkarim, a name that he stopped using long ago, Ramzi Yussef was born in Kuwait in 1968 to a family that came from Pakistani Baluchistan. He is thought to have been in contact with associates of Osama bin Laden beginning in 1988, in Afghanistan and Pakistan, while he was living in the Beit a-Shuhada (house of martyrs) guest house in Peshawar, and he is thought to have learned how to put together homemade bombs in several camps financed by bin Laden. Following a 1991 meeting in Peshawar with Abubakr Janjalani, founder of the Philippine group Abu Sayyaf, then partially financed by bin Laden, Ramzi Yussef is believed to have deliberately chosen the path of terrorism.[10] Because of his talents, he was recruited as a technical adviser to the Abu Sayyaf group, which was expert in seizing hostages and specialized in the protection of drug shipments through the airports on the islands of Basilan and Jolo. Journalists for the *Philippine Daily Inquirer*, in an article of August 23, 1998, established the fact that Osama bin Laden had in recent years been a frequent visitor to the group, particularly in their Mindanao stronghold. Around the same time, several Philippine officials, including the president's chief of staff, explained that Osama bin Laden was known for his philanthropic activities on behalf of several Muslim organizations in the southern part of the country. According to the same journalists, bin Laden's brother-in-law, Mohamed Jamel Khalif, head of a Saudi NGO, had made a financial contribution to Gamaa Islamiya , which claimed responsibility for the massacre of sixty tourists at Luxor, Egypt, on November 17, 1997.

From the 1991 meeting on, Ramzi Yussef is said to have become one of Osama bin Laden's "soldiers." It is not certain whether he ever met the Saudi, but it has been established that he was involved with the Bin Laden Brotherhood from 1988 until he was sentenced to life in prison in the United States.

Another member of the family, Zahid el-Sheikh, Ramzi Yussef's maternal uncle, is also known to have ties to Osama bin Laden. Like bin Laden, he had fought in Afghanistan, where he lost a brother in the fighting, before going to work for a Kuwaiti charitable NGO, Mercy International. Originally from Baluchistan, he is said to have also been involved in arms smuggling in Pakistan; according to the testimony of a Ramzi Yussef associate, some of these weapons were intended to assassinate Benazir Bhutto during an election campaign. According to other sources, Zahid el-Sheikh has also had close connections to one of his nephew's financiers and mentors, a Saudi identified under the name of Abdul Majid Madni. He was also known for his relations with Osama bin Laden, who is said to have used him on several occasions as a liaison, notably with Ramzi Yussef. During a search of Zahid el-Sheikh's house in Islamabad, investigators found a request for a passport for Abdel Basit, Ramzi Yussef's real name, and established a number of troubling connections: photographs of el-Sheikh in company with President Zia and Prime Minister Nawaz Sharif proved that Ramzi Yussef's uncle had friendly relations with the Pakistani political establishment.

The Algerian Islamists of Hassan Hattab's group (see appendix, document 19), notably their European networks, have been approached by bin Laden associates. They seem to have received new financial resources, with associates of the GIA entrusted with maintaining regular connections. The UCLAT, under the authority of the French Ministry of the Interior, was concerned in a November 25, 2000, report by the presence of imams supporting bin Laden's positions in mosques in Paris, London, Brussels, and Germany.

With regard to the Algerian network close to Osama bin Laden, it has been learned that it too went through Afghanistan. Ahmed Ressam, the Algerian arrested entering the United States from Canada on December 14, 1999, in possession of one hundred pounds of explosives, was part of a network of mujahedeen who had fought in Afghanistan and Bosnia.[11] The network was directed from Montreal by Fatah Kamel, who was extradited to France on May 16, 1999, in connection with a case involving the Islamists of Roubaix. Fatah Kamel had established a rear base for Algerian Islamists in Jordan. They would travel to Canada as students or asylum seekers. After Ressam's arrest, the head of the Canadian intelligence and security service acknowledged that his country had harbored many associates of the GIA. In 1997 bin Laden was in contact with the Canadian organization Human Concern International. One of its members, Ahmed Saïd Khadr, had met bin Laden in Kandahar in July 1996 (at the time, bin Laden was openly building a large villa). The Canadian connection began at this time. One of the key members of this network, Said Atmani, also known as Abu Hisham, had Bosnian and Moroccan passports and had been trained in the cells of the Egyptian Gamaa Islamiya and then fought in Bosnia in a battalion of Arab mujahedeen, under the orders of Abdelkader Mokhtari, commander of the seventh brigade of Zenica. In late September 1995 Ressam settled in Canada with the status of political refugee. These suspicions of the connections of Algerian fundamentalists to Osama bin Laden were confirmed in October 1999, when the Algerian general Mohamed Lamaari transmitted to the Saudi authorities a list of Islamists from Algeria and other countries of the Maghreb who had been trained in Osama bin Laden's camps.

In May 1995, bin Laden's right-hand man, al-Zawahiri, organized a meeting near Geneva with Egyptian Islamists and two Algerian ideologues close to the GIA. (The Saint-Michel metro attack, carried out by Algerians, took place on July 26.) One of the reasons for this secret meeting was to establish ties between Egyptian Islamists and "Afghan Algerians." In return for his aid to a GIA fringe group, al-Zawahiri wanted its support in hatching a plot against Egyptian president Hosni Mubarak, who often came to France on official and private visits. Several attempted assassinations of the Egyptian president are reported to have been aborted. According to Yossef Bodansky, a consultant to the U.S. Congress and author of the book, *Bin Laden, the Man Who Declared War on America*,[12] al-Zawahiri traveled secretly in Europe in 1997 for the sole purpose of creating networks of sleeper Islamic terrorists. He is also said to have promised his support to the GIA, which dreamed of organizing attacks in France during the World Cup soccer tournament in 1998, an idea originating with Hassan Hattab's group. On July 16, 2000, this group sent two threatening letters to Paris; those in charge of the antiterrorist struggle took them very seriously because of the links between these Algerians and bin Laden. Accomplices were uncovered in French prisons, where members of the GIA are incarcerated and where pro-bin Laden graffiti appeared. Paris preferred to keep these threats quiet.

Late in 2001 Algeria learned that the Hattab group was shaken by dissension, because some of its members had been "turned" by anti-bin Laden Saudi clerics.

Bin Laden himself traveled to Manchester and the London suburb of Wembley in 1994 to meet associates of the GIA, notably those producing the *Al-Ansar* newsletter. Financed by a bin Laden intermediary, this newsletter called for a jihad against France in 1995, the opening salvo of which was the Saint-Michel metro attack.

Finally, Bosnia, from 1992 until the Dayton Accords of November 21, 1995,[13] leading to the closure of Muslim volunteer camps and the dismantling of their units, provided new prospects for the commitment of the mujahedeen who were reluctant to return to their native countries. At least one thousand fighters from the Maghreb, Iran, Lebanon, and Turkey are believed to have fought in the former Yugoslavia, beginning in 1992. For example, most of the Algerians in Bosnia at the time belonged to the Abdallah Anas group, an organization financed by Yemeni companies owned by Osama bin Laden. But the fighters came from throughout the Muslim world, or even from France, like Lionel Dumont, the youngest of eight children, born in the north of France in 1971, who joined the cause of the jihad after converting to Islam in 1992. Drafted into the fourth RIMA (French Marine Corps) of Fréjus, this ordinary young Frenchman, who had had an untroubled schooling, served in Djibouti during the humanitarian operations in Somalia in 1993, before plunging into fundamentalist Islamism. Between 1993 and 1995 he frequently traveled to Bosnia, where he participated in humanitarian convoys in support of Muslims and then put in place a network for arms smuggling. He ended up fighting against the Serbs in battalions of the Islamic Legion officered by Afghans. Having married a Bosnian woman, he changed his name to Abu Hamza. Plunging into common criminality, he was arrested after a service station robbery, in the course of which one of his two accomplices, a North African, was killed.

According to Arab sources, the highest estimates placed four thousand mujahedeen in Bosnia. Once there, these experienced "Afghans" served as instructors for new or recently converted Muslim recruits, who had arrived directly from Western Europe under cover of humanitarian organizations, which, rather than calming the situation, fanned the flames and transformed the Bosnian ethnic conflict into a jihad.

One of the major Islamist figures in Bosnia was Abu Abdel Aziz, known as Barbarossa because of his henna-dyed beard. In Afghanistan, he had been an instructor for Abdallah Azzam's special commandos. In Bosnia, he made a display of his cruelty, parading around with the severed heads of Serbs. With finances from bin Laden, Barbarossa recruited several groups for him. But bin Laden's Egyptian associates warned him against Abu Abdel Aziz's instability and the risks that it might create.

The creation of the "independent battalion of mujahedeen" had been announced in the fall of 1993 in mosques in France, Germany, and Great Britain by a newspaper printed in Bosnia, *The Call to Jihad*. This volunteer unit, trained in camps near Zenica, was thought, however, never to have had more than a few hundred fighters at any one time. Nonetheless, this new European jihad made possible the formation of a new generation of Islamist militants, younger and as well trained as their predecessors. And it was the breeding ground for the forces that have taken up the cause of the current international Islamist movement. The passage through Bosnia, moreover, restored a certain virginity to veterans of Afghanistan, who were able to acquire Bosnian citizenship through marriage, thereby renouncing, officially at least, a sometimes troublesome past.

After the conclusion of the Dayton Accords and the departure of a large number of mercenaries, the bin Laden networks grew on the fertile Bosnian soil. Through an Islamic charitable organization, the Saudi High Commission (SHC), Osama bin Laden managed to resume his activities in Bosnia as early as 1996, a few short months after the removal of foreign fighters. According to a French source, most of the leadership of the SHC supported Osama bin Laden, even though, or perhaps because, most of the funds came from Saudi Arabia. Officially listed with the U.N. High Commissioner for Refugees (UNHCR), the organization is structured like an army: "Hierarchies are clearly defined and rarely challenged," to quote an intelligence agent who managed to infiltrate the organization. At the top of the pyramid is Sheikh Nasser, a very authoritarian leader located in Sarajevo, where he enjoys high-level political support. Sheikh Nasser is a key point of passage in and out of Bosnia. His orders are usually faxed throughout Bosnian territory once a week. But as in many other Western countries, the SHC very often uses the network of mosques at Friday prayers. These orders apply to the management of supplies and the truck transport of the humanitarian aid distributed by the association. When convoys are organized, the locally recruited drivers, who are not paid until they reach their destination, receive instructions only at the last minute. Most often, when they cross from Croatia into Bosnia, drivers are replaced to ensure the confidentiality of the mission and to keep them ignorant of what they are transporting. The personnel managing supplies, on the other hand, is made up of young Arabs that the organization also uses for other tasks; the young men working in supply depots are said to be in reality mostly mujahedeen also used to secure and distribute illicit goods, drugs, and weapons.

The SHC is a powerful organization covering the entirety of the territory of the Muslim-Croatian federation of Bosnia. The cities of Mostar, Zenica, Bihac, Tuzla, Jablanica, Gracanica, and Goradze all have SHC warehouses. It is well established in Sarajevo. It even has locations at the port of Ploce and the airport in Split, two of the most important centers for transit, loading, and unloading. The organization, whose management was close to Osama bin Laden, cautiously manages its cover and scrupulously adheres to its official charitable mission; very significant quantities of dates, flour, sugar, rice, and wheat are located in the various warehouses of Ploce and Split. In addition to this food aid, there is material earmarked for hospitals, particularly the one in Mostar, which Osama bin Laden took care to supply regularly.

According to various sources who have carefully scrutinized the activities of the SHC, it seems that the organization functioned as a logistical base for Osama bin Laden's activities, with the blessing of its leaders or without their knowledge. It has been established that weapons, including mines, explosives, and assault rifles, were concealed in shipments of food and medicine. In order to avoid customs posts and Croatian police inspections, SHC drivers were compelled to follow unusual itineraries to Mostar, traveling in particular on less frequented mountain roads through the towns of Cvirni Gam, Ljubuski, and Citluk. With a network of accomplices paid in cash every time through, combined with clever disguise of the vehicles, the mujahedeen managed to supply their companions in arms. The method was confirmed when a convoy was thoroughly searched; weapons were found in the fifth, sixth, and seventh trucks of a first convoy and the sixth and seventh of a second.

The organization has also taken on the fostering of war orphans since April 1996. Medical material and books have been specially allocated to orphanages. The teaching provided in these establishments devotes a good deal of time to Islam; the young victims of the civil war, disoriented and easily influenced, provide a unique breeding ground. Religious training emphasizes the brotherhood among Muslim countries and particularly the ties that bind Bosnia to the Arab world. Osama bin Laden made regular donations to these orphanages. This campaign of Islamization of the young is very similar to those organized in the madrasas of Afghanistan, Pakistan, and Nepal.

Simultaneously, the organization is intent on establishing a visible presence for Islam by helping to build mosques. These buildings serve a dual purpose: they support a failing economy and they leave "concrete" evidence on Bosnian soil of the faith of the generous donors. This ubiquity is strengthened by cohorts of young men, chiefly from Yemen, Syria, Libya, and Jordan, who are the principal agents proselytizing the unemployed young. These mujahedeen, however, do not venture into any activities that might expose them; it is clear that they have a mission different from that of the ordinary personnel of the organization. They observe the greatest discretion, to the point that they never go on leave and do not go off their bases. When the Dayton Accords came into force, the "Arab brothers" apprehended in the warehouses were nevertheless able to slip through the cracks by means of a vast traffic in counterfeit papers and thanks to strenuous efforts by their political connections. Some even meekly left the country, only to return a few days later with new identities. According to a May 20, 1997, report of the Office of Military Intelligence of the French Ministry of Defense, "the Saudi High Commission, under cover of humanitarian aid, is helping to foster the lasting Islamization of Bosnia by acting on the youth of the country. The successful conclusion of this plan would provide Islamic fundamentalism with a perfectly positioned platform in Europe and would provide cover for members of the bin Laden organization."

According to the Serbian publication *Dani*, this commitment is so little subject to doubt that bin Laden was even offered a passport in 1993 by the Bosnian embassy in Vienna. The magazine was so certain of its sources that it published the document's serial number, 0801888, and its expiration date, September 14, 2003. This is not surprising, because the Vienna embassy was known for its activism in the search for funds.

In April 1999 suspicions concerning Osama bin Laden's involvements in Europe were confirmed by another episode. A report of a European intelligence service asserted that al-Qaeda had provided financial support to the UCK, the Kosovo Liberation Army, and had trained some of its officers in camps in Afghanistan.[14] According to the authoritative *Jane's International Defence Weekly,* documents found on the body of a UCK soldier revealed that he was a smuggler of combatants and that his group was made up in part of mercenaries of Saudi origin, all of whom had Albanian passports.

The report emphasized that the UCK was largely financed by drug trafficking. The distribution network known as the "Balkan Route" was said to bring into Europe narcotics produced by the cartels of Afghanistan with the blessings of the Taliban.

According to the Obervatoire Géopolitique des Drogues in Paris, the UCK had shipped into Western Europe more than $2 billion worth of heroin and cocaine a year. These transactions provided more than $10 million profit to the organization, allowing it to completely rearm before its spring 1998 offensive.

In this way, the fate of Osama bin Laden is indissolubly linked to this shadowy Islamic army and to its criminal satellites, from Pakistan to the frontiers of Europe. One of the original founders of the Islamic Legion with his substantial provision of fighters to it at the time of the anti-Soviet crusade, bin Laden became one of its heirs. Perhaps he was for a time even the sole heir, because he gave new meaning to the combat of all these men, ready for every sacrifice but lacking an enemy. Osama bin Laden pointed them toward the United States and the West, offering them a new crusade. Recall the Air France Airbus hijacked in Algiers by the GIA in December 1994. It was supposed to explode over Paris. In February 2001 the Algerian daily *El Youm* published an interview with the leader of the operation, Omar Chikki. Because the Algerian police had arrested six of its members, the commando group had been reduced to four, explaining its failure and the Group d'Intervention de la Gendarmerie Nationale (National Gendarmerie Intervention Group, or GIGN) assault at the Marseille airport.

6 / The Anti-American Crusade

Osama bin Laden officially identified himself to the West as a terrorist with his August 23, 1996, proclamation of the jihad. Until that date, his focus had been on support of the Afghan Muslims and the general renewal of Islam, but he had uttered no clearly anti-American attack. The August 23 fatwa[1] was unambiguous; Osama had crossed the Rubicon: "The walls of oppression and humiliation can be torn down only by a hail of bullets."

Osama bin Laden was referring to the American forces in Saudi Arabia and was clearly encouraging Muslims to take arms against the Americans. He took a further step at a meeting of Islamists in Afghanistan in February 1998, calling on Muslims to attack American interests everywhere in the world. Six months later, on the morning of August 7, 1998, the American embassies in Tanzania and Kenya were attacked. The explosion in downtown Nairobi of a bomb set off in a parking lot behind the embassy at the corner of Arap Moi and Haile Selassie Avenues killed 212 people (a dozen Americans, the rest Kenyan employees of the embassy) and injured 4,650. The attack in Dar es Salaam a few minutes later killed 11 and injured 72.[2]

President Bill Clinton decided to react by firing missiles on Afghan camps. It should be noted that bin Laden's associate Ayman al-Zawahiri called the Pakistani journalist Rahimullah Yusufzay from bin Laden's cell phone on August 20, 1998.[3] The conversation lasted for forty minutes. Twenty minutes later, the first missiles landed on bin Laden's camps in Afghanistan. The next day, al-Zawahiri called the journalist again to tell him that bin Laden was alive. His group felt so sure of itself that it was not afraid to use satellite telephones, even after the bombardment. According to a source close to bin Laden, he had been warned that the attack was imminent, perhaps by members of the Pakistani armed forces. It is obvious that the Pakistani journalist's phone was tapped. He told me that during one conversation with bin Laden, a third person had suddenly interrupted, asking in English: "Who are you talking to? Who are you talking to?"

In the hours following the American attack, the ISI gave false information to its government, claiming that one of the American missiles had struck Pakistani territory and caused numerous deaths. Pakistan protested, only to retract the protest a few hours later. The head of the ISI, Manzoor Ahmed, was dismissed after this deception. In fact, a few minutes before the missile launch, the Pentagon had sent a secret message to Pakistan to avoid the mistaken impression that it was under attack from India. In the state of Indian-Pakistani relations, such an error could have been fatal, unleashing an atomic alert.

The series of attacks in Africa might have been even more deadly. In fact, according to information made public on October 20, 2000, by one of the organization's militants, other foreign interests in Nairobi were targeted by the bombers of the Bin Laden Brotherhood, including the French embassy and the French cultural center. This information was revealed in New York by a former U.S. Army sergeant, Ali Mohamed, who admitted having worked for Osama bin Laden.[4] He was later indicted for conspiracy and for helping to establish the Bin Laden Brotherhood's networks in Kenya, but the confession confirmed for the investigators that, beyond American interests, Western interests in general were targeted and that the threat was perhaps more widespread than had at first appeared. (See documents 22, 23, and 24 in the appendix, justifying the attacks in Nairobi and Dar es Salaam.)

A few days after the attacks in East Africa, the 375 special FBI counterterrorist agents who landed in Nairobi had a nearly impossible but essential mission to accomplish: putting together the pieces of a puzzle scattered over four continents. They succeeded, thanks in part to cooperation from the Kenyan and Tanzanian police.[5] Preliminary results of the investigation showed that the bombs used against the Nairobi and Dar es Salaam embassies were very large time bombs, containing more than a ton of TNT detonated by caps and small plastic explosives, the work of professionals.

According to experts, the bombs were of "Middle Eastern" manufacture, as evidenced by the fragments of small oxygen and acetylene cartridges incorporated in the device, the "signature" of several explosives experts known to the espionage services. Detonating caps identical to those used in Nairobi were found in Dar es Salaam in the house of Rashid Saleh Hemed, one of the suspects arrested by the Tanzanian police. This demonstrated that a veritable network was involved in the operation, that it was not the work of isolated individuals. The logistics of the attacks relied on financial resources provided by a Saudi bank in Dar es Salaam, the Greenland Bank, and by Islamic charitable organizations in Nairobi.

Another investigation, focused on the Dar es Salaam truck bomb, of which nothing remained but the license plate, made possible an identification of the vehicle on the basis of a few pieces of metal. It had been a 1987 Nissan refrigerated truck, and the explosives had been soldered underneath the chassis. Through the Nissan factory in Japan and the Tanzanian importer, the FBI was able to trace the last owner of the vehicle, one of the bombers. More than three tons of evidence were collected at the sites of the explosions and sent to the FBI laboratories, along with pounds of papers abandoned by the terrorists in their hideouts. The members of the bin Laden network were evidently very bureaucratic or were dealing with a demanding and nit-picking "administration." They kept records of all their transactions, all their purchases, and even their telephone calls.

Luck and chance often help in the successful completion of complex investigations, and the FBI was very lucky. On the day of the attacks, an alert immigration officer at the Karachi airport apprehended a respectable-looking, clean-shaven passenger, carrying a valid Yemeni passport with the photograph of a bearded man. The suspicious passenger had arrived on Pakistani International Airways flight 746 from Nairobi and was traveling to Peshawar. Intrigued, the immigration officer questioned him and, because of his confused answers and counterfeit papers, turned him over to the police. After three days of interrogation, Mohammed Sadik Odeh confessed that he had participated in the Nairobi attack and that he was on his way into hiding in Afghanistan.

Although the Nairobi cell had so carefully prepared the logistics of the attack, it had neglected this point of "detail": the counterfeit passport of one of its agents was badly doctored. Odeh was discreetly brought back to Kenya by the Americans. In Nairobi, the suspect was again questioned by the Kenyan police and the FBI; he resisted for two days, claiming that his confession in Karachi had been extracted under duress, but confronted with evidence found in his Nairobi house, he was shaken and offered a flood of details to investigators, from the setting up of their headquarters in the Hilltop Hotel in Nairobi, through the making of the time bomb in an empty house at number 43, Rundu Estates, rented by one of the members of the commando group, and finally to their departure from Kenya before the explosion.

Odeh turned over the names of his accomplices: al-Owhali, Fazzam, and Fazul Mohammed, who he claimed were still in Kenya, as well as two others: a Sudanese, Mohammed Saleh, and a Saudi, Abdallah, who had already gone to Afghanistan.[6] Odeh even divulged the name of his organization, al-Qaeda, and of its head, Osama bin Laden. He obligingly explained how he helped set up the cell in Nairobi. A Palestinian from Jordan, he had first settled in Mombasa on the Indian Ocean, where he had bought a trawler with funds given to him for that purpose. His fishing business allowed him to provide financial support to the network in formation and to no longer have to depend on subsidies from the Brotherhood.

The investigators had the sense that they were reaching their goal. In the next few hours, some of the four hundred federal special agents who had been combing Kenya for several days searched the addresses divulged by Odeh, including Fazul Mohammed's house in a fashionable neighborhood of Nairobi, where they found traces of the explosive. They also learned that Fazul had been born in Moroni, Comoros, on August 25, 1972, and that he had met Osama bin Laden in Khartoum. But when the FBI arrived, the suspect had already left the premises; according to information verified by French intelligence services, he arrived on Grande Comore on August 14, 1998, on an Air Madagascar flight from Nairobi, carrying a Nairobi-Moroni-Dubai-Karachi ticket, and he left Moroni on August 22 on an Emirates flight, probably for Pakistan, from which he could easily slip into Afghanistan. At the Hilltop, which turned out to be a shabby furnished apartment rented for ten dollars a night, located above a hardware store, the FBI learned that the terrorists had made phone calls to Comoros. This trail led them to Moroni on the track of Fazul Mohammed. But the investigators arrived too late. The terrorist was again one step ahead of them and had just taken a flight, probably via Dubai, one of the United Arab Emirates, one of the few countries that had recognized the Taliban regime. In a computer file found in the fugitive's home, the FBI found various documents concerning his relations with al-Qaeda and particularly a document mentioning the name of Wadih al-Haj, an American living in Texas. This opened a new trail, but the American was already known.

For his part, Mohammed Rashid al-Owhali, whom the FBI was able to trace through the testimony of doctors in a Nairobi hospital who had treated his suspicious wounds caused by the explosion, also admitted to being part of Osama bin Laden's organization and said that he had come from Lahore on July 31 to reconnoiter. His mission was to drive the booby-trapped vehicle to the parking lot behind the embassy and to die on board when it exploded. The attack turned out differently: al-Owhali, giving up martyrdom at the last moment, set off the explosion with a grenade after jumping from the truck. In the explosion, one of the terrorists, Azzam, who had not been able to get away quickly enough because he was covering al-Owhali, was pulverized, and investigators found his remains in the branches of a tree. The buildings next to the embassy, the Cooperative Bank House and the Ufundi Cooperative Building, were also destroyed by the explosion.

Once it had completed its investigation, the FBI issued international arrest warrants in six countries, against Odeh, al-Owhali, Fazul Mohammed, Osama bin Laden, and Wadih al-Haj, for conspiracy in the Nairobi and Dar es Salaam attacks. Cooperation from the South African police led to the arrest and extradition of Khalfan Khamis Mohammed, one of the suspects in the Dar es Salaam attack, in October 1999. This twenty-six-year-old terrorist of Tanzanian nationality had gone into hiding in the Cape region under the name of Zahran Nassor Maulid. Investigation revealed that Khalfan had met the other terrorists identified by the Tanzanian police and the FBI in a house in Dar es Salaam that he had rented in his name in June 1998.

One month after the attacks, the American citizen whom the FBI had traced in the United States, Wadih al-Haj, was arrested at the conclusion of a grand jury session at the district court in Manhattan, where he had been accused of perjury. In a fifty-page document, the grand jury summarized the presumed life of Osama bin Laden and his associates and began its indictment in these terms:

> At all times since about 1989 to the date of this indictment, an international terrorist group has existed with the mission to oppose non-Islamic governments with force and violence. This organization

> came out of the Mekhtab al-Khidemat (the services office), an organization that maintained offices in various places in the world, notably in Afghanistan and Pakistan (particularly in Peshawar), as well as in the United States, in particular in the al-Kifah Refugee Center in Brooklyn, New York. The group was founded by the defendant Osama bin Laden and Mohammed Atef, with Abu Ubaidah al-Banshiri and others. From that date, around 1989, until today, the group has been called al-Qaeda. From 1989 to 1991, the group had its headquarters in Afghanistan and in Peshawar, Pakistan. In or around 1991, the leadership of al-Qaeda, including its emir (or prince), the defendant Osama bin Laden, took up residence in Sudan. Al-Qaeda had its headquarters in Sudan from about 1991 to about 1996, but maintained offices in several places in the world. In 1996, the defendant bin Laden, Mohammed Atef, and other members returned to Afghanistan.

The indictment also asserts that Osama bin Laden had openly opposed the American presence in the Gulf; that he maintained constant contact with many Islamist terrorist organizations throughout the world, including the Philippines; and that he had recruited American citizens, notably Wadih al-Haj, who had become his secretary in Sudan, to serve his cause, carry his messages, and conduct financial transactions. In the second part of the indictment, it seems that Wadih al-Haj was to be indicted for perjury following questioning in the course of which he stated that he knew nothing of bin Laden's anti-American declarations:

> The judge: "When did you learn that al-Qaeda had begun to target the United States?"
> Wadih al-Haj: "In Osama bin Laden's last interview on CNN."
> The judge: "About how many times previously had you heard bin Laden make the statement he made on CNN that the United States was now a target?
> Wadih al-Haj: "When I came back from Nairobi around three weeks ago."

After several hearings, Judge Leonard Sand refused to free him on bail. Wadih al-Haj was detained in the Metropolitan Correctional Center in New York until he appeared before a federal court in Manhattan in February 1999 for a preliminary hearing.

The career of Wadih al-Haj, a Lebanese who became an American citizen, reveals the subtle recruitment mechanisms that are characteristic of the Islamist networks.[7] He was born to a Catholic family in Sidon in 1960. He spent part of his life in the capital of Kuwait where his father worked for an oil company. Against the advice of his family, Wadih al-Haj converted to Islam when he was still a teenager; a Kuwaiti sheikh took charge of his education in the United States until he graduated from high school. Beginning in 1978, he attended Southern Louisiana University in Lafayette, supporting himself by working in a fast-food restaurant. In 1979, he flew to Pakistan to participate in the jihad along with thousands of mujahedeen. In Peshawar, al-Haj was in contact with Sheikh Azzam, the Palestinian who was the chief recruiter for the Office for Services for the Mujahedeen, and this was how he made the acquaintance of Osama bin Laden.

In January 1985, Wadih al-Haj returned to the United States and married a young American Muslim named April, whom he had heard about at the Tucson mosque. It was an "arranged" marriage of a sort, Wadih having written to the family and then married the girl a month later, but the young people apparently really liked each other. They had seven children. Shortly after graduating from Southern Louisiana University, Wadih al-Haj left for Pakistan again with his wife and his in-laws. They all contributed to the jihad: his mother-in-law was a nurse in the Afghan Surgical Hospital and his father-in-law distributed Korans in schools. But the family returned to the United States, and Wadih al-Haj became an American citizen in 1989. He settled first in Arizona and then moved to Arlington, Texas.

In 1991, Wadih al-Haj was called to New York to take over the al-Kifah Refugee Center, a charitable organization located on Atlantic Avenue, one of the main arteries in Brooklyn, whose mission was to collect funds for Afghan veterans. Soon after his arrival, he was involved in a murder investigation; the mutilated body of Mustafa Shalabi, director of the al-Kifah Refugee Center, was found in his Brooklyn apartment. According to investigators, a dispute about the use of the organization's funds ended in a killing.

In 1992, Wadih al-Haj was arrested in Arlington on a bad check charge. In his car at the time of his arrest was a man called Marwan Salama. A few years later, the investigation of the 1993 World Trade Center attack revealed that Salama had been in telephone contact with the bombers. Wadih al-Haj was keeping dangerous company.

In early 1992, he made things worse by going to Sudan with his family to go to work for bin Laden. But oddly, whenever he traveled, Wadih al-Haj always took the precaution of registering himself and his family with the American consulate. Whether out of shrewdness or naïveté, he never tried to hide.

In Khartoum, he became Osama bin Laden's secretary, officially international director of marketing and purchasing. At the time, according to his family, Wadih al-Haj worked for the farms and construction companies of the bin Laden group; he was very active and often traveled to Europe. But according to American investigators, during his stay in Sudan he became in reality one of bin Laden's principal collaborators. He was the point of entry into bin Laden's office, and he managed the leader's schedule. Bin Laden urged al-Haj to take another wife while he was in Sudan, but April, as much American as Muslim, rebelled; she urged him to quit his job with bin Laden, which he did in 1994.

The al-Haj family then moved to Nairobi, where Wadih al-Haj took over the management of a charitable organization, Help African People, devoted to the fight against malaria. In Kenya, Wadih al-Haj maintained contact with some bin Laden associates, such as Ubaidah al-Banshiri,[8] who died in a ferry accident on Lake Victoria in May 1996.[9] Wadih al-Haj was also in contact with another bin Laden associate, Mohammed Fazul. With no known residence or resources, Fazul moved in with the al-Haj family and became Wadih's secretary. Another terrorist implicated in the Nairobi attack, Mohammed Sadik Odeh, admitted under questioning that he had also been in contact with Wadih al-Haj.

Exactly one year before the attack on the Nairobi embassy, Wadih al-Haj was questioned by FBI special agents investigating bin Laden's associates. At the time of the first search of his house, shortly before this questioning, al-Haj was in Afghanistan, officially buying precious stones, an activity far removed from his humanitarian occupations. Kenyan security agents confiscated his computer and suggested to April and her mother that they would be well advised to pack up and return to the United States. According to the two women, this was a barely disguised threat. In the computer, agents found a letter, probably written by Mohammed Fazul, describing an "East African cell" in relation to Osama bin Laden and explaining that its security was threatened. The following extracts attempt to preserve the tone and style of the original document:

We can now state that the security position of the cell is one hundred percent endangered. In this report, I will try to explain the reasons why we feel we are in danger. I will also try to offer my recommendations to our wise and honored supreme commander, who I know understands everything, and we hope he will find the best solution. There are several reasons that have led me to believe that the members of the East Africa cell are in great danger, which leaves us no choice but to think and work hard to counter the plans of the enemy, who is working day and night to capture one of us and to gather more information about all of us. Whoever takes a serious interest in questions of security will take nothing lightly, neither important nor minor points, but will take everything seriously. As we have heard, seen, and read, the haj has declared war on America and that was confirmed when we saw the interview that took place in Jalalabad, in which the sheikh made the following statements: that he was declaring war on America because it had proclaimed itself the world's policeman; that he had had nothing to do with the two explosions in Saudi Arabia but was delighted that they had taken place; and that his future plans would be heard on the radio.

This was in addition to other points which pleased us all, thanks be to God. In fact, the aim of America in this interview was to slander the sheikh in the minds of the American people and to open the way to a new attack.

The same CNN network also broadcast a film on the sheikh on August 10, 1997. From all this discussion, we have understood that America wishes to undertake something against the sheikh or against those associated with him. After that, a good deal of information about the haj and his supporters was broadcast on the radio and published in magazines. We later heard the news that he and his family had moved from Jalalabad to Kandahar; they even gave the name of the village where he is living with his family. We were surprised to read in an English newspaper that America had sent a multinational force of one thousand mercenaries to Pakistan to try to capture the sheikh or Mr. Atef.

From all these developments, we have determined that there is a war in progress and that the situation is dangerous, and that whoever is associated with the haj, whatever his position or nationality, is taking risks. Thus, American forces conduct kidnapping operations against anyone who threatens American national security and American citizens, and we have already seen the case of a Pakistani seized while asleep in one of the frontier villages who found himself the next morning in Washington.

My recommendation to my brothers in East Africa is not to be lax with security and that they should know that they have now become America's primary target, and they should also know that there is American, Kenyan, and Egyptian intelligence activity in Nairobi directed toward identifying the names and addresses of members associated with the sheikh, because the Americans are well aware that the young men who were living in Somalia and are members of the sheikh's cell are the ones who killed Americans in Somalia. Because Kenya was the principal point of entry for those members, they know that there must be a center in Kenya. Ahmed [Tawi] has told me that he would speak to Taysir about changes, because we are really in danger. Our greatest problem is that our security is very weak. I told him that the network would appreciate the changes because we are one hundred percent convinced that Kenyan intelligence is aware of our existence and that in fact our security situation is very bad.[10]

The author of this document had a rather accurate picture of the situation. Two days after the search of his house, Wadih al-Haj, back from Afghanistan, was questioned by the Kenyan police, who repeated the recommendation made to his wife to leave the country. He did so a month later, in September 1997, returning to the United States without trouble; the matter seemed to have been buried. According to American antiterrorism experts, sending Wadih al-Haj back to the United States without charging him was a strategy designed to break up the bin Laden cell in Nairobi shortly after it had been set up.

On their return to the United States, the al-Haj family moved to a suburb of Arlington, where Wadih found a job in the Lone Star Tire Store. The family returned to a conventional life: the children attended a Muslim school, and the family went to the mosque every Friday. Wadih al-Haj was almost an imam in his community, and he sometimes led prayers. He was well respected, and his arrest several months later was so surprising to everyone that his American friends offered to contribute the money for his bail.

Two weeks after the Nairobi attack, Wadih al-Haj was now on the FBI's hot seat, and the Bin Laden Brotherhood began to get worried. The FBI intercepted internal messages in American Islamist circles stating that the American "Food and Beverage Industry" was very interested in the bin Laden networks, a barely veiled allusion to the FBI. On September 15, 1998, Wadih al-Haj testified to the grand jury that he did not know that al-Banshiri was dead; he also claimed not to know Odeh or other bin Laden associates. Accused of perjury, he was arrested and then charged with conspiracy "aimed at killing Americans."

The al-Haj episode is indicative of the importance of Africa in the bin Laden networks. It showed that East Africa had been chosen by bin Laden to hide explosives and to recruit suicide commandos (he had gone to Zanzibar himself in 1992). But bin Laden had not forgotten Francophone Africa, with contacts particularly in Niger and Chad.

In the north, with his Egyptian friends, bin Laden intended to maintain surveillance over maritime traffic from the Horn of Africa. He held the threat of terrorist action over ships using the Red Sea, and terrorists were trained for suicide operations in bases in Yemen and on the island of Socotra. These threats were finally carried out.

In October 2000, another spectacular attack shook the American public. The *U.S.S. Cole,* a 154-meter destroyer launched on June 8, 1996, with a crew of three hundred, put in at the Yemeni port of Aden to take on fuel before sailing to the Persian Gulf to strengthen the forces of the Fifth Fleet charged with enforcing the embargo on Iraq. At 12:15 P.M. on Thursday, June 12, while the crew was on Bravo alert status, the maximum alert level in the U.S. Navy, a small rubber boat loaded with explosives slipped through the fleet of tugs bringing the ship into the port of Aden and crashed into the American vessel. The explosion ripped a hole twelve meters by twelve meters in the left side of the hull between the front and rear engine rooms. The casualties were heavy: seventeen dead and thirty-eight wounded, one of the highest casualty levels for American forces since the attack on the U.S. Air Force barracks in Saudi Arabia in 1996.

The preliminary conclusions of the hundred FBI investigators sent to Aden after the explosion were troubling. The terrorists were well informed about the port's entry procedures and they had set up a plan of attack against which it was almost impossible to defend, with the *U.S.S. Cole* in a particularly vulnerable position at the moment of the attack. The explosive charge delivered by the two members of the suicide commando was at least 180 kilos of TNT. As is often the case, fragments of the detonator allowed identification of the attack's signature, but it took weeks, if not months of work by specialists in police science laboratories to reach a conclusion.

Although the FBI is still very reserved about this attack, the Yemeni police have made some revelations in its reconstruction of the facts. According to testimony from neighbors in the Medinat Ash-Shab neighborhood, where the group's first hideout was located, they did a lot of work on the boat, in particular with a soldering iron. Several weeks after fitting out its boat, the gang moved to the residential neighborhood of Kud Namir, where the police later found residues of the explosive. On the day of the attack, two new commandos came to launch the boat under a bridge in another neighborhood of the Little Aden peninsula, facing the harbor. As they set out on this last voyage, the terrorists oddly asked a twelve-year-old boy to watch their car for a few rials. The testimony of this boy made it possible to follow the trail. The police searched the abandoned car that had counterfeit Yemeni plates and found the addresses of at least five other hideouts and some diving equipment.

A few weeks later, a document published in Arabic, probably geared for Egyptian Islamist circles, revealed that the attack cost between five and ten thousand dollars, emphasizing that the fighters of the jihad had no need to be rich to take on Uncle Sam. (See appendix, document 25.)

Yemeni president Ali Abdallah Saleh at first stated that there were no terrorist elements in Yemen. But Washington's antiterrorism experts already saw the shadow of Osama bin Laden. Indeed, Yemen was hardly unknown territory for bin Laden. He had long had connections there: networks, friendships, and even a few commercial enterprises, often run by Afghan veterans. In 1992 his sympathizers had already tried to blow up a building in Aden housing American soldiers.

There were strong presumptions against bin Laden that would be confirmed by privileged information gathered by intelligence agents in Afghanistan. A few days before the attack, a meeting of the inner circle of the Brotherhood had taken place in one of its centers in Afghanistan: Osama bin Laden, Dr. al-Zawahiri, and Rifai Taha, the organizer of the attacks on tourists in Luxor. Now considered one of the major figures in the Brotherhood because of his dual image as intellectual theoretician and "operational technician," Taha is said to have reminded the leaders of the Bin Laden

Brotherhood that the movement had made no public showing for several months and that it was necessary to consider actions in response to the dramatic events in the Middle East. At the time, the tension between Israeli prime minister Ehud Barak and Palestinian leader Yasser Arafat was extreme, and no compromise seemed in sight, while the Jewish and Arab communities were engaged in violent confrontations on the ground. The meeting then decided on a series of attacks in Egypt and against American interests because of Washington's unconditional support for Israel.

And indeed, one of the suspects in the attack against the *Cole* confessed to Yemeni investigators that he had been trained in Bosnia and Afghanistan by the bin Laden organization. Another suspect, Fahdal Quoso, admitted receiving money from the same network; he was supposed to film the attack for later use as propaganda. The operational leader of the network, Mohamed Omara Harazi, is an explosives specialist.[11] Conversations intercepted from mobile telephones prove that his team maintained communication with the bin Laden networks in Somalia, Eritrea, Kenya, and Tanzania, while at the same time trying to recruit Islamists in Brooklyn. The American judicial authorities have evidence that one of the military chiefs of the Bin Laden Brotherhood, Tufik al-Atach, had in May 1999 ordered Jamal al-Badawi, one of the suspects arrested in Yemen, to buy two dinghies. They were intended to be used as suicide boats against the American warship.

7 / Target: Bin Laden

The most-wanted list of the FBI describes Osama bin Laden as a giant, six foot five inches tall, thin and stooped, leaning on a cane, his emaciated face framed in dark hair; brown-eyed, olive-skinned, with a bushy salt-and-pepper beard. In the rare photos of him in circulation, he most often has a feverish, distant look, head wrapped in a red keffieh, wearing a khaki or brown robe or battle fatigues; he is nearly always sitting in a thoughtful attitude, dignified but rather sad, despite the Kalashnikov rifle across his knees or hanging from one of the stands of a bookcase full of leather-bound books. Even in photos he approved for publication, such as those of the Palestinian journalist Abdel Bari Atwane, taken in his secret operations post, Osama bin Laden projects the image of a martyred warrior prophet, doomed to live weapon in hand for his own safety.

Security was indeed an obsession for bin Laden; he felt seriously threatened, though he insisted that he trusted his bodyguards completely, claiming that none of them would sell him to the infidels. According to one of his intimates, his Stinger-missile-armed bodyguards were looking for a doppelganger of their chief to serve as a decoy in case of an attack; they were copying Iraq's Saddam Hussein. At one point, Osama bin Laden suspected Prince Salman Abdel Aziz, brother of King Fahd, of having offered a reward of $300,000 to three Palestinian activists if they eliminated him. When he learned of this threat, he surrounded himself with bodyguards of different nationalities and put in place a new, tight security apparatus recruited by his old friend Mollah Hafizdin Akhawandi, the Taliban military official. He also relied on the advice of some retired Pakistani officers once close to President Zia.

In the spring of 1999 a Jordanian of Palestinian origin, Mohamed al-Bayid, was arrested in Afghanistan as he was getting ready, according to bin Laden's associates, to assassinate him. Condemned to death by the Taliban, the hired killer was nevertheless sent back to Jordan. In fact, he was a close associate of Mullah Omar, the chief of the Taliban, and the incident created considerable tension between the Taliban and Osama bin Laden. After that, bin Laden brought Gulf nationals to protect him, headed by Hassan al-Shaeri, one of the chiefs of the Rikhor camp in the south of Kabul, where bin Laden himself got his start in the eighties. Although bin Laden claimed not to be afraid of death, before each meal several of his guards had to taste what he would eat.

The few psychological portraits of bin Laden making the rounds of Islamist circles describe him as a rather shy man of few words, naturally grave, who makes an effort to smile. (See appendix, document 1, a sympathetic portrait of bin Laden.) They say he is intelligent and observant, with a sharp sense of repartee. But they also describe him as hesitant, slow to take decisions and to judge. According to these sources, Osama bin Laden is not impulsive; he takes his time, supposedly not because he is unsure of himself, but because he likes to consult the ulemas, which can be complicated for security reasons. This attitude is the source of delays with which he is sometimes reproached. But for his uncritical supporters, his slowness is a sign of wisdom.

Several sources describe the rebel as weakened and ill. According to some he has severe back pain and his spinal column is fragile; according to others, he suffers from a deficiency in white blood cell count or even, according to Pakistani informers, from cancer. But Osama bin Laden betrays none of this.

Late in 1998, Osama bin Laden agreed to be interviewed by the Pakistani journalist Rahimullah Yusufzay from the daily *The News* in one of his hiding places in Afghanistan. (When I met Yusufzay in Peshawar in 1999, he was hoping that bin Laden would contact him again for another meeting.) After several hours' journey through the desert, the journalist met bin Laden in a small encampment of three tents.

To Yusufzay, Osama bin Laden claimed that he was in good health, contrary to rumors. He did not have cancer, he liked to ride horseback, and he devoted time to his wives and his children. Once these pleasantries were over, bin Laden, holding a Kalashnikov in his lap and punctuating each sentence with a blessing, turned to the heart of the matter: "If the fact of carrying on holy war against the Jews and the Americans in order to liberate the al-Aqsa mosque and the Holy Kaaba is considered a crime, then let history call me a criminal."

The tone had been established. Osama bin Laden explained that his work was to increase the awareness of the faithful and that, God be thanked, some of them listened to him. His remarks were anti-American, but he did not lay claim to the Nairobi and Dar es Salaam attacks, merely congratulating those who had carried them out. Concerning the death of American soldiers in Somalia, bin Laden admitted: "God is my witness that we savored the death of American soldiers."

On December 22, 1998, Osama bin Laden granted an interview to another journalist, Jamal Ismail, a Palestinian who writes for *Newsweek*.[1] The Saudi was accompanied by two of his sons but complained that part of his family had been unable to join him in Afghanistan. Again holding a Kalashnikov on his lap and calling on God, bin Laden stated:

> I gave no orders [for the attacks in East Africa], but I am very happy about what happened to the Americans there. . . . If the Americans kill little children in Palestine and innocents in Iraq, and if the majority of Americans support that perverted president, that means that the American people are at war with us and that we have the right to take them as targets. . . . The doctors of the faith have issued a fatwa against any American who pays taxes to his government. He has become our target because he is providing assistance to the American war machine against the Muslim nation.[2]

There was no ambiguity. Like an ancient prophet, Osama bin Laden pointed his finger at the enemy. In doing so, he dirtied his hands only slightly, since he ordered nothing. Nothing in his language resembled a military directive or even a call to arms. He was nurturing his image as a thinker who inspires without giving orders. In that lay his strength.

Often simplistic, as in these two examples, and directed to a predominantly poorly educated rank and file, Osama bin Laden's language can also be more elaborate in order to increase the awareness of another category of sympathizers, fundamentalist intellectuals. Speaking to them, Osama stated: "The fact that the Americans have weapons of mass destruction matters to no one. Everyone is in agreement with the Jewish state having those same weapons. But when a Muslim country like Pakistan tries to defend itself against Hindu hegemony in South Asia, everything is done to prevent it. . . . We do not think it a crime to try to obtain nuclear, chemical, and biological weapons. Our Holy Land is occupied by American and Israeli forces. We have the right to defend ourselves and to liberate our Holy Land."

On November 4, 1998, following the lead of the grand jury that had issued its indictment earlier that year, Mary Jo White, the federal prosecutor in the Southern District of New York, launched a prosecution against Osama bin Laden.[3] The Saudi's anti-American crusade had gone too far. In a fifty-page indictment, the prosecutor accused Osama bin Laden, the head of the organization, Mohammed Atef, and twelve other Islamists of belonging to al-Qaeda. According to the indictment, al-Qaeda had designated the American embassies in Kenya and Tanzania as targets, as well as military establishments in Somalia and Saudi Arabia. The organization was also accused of training and hiding terrorists, of raising funds to conduct its violent actions, and of calling for the murder of Americans.

> On August 23, 1996, in the mountains of the Hindu Kush, Osama bin Laden signed and published a declaration of jihad entitled: Message of Osama bin Laden to his Muslim Brothers around the world and especially in the Arabian Peninsula, declaration of holy war against the Americans occupying the land of the two holy mosques; expulsion of the heretics from the Arabian Peninsula. . . . The declaration of jihad contains statements declaring that efforts should be united to kill Americans and to encourage others to join the jihad against the American enemy.

It took only a few flaws in the mechanism of operations and a few arrests and desertions among agents to permit at least a partial understanding of the functioning of the Bin Laden Brotherhood's structure. As in the Kenya investigation, unexpected and unhoped-for events sometimes enlightened investigators. Around the same time, for example, during a closed-door session, a Sudanese informer, Jamal Ahmed al-Fadl, admitted his involvement in the attacks in Africa and agreed to testify against Osama bin Laden and eight of his accomplices who had already been indicted.[4]

The arrest in Germany of Mandouh Mahmoud Salem, a bin Laden associate, gave some indication of the Palestinian connections of the Bin Laden

Brotherhood. According to Salem, known as Abu Hajar in the organization and considered bin Laden's finance director, the Saudi had already put together the structure of his organization long before going to Afghanistan. His plan of action included using Islamist agents recruited in Indonesia, the Philippines, and Comoros. But behind this ill-trained "cannon fodder" stood the true professional terrorists, former Palestinian officers from the PFLP-GC of Ahmed Jibril. Most of these officers, semiretired because of the advanced age of their leader (who has now retired), asked for nothing better than to return to the fight. Not fundamentalist Islamists but Muslims devoted to the Palestinian cause, they set up sleeper cells ready to take action. In order not to neglect the ideological component important to these veterans, Osama bin Laden then added the fight against the Jews to his program.

Confronted with bin Laden's anti-American crusade, as threats and fatwas followed one another, the United States established a plan for evaluating and countering risks. A veritable cell of investigators began following the trail of bin Laden's transactions through his known bank accounts. They reported daily to the National Security Council in the White House.

The National Security Agency (NSA), established in 1952 and located at Fort Meade, Maryland, not far from Washington, also plays a significant role in the struggle against terrorism. Headed by Air Force Lieutenant General Michael Hayden, the NSA specializes in the protection of American information and communication systems, but it also has the task of collecting and analyzing foreign intelligence. Developing or breaking secret codes and the use of documents in even the most obscure and unexpected foreign languages make up the task of one of the divisions of the NSA, SIGINT (Signals Intelligence). Most communications from Osama bin Laden and his subordinates are subject to detailed intercept reports, particularly calls over satellite phones. The NSA has several thousand employees assigned to the "big ears" in Arab countries who maintain permanent surveillance over the air waves with fixed and mobile listening systems. Filters using keywords make it possible for thirty voice recognition computers to make a preliminary selection from the mass of communications that have encumbered the air waves since the advent of a mass market in cellular and satellite telephones. Words such as jihad, missiles, chemical weapons, or names of people can automatically activate recorders. The messages are then worked on by translators and authenticated by software comparing tones of voice or inflections. Along with these communications intercepts, photographic surveillance is also made possible through Photint (Photo Intelligence) satellites, which can produce a high-resolution image with a precision of a few feet on the ground, depending on the position of the satellite in orbit. These spy satellites endowed with vision were created in the 1970s under the code name Kennan. The KH11 and KH12 satellites rotate around the earth on an elliptical orbit with a maximum altitude of four hundred kilometers and a minimum altitude of two hundred forty kilometers. The advantage of these satellites over their predecessors is that they function in real time, like a television camera, provided they are not blocked by clouds. But each of these satellites costs more than a half billion dollars and the United States has launched only seven of them since 1976. These same satellites helped to defeat Saddam Hussein in the Gulf War. We can assume that they have photographed many of Osama bin Laden's various hiding places in Afghanistan.

In a sixty-four-page report presented on June 9, 2000, Paul Bremer, head of a special congressional committee set up after the attacks on the American embassies in East Africa, recommended that President Clinton shift direction of the fight against terrorism on American soil from the FBI to the army. The report also proposed that all foreign students coming from countries such as Greece and Pakistan, among others, be subject to rigorous checks. As a final point, Bremer suggested that the CIA broaden its recruitment criteria in order to be able to infiltrate terrorist organizations more easily.

The worst scenario that the experts imagined was that bin Laden might successfully launch a missile on Washington, for example. Most existing studies agree that a missile must be detected within five minutes of its launching and destroyed within the next five minutes. Pentagon strategists have in part prepared against this threat on the part of so-called rogue states, including Iraq, Iran, Libya, North Korea, and Afghanistan. The terrorist threat from Islamist extremists is of the same nature as that from rogue states, and the relative ineffectiveness of Patriot missiles against the fairly primitive Scud rockets used during the Gulf War has driven the United States to conceive of more effective antimissile defense systems; these systems are effective primarily for the interception of short-range missiles. A more potent national missile defense system (NMD) that would protect against intercontinental missiles was proposed by President Clinton, but this missile shield would cost $60 billion for two hundred missiles deployed in Alaska and North Dakota. For the moment, rogue states and terrorist organizations do not have the ability to manufacture rockets able to reach the United States, but the Americans have chosen to anticipate the worst.

France, Great Britain, and Germany, for their part, have developed a new air-ground cruise missile that might be able to deal with the interception problem. This missile, called SCALP, has a range of 250 kilometers, follows the contours on the ground, and is guided by a telecommunications satellite. With a conventional explosive charge, it could destroy a missile silo in a terrorist base.

For many Western diplomats involved in the debate on the arms race inevitably provoked by the NMD plan, a question remained: would terrorists resort to using conventional weapons, including missiles, when it is in the very nature of terrorism to resort only to unforeseeable methods or techniques, if necessary calling on fanatical fighters ready to give up their lives to reach their target?

Osama bin Laden in the Afghan mountains.

Osama bin Laden, armed with his dagger. From a clandestine video shot in Afghanistan, 1999.

Ayman al-Zawahiri, Osama bin Laden's right-hand man. From a clandestine video shot in Afghanistan, 1999.

A press conference given by Osama bin Laden (Ayman al-Zawahiri is at his right), in front of a banner proclaiming the Muslim profession of faith: "There is no god but Allah, and Mohammed is his prophet."

Osama bin Laden conferring with members of his organization in an Afghan cave.

Ayman al-Zawahiri, as a doctor in Cairo.

Bin Laden and Abu Atef, the military leader of bin Laden's al-Qaeda organization.

Ayman al-Zawahiri, in a more recent photograph.

Abu Atef.

Ahmed Ressam, an Algerian arrested in Canada.

Sheikh Omar Rahman, the blind imam, organizer of the 1993 attack on the World Trade Center.

Wanted poster in the FBI Heroes campaign, offering a reward of $5 million for Osama bin Laden.

Interpol

7 January 2001

Wanted by Interpol

BIN LADEN, Usama

Legal Status	
Present family name:	**BIN LADEN**
Forename:	**USAMA**
Sex:	MALE
Date of birth:	10 March 1957 (43 years old)
Place of birth:	JEDDAH SAUDI ARABIA
Language spoken:	ARABIC

Physical description	
Height:	1.96 meter <-> 77 inches
Weight:	65 kg <-> 143 pounds
Colour of eyes:	BROWN
Colour of hair:	BLACK
Distinguishing marks and characteristics:	FULL BEARD, MOUSTACHE, MAY WALK WITH A CANE

Offences	
Person may be dangerous.	
Offences:	COUNTERFEITING , MURDER , TERRORISM , TERRORISM CONSPIRACY , THEFT WITH VIOLENCE
Arrest Warrant Issued by:	SOUTHERN DISTRICT OF NEW YORK, NEW YORK / UNITED STATES , TRIPOLI / LIBYAN ARAB REPUBLIC

Interpol's wanted poster for Osama bin Laden, January 7, 2001

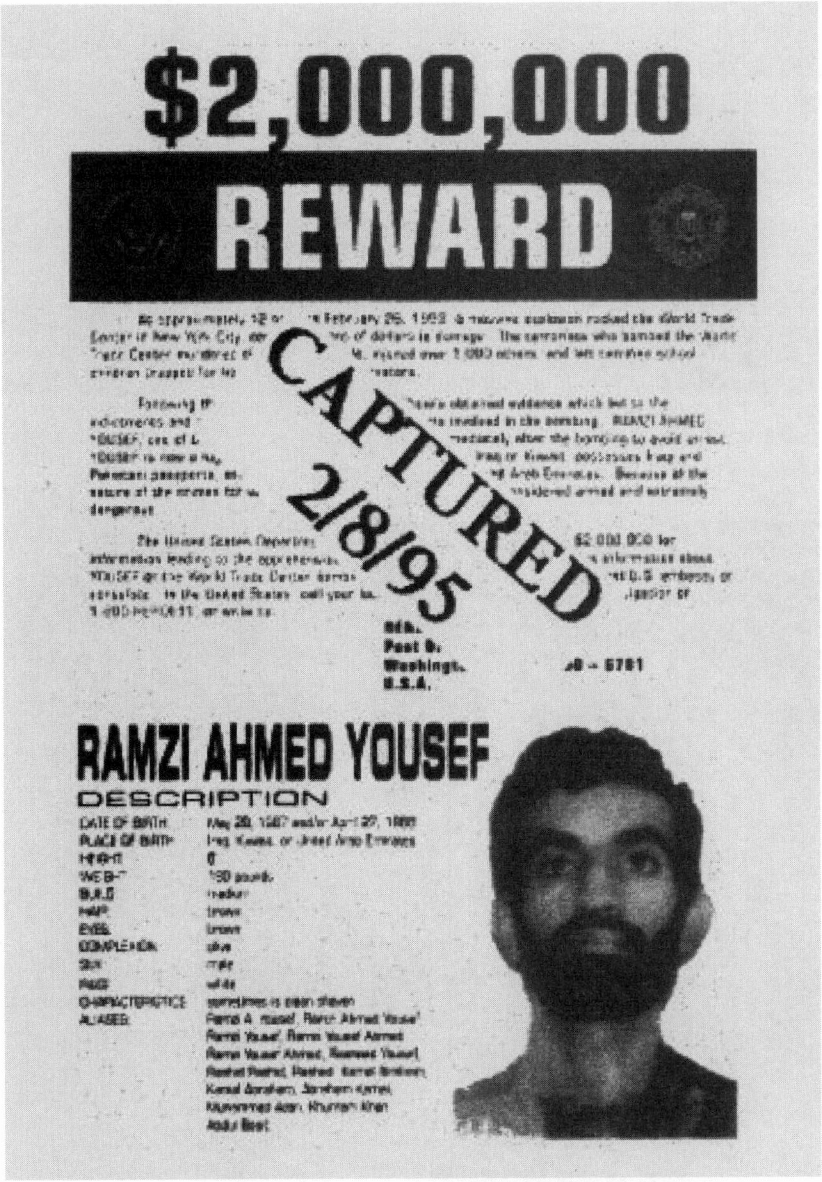

Wanted poster for Ramzi Yussef, who set off the World Trade Center bomb in 1993. He was captured on February 8, 1995.

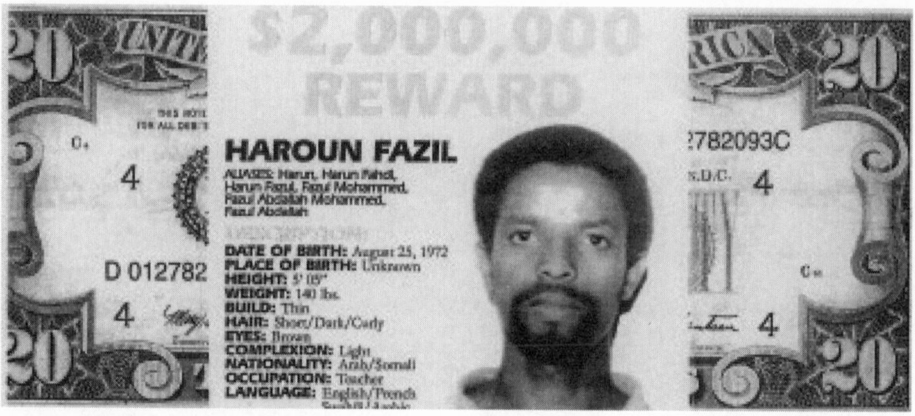

Harun Fazil, who bombed the American embassy in Nairobi. A fugitive.

Wadih al-Haj, an accomplice in the Nairobi embassy bombing, in American custody.

Abu Abdel Aziz, known as "Barbarossa," displaying the head of a Serb in Bosnia.

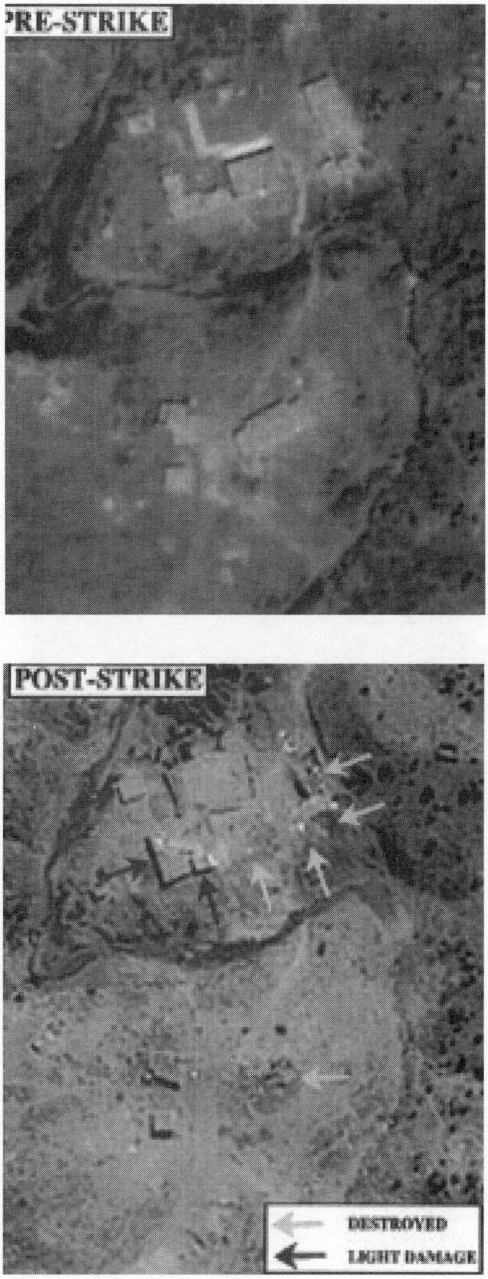

Zhawar Kili al-Badr, one of bin Laden's principal training camps. Photos taken before and after the 1998 American bombardment.

How to fire Stinger missiles: a mujahed in training.

8 / Osama bin Laden Confronts the Arab World

There is no doubt that Osama bin Laden is the chief enemy of the Americans, but that is not all that he is. Seeing him only as a "banker of the jihad" or a leader of the Islamic Legion would be to forget that he is first of all a Saudi, even though he has been stripped of his citizenship, and that he is in addition a particularly virulent opponent of King Fahd. According to him and his associates, his anti-Americanism is connected to what he denounces as "the accursed alliance between Riyadh and Washington since the Gulf War." His opposition to the Saudi government is a particularly powerful motive for his activity. A better understanding of this aspect of his personality would make it easier to understand how and why bin Laden entered upon the anti-American crusade that he considered so legitimate and justified.

As the months went by—in large part because of the increased surveillance of the opposition in Saudi Arabia following Osama bin Laden's flight to Sudan and then to Afghanistan—other members of the Saudi opposition in exile in London, some of whom were very close associates of bin Laden, became his points of contact with the rest of the world. These exiles also began to denounce in the English media the "drift of the Wahhabi monarchy."

The most important and mysterious of these bin Laden emissaries is Khaled al-Fawaz, a short, plump man with a pleasant face and a carefully trimmed beard. Smiling and easily approachable, always dressed in traditional costume, this forty-year-old Saudi, who took up residence in London in 1994, did not speak a word of English when he arrived in the United Kingdom. Today he expresses the thinking of Osama bin Laden in elegant, precise English, and he often does so with great patience and consideration when he makes statements difficult for a Westerner to understand or accept on the virtues of sharia, particularly on questions of justice. Khaled al-Fawaz is a perfect example of a brilliant intellectual engaged in extremist political combat, but one who never gets excited; he never loses the thread of a logical explanation intended to reassure his listeners. This talent is no doubt the source of his success in London, where he has played an important role among Arabs, as well as among journalists and politicians, with whom he has shown himself to be an unparalleled lobbyist and influential voice. From his modest house in the Dollis Hill neighborhood of London, where he lived with his family and where I visited him on several occasions, he repeated and interpreted the latest messages of Osama bin Laden until his arrest by Scotland Yard in September 1998. Given the conclusions of the federal grand jury in New York, his arrest might lead to his extradition to the United States to join Wadih al-Haj, Ramzi Yussef, and Sheikh Abdul Rahman of the Brooklyn mosque. There is no doubt about the links between Khaled al-Fawaz and Osama bin Laden; he himself openly admits them.

Until just before his arrest by Scotland Yard, Khaled al-Fawaz explained that the final break between the rebel and the monarchy occurred in 1990, during the Gulf War, with the arrival of American and other Western forces, infidels, in Saudi Arabia. This "invasion of the Holy Land" by foreign soldiers was, in bin Laden's view, not only a surrender of the kingdom's sovereignty but above all pure and simple apostasy. According to Khaled al-Fawaz, although Osama bin Laden was for a time Washington's ally in organizing the jihad against the Red Army, he now holds an irrevocably negative view of the Americans, inspired by his "horror" at having seen them on magazine covers and television screens around the world bearing arms and trampling on the sacred soil of Arabia.[1] Khaled al-Fawaz, repeating in part the terms of Osama bin Laden's declaration of war on the United States, asserted that never before had Saudi Arabia allowed a non-Muslim soldier, much less a female soldier, to set foot on its sacred soil, as the Americans had dared to do. These remarks were tempered only by the dark humor of bin Laden and his emissaries in Europe describing the American expeditionary force as "a band of weaklings, unable to survive in the desert without bottles of mineral water." In bin Laden's eyes the American provocation was unforgivable and the "betrayal of King Fahd historic."

But Osama bin Laden was aware of the fragility of this argument and that it was for local consumption only inside Saudi Arabia, and even there only among small opposition circles. Moreover, the argument has become stale, now that the American presence has lasted more than ten years and the Iraqi threat is still present.[2] In order to attract the attention of the international media and to attempt to win over Arab political figures, the opposition to King Fahd, which was associated with bin Laden, perfected a more solid presentation based on religious and legal arguments. According to Khaled al-Fawaz, the conclusion to a long analysis was simple: King Fahd had to abdicate.

> The Saudi monarchy has become an outlaw: it does not respect the fundamental principles of sharia. The first example of this betrayal is based on the universal nature of Islamic law; because sharia is one, it cannot be modified or presented in multiple variants. But in fact we observe that the Saudi regime applies different Islamic laws depending on the persons concerned. . . . There is one law for foreigners, one for immigrant workers, one for soldiers, one for clerics, and obviously one for members of the royal family, particularly adapted to its crimes. . . . These various opportunistic forms of sharia exist only to protect the royal family and the dignitaries of the regime, who have constantly been guilty of corruption, theft, bribery, and other offenses, all condemned and punished by Islamic law. This situation is enough to outlaw the Saudi regime: the simple fact that it applies a sharia modified to cover its criminal acts makes it illegal from the point of view of Islam and justifies driving it out.[3]

In order to transmit his subversive message and secure international support for his plan to overthrow King Fahd, Osama bin Laden—having become the leader of the "crusaders" for the purification of the Wahhabi kingdom—had exercised influence through various intermediaries over a number of research and analysis organizations. The most active and visible of these institutions was the ARC, Advice and Reformation Committee. According to its members, this organization, ostensibly advocating the reformation of Saudi institutions, calls for nonviolent and advisory activities. In order to protect the Saudi population from the ferocious repression that would inevitably be provoked by an uprising or even by a mere challenge to the regime, the ARC advocates dialogue, officially. But hidden behind this approach that is apparently respectful of law and order, the militants of the ARC are implicitly urging the most radical elements of the Saudi opposition to overthrow the regime. Most leaders of the ARC are in reality firebrands. To lead Saudis to insurrection, the council of wise men, or ulema, of the ARC relies on Islamic law and the right to undertake jihad. These "doctors of the faith" are categorical: "Two Muslims may have divergent views of a single situation; it is enough that both views equally respect sharia."

According to Khaled al-Fawaz, this reference to theology justifies the recourse to violence, because holy war against an opponent is permitted if he has violated Islamic law. In the name of what they thereby define as a "point of law," the ARC and Osama bin Laden support jihad against a monarchy considered illegal. The "reformers" constantly foster their subversive action by denouncing the privileges of the king and his family and, above all, by challenging his legitimacy. With moderate language and supposedly "scholarly" religious arguments designed to impress their least educated militants, the reformers have maintained a clandestine, loyal network prepared to act according to orders.

Osama bin Laden added to these religious arguments more down-to-earth ones, coming at the end of an astonishing series of calculations. In an interview with a Palestinian journalist, bin Laden claimed that the Americans have been stealing $135 from the Arabs for every barrel of oil for the last twenty-five years. According to him, this swindle amounted to the greatest theft in the history of humanity. Bin Laden calculated that $135 per barrel for the 30 million barrels produced every day in Muslim countries means a lost revenue of $4.05 billion per day. According to the rebel, over twenty-five years, this "theft" authorizes each of the 1.2 billion Muslims in the world to claim $30 billion from America. (During the same interview, Osama bin Laden attacked the leaders of the Middle East "who have lost their virility." He also asserted that Muslim women "would refuse to be defended by American and Jewish whores.")

Without entering into the details of these baroque calculations, it is clear that bin Laden was attempting to establish connections with the claim favored by supporters of the Third World, that Western capitalists have pillaged the poor countries. "To force us to pay interest on loans, the Americans have dragged the countries of the region into a vicious circle from which it is impossible to escape except by the will of God."

According to the ARC in exile in London, the hidden resistance in Saudi Arabia includes several tens of thousands of sympathizers, all armed and mostly unknown to the Saudi security services. According to Khaled al-Fawaz, who was a particularly active advocate for the ARC in the British media until his arrest in 1998, it is a Bedouin tradition to possess many weapons, sometimes heavy weapons, such as small armored vehicles carefully maintained for forty years, antiaircraft batteries, and antitank missile launchers. It is reported that the network of "reformers" is largely and secretly financed by rich Saudis, some of whom are said to be close to the royal family, but have chosen to remain concealed and not to go into exile in order to be able to provide information to the rebellion and to hasten change. The opposition is also said to have means of communication, an intelligence service, and even a criminal court. The entire insurrectional organization is in strict accordance with sharia and entirely devoted to Osama for the overthrow of the corrupt king.

This subversive network, which was originally merely a Saudi dissident movement concerned with strictly domestic political objectives, has become in bin Laden's view an additional war machine in the service of his worldwide Islamist crusade. On the occasion of my last meeting with Khaled al-Fawaz before his arrest in London in January 1998, he explained to me that the struggle of the GIA in Algeria clearly foreshadowed future confrontations with the Saudi monarchy and that the armed rebel groups had carefully studied the methods of the GIA. This statement by one of Osama bin Laden's men in Europe was not very surprising, since it is widely known that bin Laden had always been a passionate supporter of Algerian Islamism. Among other things, he encouraged discreet contacts with GIA sympathizers in London and is said to have offered, at an early point, training sessions in several camps in Pakistan. A very active member of the GIA, Mustapha al-Jezairi, met Osama bin Laden in his Afghan hideout before being killed in April 1997 during a fight in the camp at Jalozai, the result of disputes among various factions.

The opposition to King Fahd thus fits in perfectly with the arguments for insurgency propounded by bin Laden. Driven from his country, stripped of his citizenship, banished from his place of exile in Sudan, constantly under threat in the mountains of Afghanistan where he went to ground, bin Laden learned to use any means available. He loved to spread confusion and cloud the issues. And he managed to do so by combining his battles with one another. By declaring war on the United States and launching his anti-American crusade, he took on the mantle of a Third World militant who was anticapitalist and secondarily Islamist, but in reality he was indirectly attacking King Fahd. By supporting the ARC and its militants, he was presenting himself as a Saudi dissident, but he was primarily threatening the Americans, who were worried about their allies in the Gulf; and as a final fillip, he spread panic. The multinational oil companies have nightmares about refineries in flames and sabotaged pipelines.

By circulating the rumor that he had chosen the GIA as a model of fighting for the Saudi opposition, he threw the monarchy into a panic and led European diplomats to fear the worst; indeed, no Western country would benefit if Saudi Arabia were destabilized. By financing Koranic schools and mosques in Europe and madrasas at the gates of India, he was asserting his will to create sanctuaries around the world for his planned subversive activities. By creating this carefully maintained confusion, Osama bin Laden went well beyond his image as a Saudi rebel; he had indeed created, with the naïve complicity of some journalists, the "Bin Laden Brotherhood," an informal organization much more troubling than al-Qaeda. The danger of the Bin Laden Brotherhood is everywhere, particularly because its agents are unknown, for the good reason that they will claim their allegiance to bin Laden only after their action has been carried out.

9 / The Bin Laden Brotherhood

The major question still facing us is whether Osama bin Laden was the head of a terrorist Islamist universe. If not head of a universe, was he simply the guru of a loose conglomeration of extremist fundamentalists? Or was he, as has so often been said, the banker of Islamist terror? Speculation is rife about his actual role as much as about the real size of his fortune.

In reality, Osama bin Laden was both much less and much more than all that. He was above all the man who revived pan-Islamism, a coalition builder working to bring together Sunnis and Shiis, and the spiritual leader of the "Bin Laden Brotherhood" that has made a name for itself through attempted and implemented terrorist acts. He held no official post as military leader, ideologue, or religious leader, but his influence was real and profound. He demanded nothing, but there was always a fighter burning with the desire to give him satisfaction. He never gave precise instructions, but there was always a mujahed somewhere in the world to obey blindly what he believed to be an order, or even to anticipate his wishes. If we are to believe what he said or what we read in his statements and fatwas, Osama bin Laden never explicitly ordered an attack, but he was always delighted to see Americans struck to the heart, and he readily said so to whoever was listening; it was easy to please him. To give him satisfaction, it was enough to procure a few kilos of TNT and to recruit a few "good Muslims" willing to sacrifice themselves or to live in miserable conditions until they accomplished their mission and returned to anonymity, if they were not captured or killed beforehand. Is any man more powerful than one who has no need to demand in order to get what he wants and whose authority cannot be challenged because his disciples have never met him, and most of them never will?

Who are the men and women making up this army of shadows, who even paid from their own pockets for the privilege of carrying out the judgments of the invisible sheikh? How was what seems to be an international organization of terror established? How were messages and orders transmitted? What was the source of funds, and how were they laundered when that was necessary? The analysis of information gathered from recent episodes of Islamic terrorism in Europe has made it possible to dissect often complex mechanisms and also to understand how and why Osama bin Laden was able to rely on a powerful logistical system that he did not even need to maintain or finance himself, a network that was self-sufficient, devoted, and not burdensome, if not entirely free.

The Bin Laden Brotherhood had two aspects, one in the open, the other in the shadows. Today its best-known face is obviously the one that, under the bright lights of the media, the Western secret services have been studying for months. However, the same information often goes around in circles; a great deal of the intelligence available is credible, although often speculative. But analysts have not yet achieved the precision of the antiterrorist dossiers accumulated in the 1980s on Palestinian or South American movements, or even on Carlos.

The hidden face of the Bin Laden Brotherhood, on the other hand, peopled by tens of thousands of militants, is in essence more mysterious, because most of its members are unknown or clandestine. But, paradoxically, we know more about this second circle, which might be called bin Laden's breeding ground, than about its inner circle, because Islamist organizations have long been the subject of detailed study by various intelligence services in Europe and the United States. And this detailed knowledge of pan-Islamist extremist networks is what makes it possible to fight back effectively.

Osama bin Laden's inner circle was quite obviously very closed. Testimony from various witnesses suggests that it was limited to a number of loyal followers that can be counted on one hand. The most wanted among them, after Osama bin Laden himself, was Sheikh Tassir Abdullah, otherwise known as Abu Afez al-Masri al-Khabir, also known to the FBI as Commander Atef or Mohammed Atef. He is thought to have been head of military operations for bin Laden, a position he is thought to have shared with Abu

Ubaidah al-Banshiri until the death of the latter in 1996. According to American prosecutors, Atef was implicated in the Nairobi and Dar es Salaam attacks. There was a price on his head with $5 million in the FBI's Heroes program,[1] a "patriotic" program encouraging citizens or any informers to provide information to the FBI making an arrest possible.

In May 1998, a few weeks before the attacks against the American embassies in Kenya and Tanzania, one of my collaborators met Mohammed Atef, or Abou Atef, as he was also called. The meeting was organized in Peshawar, Pakistan, in a madrasa. We did not know who he was; we just had the assurance of our intermediary Khalel al-Fawaz, a Saudi based in England, that it would be an "exceptional and interesting" meeting. Today, al-Fawaz is in prison in London for his alleged role in the logistics support of the bin Laden networks, and our interview subject Abou Atef, who was then going by the name of Sheikh Tassir Abdullah, died November 18, 2001, in a bombing raid on an al-Qaeda barracks in Kabul. What did we learn from this former Egyptian policeman, head of bin Laden's security and number three in the terrorist organization?

"Our duty is to struggle against the enemies of God; our duty is to put an end to the humiliation of the people of Islam that has lasted too long." He added later: "America thinks it is strong, that it controls everything, but what can it do, one day, against our young martyrs?"

The message to be gleaned from this is that destroying America, for the fundamentalists, was earning visas to paradise. It also occurred to me, in retrospect, that his statements implied that civilians would be targeted. "Civilians must impose the just cause on their corrupt and infidel governments; otherwise they will be even more accountable," said Sheikh Tassir to my envoy.

Sheikh Tassir, of course, denied American charges concerning his responsibility in the East African attacks. Tassir was in charge of security during bin Laden's interview with the Pakistani journalist Rahimullah Yusufzay of the *News* on December 22, 1998. During the interview, Osama bin Laden even occasionally sought his approbation in answering embarrassing questions. In February 1998, during the press conference at which bin Laden announced the creation of the International Islamic Front for the Jihad against the United States and Israel, he presented Sheikh Tassir as his right-hand man. Dressed like an Afghan dignitary, with a beard and a turban, Tassir had undoubtedly become one of the pillars of the Bin Laden

Brotherhood. Trained in the Egyptian police in the 1970s, Tassir arrived in Peshawar in 1983 to participate, like his co-religionists, in the holy war. According to several sources, he was then in close contact with Abdallah Azzam, the Palestinian master recruiter. According to some informers, Tassir was the source of Azzam's move from the university to militancy. During the same period, Tassir is thought to have met Osama bin Laden.

Perhaps the most prominent member of the inner circle of supreme leaders is Dr. Ayman al-Zawahiri, one of the founders and leaders of the Egyptian organization Islamic Jihad. Al-Zawahiri's profile makes for an unlikely Islamist: the scion of a family of medical doctors on his father's side and a clan of diplomats and statesmen on his mother's, he grew up in the affluent, cosmopolitan neighborhood of Maadi. Like his father, his uncle, and half a dozen relatives, Ayman and two of his sisters followed in the family footsteps and became doctors. His mother's family, the Azzams, is even better known in Egypt and has long-standing connections to the Saudi royals. His maternal grandfather, Abdelwahab Azzam, was Egypt's ambassador to Saudi Arabia; upon retiring he was entrusted with establishing Riyadh (King Saud) University and became its first administrator. Another kinsman, Abdelrahman Azzam Pasha, was the Arab League's first secretary general; his daughter married the son of King Feisal of Saudi Arabia. Well-connected as he was in a country where connections matter, Dr. Ayman al-Zawahiri turned his back on his attractive prospects and became involved in the rising Islamist trend during the last years of Sadat's regime. When Sadat was assassinated in 1981 at the hands of a member of Islamic Jihad, an organization few had heard of in Egypt at the time, Ayman al-Zawahiri was one of those indicted and tried. He served three years in jail, where it is reasonable to assume he was radicalized and embittered, and on his release he left for Saudi Arabia and from there to Pakistan. It was while practicing medicine in Peshawar that he met Osama bin Laden, the black sheep of his own family. According to several Arab and Western sources, al-Zawahiri and his family have spent nearly seventeen years in Afghanistan. After Osama bin Laden, Ayman al-Zawahiri was at the top of the FBI's most-wanted list and for the same charges as Osama bin Laden.

Two other militants of lesser importance, but symbolic because of their connection, also gravitated around Osama bin Laden. They are the sons of Sheikh Omar of the Brooklyn mosque in prison in the United States. Mohamed and Abu Asim were recognized in the company of Pakistani journalists on the site of one of bin Laden's bases bombed by the Americans, at al-Badr, near Khost. Mohamed made no secret of the fact that the arrest and detention of his father would sooner or later bring about reprisals against the Americans.

Two other lesser known figures, Abu Yassir Rifai Ahmed Taha, an Egyptian disciple of Sheikh Omar who is said to have written some of bin Laden's fatwas, and Shawki al-Islambouli, the brother of Khalid, assassin of President Anwar Sadat,[2] are also presumed to be close to bin Laden.

Beyond this inner circle living in hiding, about which information is scanty, police have uncovered preliminary information making it possible to follow the various operational channels among rank-and-file militants. Events of the last ten years have been very instructive for the antiterrorist battle, ten years during which the Western police and intelligence services, including the FBI, have centralized all information available in order to analyze the modus operandi of organizations and individuals to prepare profiles of terrorists, propagandists, recruiters, and useful idiots, a category dear to Lenin, which hard-line Islamists do not fail to use. The following episodes made it possible to make some edifying connections.

The attack on the World Trade Center in February 1993 led the FBI to arrest four Palestinians, one Egyptian, and an Iraqi. Soon thereafter, on the occasion of a second thwarted attempt, six Sudanese and five Egyptians were in turn arrested. On August 25, 1995, in Rabat, the Moroccan police arrested a commando group of French Muslims and hoodlums that had been put together in France to commit a series of attacks in Morocco; the young terrorists had been able to carry out only one of their planned attacks. In 1997 the dismantling of the Islamist network set up by Mohammed Shalabi in the Paris region led to the arrest of several French converts to Islam. The latter had been providing logistical assistance to GIA militants who had infiltrated into France.

With theaters of operation separated by several thousand miles, with militants from all continents and various backgrounds, these three examples reveal that the establishment of Islamist networks or loose associations is internationalist. If we study all the information related to the networks that have been dismantled or are under surveillance in Europe as well as to the attacks that have already been committed, five common points appear clearly. A loose Islamist terrorist association manifests more often the characteristics of a decentralized transnational mafia than the centralized structures of a genuine organization. It is not dependent on a single source of funds and most often generates its own resources. It is always linked to one or more charismatic leaders who are also in its view victims or martyrs. It is violently anti-Western, anti-American, and hence anti-Jewish in its language and is systematically opposed to the peace process in the Middle East. Finally, for the operational aspects of its holy war, a loose Islamist association relies on Afghan and Bosnian recruitment and training networks that supply it on demand with weapons and experienced fighters.

The Bin Laden Brotherhood met these five criteria.

Religious terrorism, based on extremist Islamic militancy, has replaced the political violence of the 1980s, which was based on nationalist or separatist demands, such as those of the Basque Euzkadi Ta Azkatazuna (ETA), the Irish Republican Army in Northern Ireland, the FLNC in Corsica, and the FLB in Brittany, and often on an ultraleft ideology that was rudimentary but coherent, like that of Action Directe in France. Compared to the political lines of the terrorist groups of the 1970s and 1980s, those of the current Islamist movements seem as a general rule to be less well-defined. Because of this ideological weakness, the Islamist universe is far from articulating demands as precise as those of organizations such as the German Red Army Faction, the Red Brigades in Italy, or the Japanese Red Army, all adherents to Marxism.

Islamist circles and the Islamic terrorist international have demands that are as vague as their apparent structures, which does not prevent them from perpetual recruiting. In many Muslim countries, the reference to unquestionable or presumably universal religious values makes this Islamic sphere sufficiently unifying and mobilizing in itself so that its leaders have no real need to specify their aims, and even less to provide a calendar. There are no pending elections, no concrete proposals. The militants themselves generally have no precise political demands concerning their future, except what is prompted by their leaders, notably basic themes like the establishment of Islamist regimes in Arab countries and a total rejection of American culture. They do, however, often demand the release of prisoners, and bin Laden himself has been known to articulate specific demands. But there is no concrete economic or social program that the militants could adopt. The Islamist rank-and-file fighters are, in fact, not militants in the political sense of the term; they have no manifesto or charter defining their objectives, comparable, for example, to the Freedom Charter of the ANC (African National Congress) in South Africa.

Today's Islamist extremists come together around a multitude of religious preachers, who are not all of the first order, to say the least. Through their sermons, these mullahs or imams inspire the acts of their followers, including terrorist acts, but the mullahs are nevertheless not military leaders. They deny their influence and often claim to be unaware of the violence that they provoke, while taking shelter behind the necessity of or the theological justification for holy war, a notion transcending themselves, and one that they could not possibly comment on or judge. This rallying to a sheikh is the source of the fragmented structures and the multiple tendencies that are rooted in a common interpretation of the sermons of a spiritual guide rather than deriving from precise instructions. This vagueness, which is deliberately maintained, is the source of the docility and the submissiveness of Islamist activists.

According to most Western intelligence services, these preachers, who inspire the conduct of the loose Islamic association we have been discussing, but who refuse to present themselves as leaders, now number six: Omar Abdul Rahman, Mohamed Hussein Fadlallah, Rashid Ghannouchi, Gulbuddin Hekmatyar, Hassan al-Turabi, and Mullah Omar. But their number can vary as a function of "persecutions" or an event, such as the unforeseen advent of the Taliban movement arising from a vision of Mullah Omar. One of these guides, Hassan al-Turabi, whom Osama bin Laden met in Khartoum in 1991, and from whom he moved away when he was thrown out of Sudan, has, however, lost influence recently and can now hardly lay claim to the title of charismatic leader.

The most well-known of these spiritual guides is the Egyptian Sheikh Omar Abdul Rahman. (See appendix, document 29, a demand for his release.) This imam of a Brooklyn mosque, who was charged with murder in the 1993 attack on the World Trade Center, is also suspected of having ordered or at least instigated the assassination of Egyptian President Anwar Sadat, although he was not tried on that charge in Egypt. His image as a tired and blind[3] old man behind bars in an American prison for a time invaded television screens, making him a martyr. According to the American administration the sheikh from Brooklyn bears a heavy responsibility; the attack against the World Trade Center represented a turning point in the strategy of the Islamists, who had never before dared to organize an attack on American soil. The FBI was all the more troubled because the principal suspect, Ahmed Ramzi Yussef, was also suspected of having prepared, in Thailand, Malaysia, and the Philippines, an attempted assassination of the pope, which was to have taken place in December 1994. Yussef, who had spent a good deal of time in Pakistan and Afghanistan in the mid-1980s, had been trained by the Philippine Abu Sayyaf group, which maintained relations with Algerian Islamists and with Osama bin Laden.

According to the FBI, at the time, Yussef was planning from Manila a gigantic and unprecedented attack, the simultaneous explosion of twelve American commercial airplanes over the Pacific. Yussef was arrested by the FBI in Pakistan on February 7, 1995. He was living rather comfortably in Islamabad, in a guest house by the name of Su Casa.

On February 16, under questioning by the FBI, Ramzi Yussef confirmed the information found on his computer's hard disk concerning plans for attacks on American airline companies and on Air France.[4] American investigators later learned that the network that organized the World Trade Center attack had also offered funds to two emissaries from the GIA at a secret meeting in Manila, proving—if proof were needed—that Islamist terrorists ignore borders in the name of the jihad.

In 1995, Benazir Bhutto promised the Saudis that she would exercise more control over the ISI, which supported fundamentalist groups. Some members of the Pakistani secret services obeyed: General Rehman Malik dismantled Ramzi Yussef's network involved in the World Trade Center attack. Egypt, however, remains a prolific source of Islamists, Sheikh Omar Abdul Rahman being only one of the many from that country. The principal Egyptian organization is the Islamic Jihad of Dr. Ayman al-Zawahiri, bin Laden's companion, who is known as the professor, the engineer, or the general emir of the Tanzim. Numerous investigations by Egyptian state security, and no less numerous interrogations of Islamist fundamentalists,[5] arrested in various places around the world, have made it possible to disentangle the organization of the movement, which depended on a consultative council of nine imams, called the Majlis Shoura, sitting in Afghanistan and presided by Ayman al-Zawahiri himself, and on an operational council whose members were located in Albania, Kenya, Tanzania, the United States, Great Britain, and Pakistan. Several committees divided up various duties: one for "internal civil organization" responsible for relations with imams in Egypt; one for security, maintaining constant watch on Egyptian officials and Egyptian interests abroad; one for "documents," providing airline tickets, passports, and visas; a finance committee headed by Nasr Fahmi Nasr, a bin Laden associate, responsible for collecting funds; a sharia committee, delivering fatwas and studying Islamic jurisprudence; and a media committee.

These various operational committees in reality had little autonomy and were principally cells executing orders. According to Ahmed Ibrahim al-Sayed al-Najar's testimony at his Cairo trial (see appendix, document 30), the committees were all under orders from Dr. al-Zawahiri, who strictly forbade any coordination among the heads of the committees in order to avoid the muddling of instructions. Orders from headquarters came by courier, fax, or telephone, using coded or cryptic words and phrases, but were also sometimes transmitted at meetings in other countries or during religious ceremonies, including the pilgrimage to Mecca. Al-Najar finally admitted at trial that the headquarters of his organization was in Afghanistan, although he was unable to name its leader. In fact, it appears that the security of the members of the movement was largely dependent on their anonymity, and several internal manuals and circulars explained that militants should never divulge their true identities, passport numbers, or places of residence. They were even prohibited from placing themselves in an illegal situation, for example, by traveling with two passports under different names or carrying secret documents referring to activities of the movement that might awaken the curiosity of the police or immigration services.

According to Egyptian sources, Islamic Jihad had outposts not only throughout the Arab Muslim world, in Yemen, Saudi Arabia, and Albania, but also in Austria and Germany as well as in Chicago and San Francisco. Islamic Jihad's largest training camp in Afghanistan was said to be in the valley of Konar, near the al-Mourabitoun camp belonging to another Egyptian Islamist movement, Gamaa Islamiya.

However, since the beginning of the year 2000, it seems that Islamic Jihad has been divided by a leadership battle, to the point that, according to some reports, Ayman al-Zawahiri has been dismissed or has resigned in order not to embarrass the organization. Some of its members are reported to have criticized his association with the Bin Laden Brotherhood, which had diverted Islamic Jihad from its original and principal purpose, the overthrow of the Egyptian government. Moreover, Ayman al-Zawahiri's opponents pointed out that his adherence to Osama bin Laden's anti-American cause had exposed Islamic Jihad to a manhunt that was unprecedented in the history of the organization. Several local leaders had already suffered the consequences of this fusion, and, under American pressure, had been extradited to Egypt from Tirana,[6] Baku, and Dubai. According to Muntassir al-Zayyat, a lawyer for the Egyptian fundamentalists, Ayman al-Zawahiri had not been dismissed from his position as emir; Islamic Jihad had merely undergone a reorganization. According to him, "Al-Zawahiri's resignation reflected his own objective logic and his decision to take responsibility for the failures the organization had suffered in the last few years."

Beyond these cant phrases, the members of Islamic Jihad may also recall a 1995 incident calling into question the honesty of Ayman al-Zawahiri, suspected with three accomplices of having diverted a substantial part of the funds sent by an Islamic community in New York and by the Iranian Office of Liberation Movements. The four leaders had at the time been criticized for not sending enough money to Egypt to finance the holy war against the regime.

The movement encountered further difficulties with the April 7, 2000, arrest by military police at the Dubai airport of Mohamed al-Zawahiri, Ayman's brother, known as the "engineer," who had been living in the United Arab Emirates since February (see appendix, document 31). When questioned, Mohamed al-Zawahiri revealed details about the military arm of Islamic Jihad, for which he was responsible. He had in fact been at odds with the organization since the resignation or dismissal of his brother and had gone to one of Osama bin Laden's bases in Kandahar, where he was accused of being a double agent and expelled to Peshawar. The "engineer" was reported to have feared for his safety in Peshawar and to have tried to reach Yemen through Dubai, a decision that proved disastrous for him.

Among the religious guides is also the guide of the Islamists of Lebanon, the Shii Mohammed Hussein Fadlallah, head of Hezbollah. Hussein Fadlallah was born in Iraq in 1936; he settled in Lebanon, where he founded the Circle of Brotherhood and the Islamic Legal Institute, some time before 1976. Hezbollah is unquestionably one of the best organized of the Islamist extremist organizations, an exceptional organization that stands apart from all other movements in the Muslim world. "Hezbollah" means Party of God, and the word originates in a verse of the Koran, "Wa inna

Hezbollah houm al ghaliboun," that is, "The followers of God will conquer." On February 1, 1979, this sentence appeared on hundreds of banners celebrating the triumphal return of Imam Khomeini after his years of exile in Neauphle-le-Château. Shortly after the return of Khomeini to Iran, the Iranian Hezbollah was established. In the name of the Islamic revolution, Iranian leaders at the time sought to export the Hezbollah movement to all Shii countries. Thus, in the spring of 1984, Teheran asked Lebanese Islamists to establish their own Hezbollah. This organization very rapidly distinguished itself by the violence of its actions, intended to empty Beirut and Lebanon of all foreign "Satans": non-Muslims, especially Christians, Westerners, and Jews. Whereas earlier attacks had been aimed solely at foreign interests,[7] Hezbollah generalized the spread of terror, sowing fear in the Lebanese population, which no longer knew what militias or factions to turn to. Hezbollah soon found its specialty in Lebanon: within a few months, its leadership perfected their technique of kidnapping. Beginning in 1985, Hezbollah carried out increasing numbers of hostage takings of journalists, diplomats, and religious figures, in order to attract international media attention, which it succeeded in doing. Analysis suggests that around fifteen thousand people, including Sunnis, are regularly subsidized by Hezbollah, with a core of around seven thousand, of whom five thousand are full-time employees. Financially, Hezbollah depends on no external source; its revenues come from trafficking in drugs cultivated in the Bekaa Valley and from extortion of merchants, restaurant owners, and businessmen in its area of influence, whose buildings are often bombed if they refuse to pay this revolutionary tax.

In August 1992 bin Laden's associate al-Zawahiri signed a cooperation agreement with the Iranian Shiis and their offshoots, such as Hezbollah. Thus the Sunni Islamic Legions were secretly supported by the guardians of the Iranian revolution, the *pasdaran*. But conflicts broke out because the Iranians wanted to take over control. Bin Laden nevertheless maintained excellent relations with Imad Mughneyh's group, which was responsible for the abduction of French citizens in Lebanon in 1986. Imad Mughnyeh had been recruited in the 1980s by "Department 210" of the pasdaran secret services, which specialized in hostage taking, and his network had sleeper agents in Europe and in Africa.

Hezbollah has many branches outside Lebanon, with official representatives in Saudi Arabia, Kuwait, and Iraq. There are about twenty organizations reporting to Lebanese movements such as Islamic Jihad of Hussein Mussawi and the Organization of Revolutionary Justice of Imad Mughnyeh. These two groups, open specialists in terrorism, in fact manipulate a whole swarm of small extremist groups in Lebanon, such as the Standard of Islam, the Independent Movement for the Liberation of Captive People (Hezbollah-Palestine), the Organization for Divine Justice, and finally the group best known in France, the CSAPP, Committee of Solidarity with Arab Political Prisoners. This committee, headed by a Tunisian named Fuad Ali Saleh, claimed responsibility for the attacks in France in December 1985 and February, March, and September 1986. It was dismantled by the DST, the French counterespionage agency, in 1987.

North African Islamists also have their guide, Rashid Ghannouchi. The influence of this intellectual has always gone beyond the borders of his native Tunisia, and he has always in some ways promoted Maghrebi pan-Islamism. In 1990 it was Rashid Ghannouchi himself who drafted the platform for the FIS for the Algerian municipal elections. In 1990 and 1991 the en-Nahda movement[8] sent many members to Algeria to support FIS militants in the election campaign. En-Nahda and its leader helped the FIS to establish contact with sources of funds in the Arab monarchies on the eve of the Gulf War.

Another "heavyweight" of Islamic ideology today is Gulbuddin Hekmatyar, the head of Hezb-e-Islami. When Soviet troops left Afghanistan, he became a political and religious leader of the very first rank, even occupying the post of prime minister for a time in 1995. His organization was, and remains, one of the hinges of the "Afghan network" for training Algerian and European mujahedeen. More than merely a spiritual guide, Hekmatyar is also a military leader and a rather accomplished diplomat, with a mastery of the mechanics of opportunistic alliances and reversals. Intent on recovering a place on the Afghan chessboard, he recently established contact with his old enemy Massoud. In 1988, despite his doubts and hesitations, he had already presented the image of an essential leader, in some sense a visionary about the future of Afghanistan, one of the key countries of the Asian continent.[9] After having been long disregarded by the world, including Washington, which underestimated the Islamic uprising and the development of chaos, Afghanistan had become a geopolitical keystone, in particular because of the various smuggling operations that had long afflicted it. At the crossroads of China, Central Asia, and the intimate enemies India and Pakistan, Afghanistan under total rule by fundamentalist Islamists and drug traffickers had become the hot spot that could shatter the balance of the entire region.

Compared to these emblematic figures of the contemporary Islamist cause, Osama bin Laden is certainly not a spiritual guide; he does not have the religious competence for the role and besides lays no claim to the title. But willingly or not, because of his image as a martyr of the Americans and his perpetual flight, he has nevertheless become one of the Islamic leaders able to mobilize all the passion of Muslims around the world. His influence is exercised in a different context. Of all the figures in the Islamic world today, he is probably the most pragmatic and the most political. His language is not confused, and although his statements are sometimes convoluted—particularly when he talks about attacks attributed to him—this is essentially to avoid being accused of having caused them. Bin Laden's battle is not a battle of ideas. He did not just promise eternal paradise to his followers; he also demanded the abdication of King Fahd, the withdrawal of American forces stationed in Saudi Arabia, and recognition of the Taliban government. This appeared to be a more realistic program than the establishment of an Islamic society throughout the world or the pure and simple disappearance of Israel.

Moreover, Osama bin Laden has a well-developed political sense. He sought support and alliances and not only among fundamentalist religious guides. On a number of occasions since his time in Sudan, he attempted to interest political leaders of the Arab world in his anti-American battle, hoping to strike a sympathetic chord in his listeners. According to well-informed Western sources, not hitherto divulged, Osama bin Laden approached Iraq through diplomatic channels on three occasions in 1997. The first attempt took place in Ankara, when a Turkish businessman sent by bin Laden asked to see Ambassador Dahman al-Takriti. Osama bin Laden was eager to inform the Iraqi diplomat that he wished to establish relations with Iraq with a view toward coordinating their efforts "against the enemies of Islam, the United States, Israel, and their agents in the Gulf." Without even consulting Baghdad, the ambassador, who it seems had previous instructions, did nothing in response to the request.

Another emissary appeared at the Iraqi embassy in Cairo in June 1997. Received by Ambassador Samir Najim al-Takriti, Osama bin Laden's envoy, a Somali giving the name of Haj Ahmed Tijani, made the same proposal but supplemented it with attractive offers, including the supply of electronic equipment and spare aircraft parts, in very short supply in Iraq because of the draconian embargo under which the country has been placed since August 1990. Despite these tempting offers, Tijani's mission also failed. The next contact took place soon thereafter, still in 1997, while tension between Baghdad and Washington was at its peak. A Yemeni named Fadel Chaih al-Dalii was sent to Baghdad. He was from a family that had provided a number of mujahedeen to bin Laden's organization during the jihad in Afghanistan. Al-Dalii repeated the earlier proposals and added three new offers: to furnish the names and addresses of members of the Iraqi Shii opposition to the Iraqi secret service, to organize a lobbying network in favor of Iraq around the world in order to raise funds, and to carry on operations in concert with Iraqi forces against Anglo-American interests. This third and final approach was no more successful than the earlier ones. The Iraqis are secularists who distrust Islamists in principle, and Osama bin Laden was not credible because of his ostentatious clericalism; his word meant nothing to them. Qossay Saddam Hussein,[10] the president's son, who called Osama bin Laden an "off-shoot," did not have enough confidence in him to risk exposing the regime to renewed campaigns in the international press, where it was already subject to harsh criticism. Moreover, adventurist cooperation with the Saudi would call into question Saddam Hussein's projected reconciliation with Saudi Arabia.

It appears, however, that this version is only the publicly admissible one, the one that can pass political muster. According to the same sources, there was another scenario more in keeping with the calculating mentality of Saddam Hussein and his secret services. In 1998, after declining all offers that had come to them through official diplomatic channels, those services are reported to have established a secret operational "connection" with bin Laden in Manila and in Kashmir. It was indeed difficult for Iraq to ignore an Arab like Osama bin Laden, who "so effectively humiliated the Americans." Colonel Khairallah al-Takriti,[11] brother of the head of the Mukhabarat, the intelligence services, is reported to have been named case officer for the connection. The arrest of two Moroccan associates of bin Laden in Rabat on November 11, 1998, made it possible to establish the existence of this link with certainty. According to Western sources, the Iraqi services have sought to secure the assistance of bin Laden's networks, in case Iraq were again to be attacked by the United Sates, in order to carry out attacks against American targets in Arab countries.

According to Arab sources, in anticipation of a foreseeable reversal of alliances in Kabul,[12] bin Laden had been in discreet contact since September 2000 with associates of Oudai Hussein, another of Saddam's sons; the ground for agreement was the anti-Israeli and anti-American battle. Bin Laden and the Iraqis are said to have exchanged information about chemical and biological weapons, despite the opposition of some of the Baghdad leadership, including Tarik Aziz.[13]

Another factor favoring the flourishing of the Bin Laden Brotherhood was without a doubt the existence of a powerful Islamist network in Europe. The European public was surprised to learn, for example, that for a number of years London had provided refuge to a number of Algerians, former FIS deputies, Tunisian Islamist leaders including Rashid Ghannouchi, activists from the GIA, members of the opposition to the Saudi monarchy, and very many Egyptians of Islamic Jihad suspected of involvement in the assassination of Anwar Sadat.

The preponderant role of London as the nerve center of this informal Islamist conglomeration should not make us forget that the rest of Europe is for the Islamists not only a base camp but a field of battle. On February 17, 1995, a report prepared for the office of the president of the European Union by the "Terrorism" working group revealed the extent to which Europe as a whole was threatened by Islamist organizations. This group of experts, experienced in analyzing the behavior of conventional terrorist groups such as the ETA or the IRA, acknowledged that the fundamentalist Islamist threat was radically different: "In the Islamic context, the structure is limited to a few spokesmen and media contacts, whereas certain mosques, movements, and even charitable associations are used as a religious front by terrorist groups. Hence, in the absence of a properly political strategy, politics is identified with religion, and activism is seen as a religious duty."

It appears from this document that all Europe is infiltrated by Islamic organizations. The name bin Laden appears in the report as financier of the principal networks of violent Islamists in Europe. After Great Britain, Germany harbors the next largest number of Islamist militants, distributed throughout the country in a community of 2.2 million Muslims, although most of these are immigrants who have no wish to cause trouble. Germany is a crossroads where North Africans and Turks have for several years been developing networks of solidarity and influence in order to share the bases and the logistical resources available to the Turks who have been in Germany for decades. Indeed, in Cologne and Aachen there are groups affiliated with Hamas and Hezbollah and numerous activists associated with the FIS or the GIA, who focus on legal and open political activities. According to German investigators, it seems that Germany—under the cover of propaganda activities—is primarily a logistical and operational base, notably for the supply of arms to the GIA underground in Algeria.

Northern Europe is to a lesser extent a center of Islamist activity. Denmark has a population of eighty thousand Muslims, most of whom are peaceable refugees. There is, however, an organization known for its criminal activities, Gamaa Islamiya, whose membership is essentially Egyptian and Pakistani. One activist has been under particular surveillance by the security services: Fuad Mohammed Talat, who travels often to Australia and the United Kingdom in order to meet other Islamist leaders.

In Belgium, with a population of more than three hundred thousand Muslims, twelve thousand of whom are Algerians, radical Islam is primarily represented by the Muslim Brotherhood. The FIS, the GIA, and the Tunisian movement en-Nahda are also well established, but with small numbers. The most active Islamist network in Belgium is that of Ahmed Zawi, suspected of having hidden the elusive Tarik, implicated in the Paris attacks.

In Sweden, the Iranians and their armed wing Hezbollah dominate the scene. There are also significant centers of the FIS, the GIA, and en-Nahda. The presence of Abdelkrim Deneche in Stockholm was taken very seriously by the Swedish police. Deneche, a former editor of the journal *Al-Ansar*, was for a time director and coordinator of the terrorist networks of northern Europe, and he is strongly suspected of involvement in the Paris attacks.

Holland, with a community of four hundred thousand Muslims, including a wave of recent immigrants from North Africa, the Near East, and the former Yugoslavia, has in the last few years begun to be an area of concern.

Southern Europe contains communities that have been established for a long time, with Italy providing a classic example. The FIS is well established there, as is the GIA, chiefly in Milan, Naples, Perugia, and Rome, and their links have been demonstrated by searches, notably in Perugia in May

1994. The most active representative of the networks in Italy was Jamel Lunici, alias Zubir. Before becoming a leader of the network in Italy, Lunici had set up shop in Germany after leaving Algeria following the cancellation of elections in January 1992. In Germany, after arranging for the entry of a number of petty criminals from the Algiers neighborhood where he was born, Lunici had set up a veritable counterespionage network designed to make it possible to unmask officers of Algerian Military Security who were trying to infiltrate his organization. Depending on his audience, Lunici often changed identity, becoming in turn Salah Mustapha, Bengacem Labyed, or Whadduh Jamal. Holding a valid Italian residence permit and wanted by the police of four countries, Lunici was living discreetly south of Milan, at 62 via Trento, a middle-class street in Porto Morone. His principal responsibility was the purchase of weapons, communications equipment, and medicine, all of which were transported to Algeria through Morocco. At the time he specialized in purchasing military equipment from the Red Army, widely available in Germany. According to Judge Jean-Louis Bruguière, Jamel Lunici had become the head of the operational network of the GIA in Europe. As the result of an Interpol warrant, Lunici was arrested on November 1, 1994, following a complaint from Morocco, which had established his responsibility for an arms shipment intercepted at Oujda on the Algerian border. At the time of his arrest, Lunici was supplying weapons to the Algerian guerrilla forces of Rabah Kebir, one of the leaders of the FIS outside the country, and his associate Abassi Osama, son of the FIS leader Abassi Madani, still under house arrest in Algiers.

Jamel Lunici's arrest in Italy, however, did not destroy the network. Another, entirely official, organization took over the operation: the Islamic Cultural Institute, situated on viale Jenner in Milan and headed by an Egyptian, Anwar al-Sayed Shaabane, an associate of Gulbuddin Hekmatyar. Supported by funds coming from Kuwaiti and Saudi banks, this organization had regular contact with Islamists of the Egyptian Gamaa Islamiya, who sent to it all their communiqués claiming responsibility for attacks in Egypt. Taps on one of the institute's telephones carried out by the Italians also revealed that one of the leaders of the Islamic center was in regular contact with Sheikh Omar of the Brooklyn mosque before his arrest.

In early January 2001 Algerians led by a certain Abu Doha, intended to use a car bomb to blow up the American embassy in Rome; the embassy and U.S. consulates in Italy suddenly closed their offices for two days, and NATO bases were placed on maximum alert.

In mid-February 2001 an Algerian network of the Salifiya Movement of Preaching and Combat of Hassan Hattab, said to be the successor of the GIA, was dismantled in London, while at the same time a network was on trial in Paris for burglaries committed in northern France and for forging counterfeit papers for veterans of Afghanistan and Bosnia. One of the accused, Fatah Kamel, was in contact with bin Laden and had been one of his agents in Canada.

Around the middle of the 1990s members of the Italian network established close ties with Switzerland for obvious reasons having to do with banking, according to experts. Islamist militants in Switzerland long relied on Murad Dhina, an atomic physicist employed by CERN, the European Center for Nuclear Research, until 1994. A search by the French judicial police of Dhina's residence in Saint-Genis-Pouilly in the department of Ain, while he was in Sudan, turned up a number of compromising documents. On his return from Khartoum, Dhina took refuge in Switzerland, where he disappeared. The arrest of his correspondent in Italy, Jamel Lunici, did not lead to his discovery. Dhina chose Switzerland probably because he thought that the country had a lenient attitude toward Islamists. It is true that Switzerland has long welcomed Islamic organizations. The Islamic Center of Geneva, for example, was opened in 1961 on the initiative of Dr. Sayed Ramadan, son-in-law of Hassan al-Banna, the founder of the Muslim Brotherhood in 1945. Except for the center in Munich, the international center in Geneva was for thirty years the only platform for the Brotherhood in Europe.

This tour of the Europe of Islamist networks gives some sense of the loose collection of organizations, some of whose members were at the disposal of Osama bin Laden. It does not take into consideration the former East-bloc countries where radical Islamists are also established, but where it is still difficult to uncover credible information.

The Bin Laden Brotherhood thus had fertile soil in Europe, and it appears that nothing that happened in fundamentalist Islamist circles, in Palestinian movements, among former terrorist groups close to the PLO, or in the secret services of several countries in the Arab world was totally removed from Osama bin Laden and his Brotherhood. Although they may have been informal, the contacts were nonetheless real and the risks no less considerable.

For example, in late 2000, in addition to chemical products and documentation on explosives, the German antiterrorist services seized a videocassette in one of the two apartments shared by four Salafiya Islamists in Frankfurt. Lasting twelve minutes and accompanied by mujahedeen music, it showed the cathedral and the Christmas market in Strasbourg. The leader of the group was an Algerian born in the French town of Romans in the Drôme department in the 1970s, Fuad Sabur. Judge Jean-Louis Bruguière had identified him in 1995 as an important member of the logistical networks of the GIA in Lyon and Saint-Étienne. He was responsible for distributing the *Al-Ansar* newsletter in the Marseille region when he was arrested there in 1996. But he was released before trial. He disappeared, reached a bin Laden training camp in Afghanistan, and then returned to Germany. One of his three subordinates had counterfeit English papers, while the two others had counterfeit French documents.

The DST also established that this group was linked to Abu Doha, who was implicated in anti-American threats in Italy. He was also supposed to shelter Ahmed Ressam after his attacks in the United States but was prevented from doing this by Ressam's arrest in December 1999.

In late June 2001, Mohamed Bensakhria, an Algerian bin Laden associate, was arrested in Alicante, Spain. In mid-July, he was extradited to Paris for his participation in preparing the attack on Strasbourg.

10 / Asian Fever

Intelligence services have recently been working on a troubling hypothesis: it seems that Osama bin Laden had managed to establish some bridgeheads of his Brotherhood in China, Southeast Asia, and the former Soviet Islamic republics. China is not so far from Afghanistan, and the two countries do in fact share a small border; several of bin Laden's emissaries are said to have already gone to the region, also known as Eastern Turkistan,[1] to urge the Uygur Muslims to express their hostility to Beijing and imitate the Muslims of the former Soviet Union by demanding their independence. The Uygur, Kazakh, Kirghiz, Uzbek, Tatar, and Hwei[2] Muslim minorities have paid some attention to separatist views, in light of the discrimination they feel they have suffered. In fact, considering themselves to have been overlooked in the economic development that has benefited the coastal provinces, the Muslim Chinese are currently tempted to establish ties with their Pakistani and Afghan neighbors. In late August 1999 the Chinese security services arrested twenty armed Uygur militants who were in the process of setting up a logistical network in preparation for attacks to be carried out at ceremonies celebrating the fiftieth anniversary of the establishment of the People's Republic on October 1. After this incident, the Chinese asked the Taliban to bar Osama bin Laden from providing further training for Uygur separatists in his camps. According to a Western source who spent more than a month in Afghanistan, it is a fact that two military camps headed by a certain Tahar Jan were devoted exclusively to the training of Chinese Islamists. According to the same informant, however, the Taliban were engaged in a high-risk game in their relations with China, because they had turned over three unexploded U.S. cruise missiles to China in return for a demining operation. But the demining work had not yet begun, and the Beijing authorities perhaps had some difficulty in accepting the Taliban's double-dealing.

If bin Laden's agitators manage to fan the flames of the Chinese situation, notably by making financial contributions, they would seriously embarrass the Chinese government, because Xinjiang Uygur is a strategic region containing large oil reserves, not to mention the nuclear testing center of Lop Nur.

The problem is all the more troubling to Beijing because, with at least 35 million Muslims (150 million according to religious sources), China has the twelfth largest Muslim population in the world.[3] Moreover, Muslims of neighboring countries, Tajikistan, Kirghizstan, Kazakhstan, and Pakistan, have provided discreet but effective support to Chinese rebel Muslim movements along a not very well guarded border. In order to stifle the Muslim separatists, China has decided to encourage the Uygur Muslims to emigrate to Kazakhstan, while simultaneously implementing an authoritarian policy of Han colonization, given the name "national transmigration." The relatively underpopulated Kazakhstan, with 17 million inhabitants, would gain more than a million people, a perspective that the authorities consider rather attractive. Since 1993, moreover, Kazakhstan has permitted the Uygur separatists to maintain official representation in the capital, Alma Ata, which Beijing obviously considers as interference in internal Chinese affairs, even though the danger of an implosion in China because of a Muslim uprising is very remote.

For its part, in Russia, the FSB, successor to the KGB, has been determined to limit the influence of the Islamists, and particularly the Taliban, in Central Asia (an indication that the risk is not negligible). The head of the Russian foreign intelligence service, Sergei Lebedev, with the assistance of the Shanghai Five group, bringing together the secret services of Russia, China, Tajikistan, Kazakhstan, and Kirghizstan, intends to make life difficult for the Uygur Islamist rebels. Osama bin Laden and his advisers had obviously analyzed the situation and discovered in this region of western China a new target worthy of their ambitions.

Other Asian nations besides China were also in bin Laden's sights. Malaysia, Thailand, and the Philippines were possible targets. Malaysia was particularly promising; Islam has been the state religion there since 1967. As in China, Islam was introduced to Malaysia by merchants. Generally speaking, as an active member of the International Islamic Conference, Malaysia presents itself as a defender of Islam, for example contributing soldiers to the peacekeeping forces in Bosnia. A particularly powerful religious movement, al-Arqam, with about one hundred thousand supporters, has agitated for application of sharia and called for the establishment of Islamic regimes throughout Southeast Asia. This extremely wealthy organization (it has reportedly collected more than $120 million in voluntary contributions) gave rise to a special meeting of the ministers of religious affairs of the Association of Southeast Asian Nations (ASEAN) countries.[4] Following this meeting, al-Arqam, whose relations with the Egyptian Muslim Brotherhood had been uncovered, was banned in Malaysia. Since that date, the members of al-Arqam, deprived of organizational structure, have been acting as mavericks and provide a breeding ground of activists without a cause for the Bin Laden Brotherhood's recruiters.

Another country at risk is Indonesia, the country with the largest Muslim population in the world. In the early twentieth century, Islam was a driving force behind Indonesian nationalism and the rejection of Dutch colonialism. It is thus an unavoidable reality in the country, even though Sukarno, the father of independence, set forth the principles of a secular state in the 1930s. But since the Iranian revolution, an Islamic revival has made progress among the lower classes; the imams have been delivering more aggressive sermons and more and more women have been wearing the veil. The Gulf War of 1990 and 1991 amplified this Islamic revival, and the government began to make concessions to Islamists. In 1991, for example, President Suharto made the pilgrimage to Mecca, and in 1994 the wearing of the veil was authorized in schools, where the teaching of Islam became obligatory, even in Christian schools. These numerous signs and the flourishing of Islamic associations have led observers to think that Indonesia is running the risk of gradually sliding into fundamentalism. Finally, the Malaysian al-Arqam, banned in its country of origin, has established militant networks on Sumatra, notably in Aceh, an area of northwestern Sumatra with a large Muslim population that is calling for independence.

Thailand is another country with a significant Muslim community (nearly three million believers); it presents fewer risks of fundamentalist upheaval, but there are nevertheless problems posed by the Muslims concentrated in the south of the country. The four provinces of Pattani, Yala,

Satun, and Narathiwat have been shaken by endemic civil war demanding the liberation of Pattani, an old Muslim kingdom once dependent on Siam and now demanding to be joined to the Malaysian state of Kelantan, governed by the Malaysian Islamist party. These four provinces, 90 percent of whose population is Muslim, have a large network of mosques and Koranic schools. The Pattani United Liberation Front (PULO)[5] takes orders from and has headquarters in Mecca in Saudi Arabia and Kelantan in Malaysia. The organization has its own training camps, which members of the Bin Laden Brotherhood have passed through on several occasions.

The Philippines, finally, presents a problem with the Moro community. They number five million, around 8 percent of the population, and live in the southwestern part of the country. Some of them have demanded an independent state, but presently, the real crisis is the one opposing the army to the Abu Sayyaf rebel group, which has presented itself as a fundamentalist movement. This movement, hiding behind an extremely rudimentary political discourse and ill-defined objectives, focuses rather on organized crime activities, ranging from hostage taking to drug trafficking, with revenues of a billion dollars a year from the transport of marijuana alone through the islands of Jolo and Basilan. The group was said to be distantly and historically related to the Moro National Liberation Front that had fought for an independent Islamic state in the 1970s, but most of the members of the front, now carrying on negotiations with the Philippine government, do not recognize themselves in the extremist language and actions of the Abu Sayyaf group. Relations of the group with the Bin Laden Brotherhood were established by several events, including the case of Ramzi Yussef, who had spent time in the Abu Sayyaf guerrilla organization. But it seems that the group was heavily infiltrated by the Libyan and Philippine secret services in 1999, leading the Bin Laden Brotherhood to keep its distance and even to break off all relations with the group. The subsequent hostage takings may very well have been a means for the Jolo rebels to attempt to patch things up with Osama bin Laden by trying to show themselves to be effective partners.

If that was their purpose, the attempt of the Abu Sayyaf group must have borne fruit. On June 27, 2000, a French citizen of Algerian origin, Abdessalem Boulanwar, was taken into custody and interrogated by the DST. He had recently been deported from the Philippines, where he had been arrested on December 16, 1999 in possession of a manual on urban guerrilla warfare and a "component of an explosive charge." He was suspected of being in contact with the Afghan Algerians, bin Laden, and the Moro Islamic Liberation Front, an armed group calling for the independence of the southern Philippines. And on May 29, 2000, the head of the Moro Islamic Liberation Front stated on the German television network ZDF that it was receiving financial support from bin Laden. The following August, the Philippine intelligence services (already busy with tracking down Alfred Sirven, the covert financier of Elf, France's largest industrial company), was investigating possible ties between bin Laden and Gemma Cruz Araneta, the minister of tourism. She was suspected of contacts with the IIRO (International Islamic Relief Organization). According to the Philippine *Daily Inquirer* of April 15, 2000, under humanitarian cover, the IIRO made it possible for bin Laden associates to finance the operations of the Moro Islamic Liberation Front.

Although no real threat of Islamic destabilization is to be feared in these Asian countries, in which the problems specific to the Arab world have trouble making headway among the lower classes, there is some risk that some Muslims in Southeast Asia may prove susceptible to recruitment by fundamentalist Islamists always in search of helping hands to organize attacks or transport drugs.

Another hot spot lies in the Caucasus region of Chechnya. Osama bin Laden began moving his pawns there by providing discreet aid to the Islamist separatists. The crisis is not a new one; the Chechens have been in conflict with Moscow since the late eighteenth century. The conflict has opposed a centralizing government perceived as brutal with a population determined to preserve its cultural differences. Further complicating relations with the Moscow government, the Chechens are Sufi-influenced Sunnis and were Islamized over the course of centuries by their neighbors in Daghestan.

On October 27, 1991, a Chechen nationalist movement that had come into existence in the 1980s swept aside the Kremlin authorities. Under the impetus of a young nationalist general of the Soviet Army, Jokhar Dudayev, head of the National Congress of the Chechen People, legislative and presidential elections were organized. Dudayev won by a large margin and on October 27, 1991, Chechnya unilaterally declared independence. Grozny's secessionist move was rejected by Moscow. The authorities, who were still Soviet at the time, sent the "Chechen criminals" barely disguised threats of retaliation and declared the October 27 elections illegal. On November 7 Boris Yeltsin proclaimed a state of emergency in Grozny and sent a force of two thousand men. Two days later, in the face of an extraordinary mobilization of the population, which set up anti-Soviet militias and called for holy war against the occupier, the Kremlin retreated. On November 9 the Duma lifted the state of emergency and Russian troops went back across the border. The conflict between Moscow and Grozny had just begun; the rebel Republic of Chechnya refused to adhere to the Russian Federation treaty signed on March 31, 1992. But Dudayev, who very rapidly sank into dictatorship and nepotism, had the greatest difficulty in controlling a country governed by mafias and competing clan interests. A prerevolutionary atmosphere took hold by July 1994, and factional conflict led to a failed coup attempt against Dudayev's regime on November 26, 1994.

In Moscow's view, the crisis had become too serious, and on December 11, 1994, a Russian armored division (thirty thousand men, 230 tanks, and 450 armored vehicles) crossed over the Chechen border. The Russians claimed that this was not an invasion, but "an operation to disarm factions." The Chechens responded with a militia forty-five thousand strong. The culminating point of the fighting was the battle of Grozny, from December 1994 to February 1995, preceded by Russian bombing raids and artillery strikes. The fall of Grozny and the destruction of the city by the Russian forces had a disastrous effect on the morale of Russian troops and on public opinion.[6] But the secessionist rebels were neither crushed nor discouraged; civil war resumed in the countryside. Far from being decapitated by the death of its leader (Dudayev was assassinated on April 21, 1996), the rebellion developed such strength that the Kremlin had to send the popular general Alexander Lebed to negotiate with the separatists. The negotiations ended with the withdrawal of the defeated Russian army and a promise of reparation for the damage inflicted on Grozny.

But the defeat of Moscow did not signal the end of the war. Five years later, in July 2001, with the second battle of Grozny, which had begun on September 5, 1999, the Russian army was still bogged down in Chechnya. Once again challenging the legitimacy of the independent Chechen republic and determined to put a definitive end to "Chechen terrorism," the Russians had launched a new heavy offensive in the Caucasus. The Russian army, which had drafted more than eighty thousand men, planned this time to use against the rebels new bombs dropped from Sukhoi-27 aircraft that were adapted for urban fighting. This new technology, called FAE (fuel air explosive), consists of creating a blast effect and a column of heat by means of the combustion of a cloud of gas sprayed in the atmosphere. These explosives were also fired by Metis-M and Kornet antitank missiles and Shmel mobile rocket launchers modified for the purpose.

If Moscow took the risk of committing its elite units and using the kinds of weapons that could not fail to provoke very critical international reactions, we must conclude that the Russians were deeply concerned by the Chechen situation, insofar as the example of this small rebel republic could spread, to neighboring Daghestan, for example.[7]

Against a background of holy war against the Russian occupier, the Chechen crisis bore a good deal of resemblance to the Afghan crisis of the 1980s: the Russian army was humiliated by a Muslim resistance. Indeed, most Arab countries sent mujahedeen to Grozny, an action denounced by Russia, which called this foreign assistance direct interference in internal affairs. Clear messages were sent to Pakistan and to several Gulf countries. The Kremlin was right to be worried, because the Pakistani extremist fundamentalist group al-Badr, led by Emir Bakht Zamin Khan, had recently exhorted the Islamic nation in the broadest sense to send military forces to fight beside the Chechens. Moscow, moreover, recently established a list of more than twenty Arab and Islamist charitable associations that have provided financial support to the separatists since the beginning of the conflict. Russian intelligence services include the Bin Laden Brotherhood among those organizations and remain fearful of attacks on Russian soil like the one of August 8, 2000 (twelve killed and one hundred wounded), in an underground passage on Pushkin Square in Moscow. Even though Chechen president Aslan Maskhadov asserted that the attack had not been ordered by Chechnya, Russian secret services have few doubts about the involvement of the separatists.

Russian and Western intelligence services are vigilant, but like Afghanistan in the 1980s, the distant islands of the Philippine archipelago or of Malaysia, Xinjiang Uygur, Daghestan, and Chechnya are areas sometimes undermined by endemic conflicts punctuated by explosions of violence. It does not seem difficult for the men of the Bin Laden Brotherhood or like-minded agitators to lay their foundations there while patiently awaiting the propitious moment to activate their networks. This is all the more the case since Islamists launched offensives in the fall of 2000 to seize control of the drug routes in Central Asia. In Uzbe-kistan, the Islamist leader Jumaboi Namangani is said to have received instruction and modern weapons from bin Laden, in return for which he attempted to supply bin Laden with chemical and biological weapons coming from the former Muslim republics of the Soviet Union. Reportedly, he had also offered a fallback base in the valley of the Fergana, in case "Brother Osama" needed a refuge outside Afghanistan.

11 / The Bin Laden Network's Billions

Once we have analyzed why an Islamic network was able to emerge from the void and how it is able to forge international alliances, the question arises as to how they go about it, particularly how these internationalist militants go about financing their activities.

In becoming one of the heads of the Islamic Legion, Osama bin Laden also inherited the title of financier of international Islamic terrorism. For several years his fortune has been the subject of interminable speculation. Osama bin Laden is without a doubt a wealthy man. His father had become head of the largest construction business in Saudi Arabia, a fortune built according to the American press "by recycling petrodollars into construction." Today, the bin Laden family is still in control of a fortune estimated at more than $5 billion, and in the 1990s, the personal holdings of Osama bin Laden were assessed at $300 million. According to his detractors, he made his personal fortune in part through the "solidarity funds" that he was in charge of at the time he controlled the network of Afghan Arabs on behalf of the Saudi secret services. These funds were made up in large part of money allocated for the Afghan resistance by the West and the Gulf monarchies.

Osama bin Laden is still unquestionably wealthy but probably much less so than in the past. Well-informed sources credited him with $800 million in liquid funds at the time of his exile, not to mention his real estate and industrial investments, perhaps not all of which were convertible into cash. His sudden flight from Sudan is said to have cost him more than $150 million, with the renting of a plane (a Hercules), the surrender of claims on uncompleted contracts in Khartoum, the hasty liquidation of his real estate holdings, and the costs of setting up residence in Afghanistan. Some of his associates are even said to have complained of not having been fully paid by the Sudanese government for certain construction projects, an assertion challenged in business circles in Khartoum. According to some sources in Islamic circles in London, the largest bone of contention has to do with payment for the Tahaddi (the Challenge) road between Shandi and Port Sudan, assessed at $200 million.

However, an anecdote reveals the extent to which, although Osama bin Laden is an astute businessman, he is capable of spending his fortune in an unbusinesslike manner. According to Pakistani sources, his capital made it possible for him to bid against the American secret services. For example, Osama bin Laden had been trying for some time to buy Stinger missiles that were distributed to the Afghan resistance in the 1980s. In fact, since 1998 there had been a race between him and the Pentagon, which was trying to recover all the missile launchers. If the American military offered $100,000 for a Stinger, Osama bin Laden would offer twice that. The Americans were obviously afraid that the missiles would be used against American or Western targets.[1]

Are the significant funds still at the disposal of Osama bin Laden carefully concealed in the complexities of the accounts of many shell corporations, such as Asma United, known under the name of Mira? Are several charitable organizations identified by the American intelligence services—the al-Rahma agency, the al-Haramein based in London, the al-Muwafak based in the Balkans, the Islamic Resurrection Foundation, and the Islamic Revival Foundation, headed by an Albanian—bin Laden financial arms? Negotiations are said finally to have begun with the Sudanese government with a view to seizing bin Laden's assets in Sudan. According to other reports emanating from Arab bankers, Osama bin Laden also placed funds in safety in banks in the sultanate of Brunei and even in some European establishments. The latter deposits are reported to have been arranged by one of the colleagues of the former head of the Arab Banking Corporation.[2] According to the intelligence services of the Arabian peninsula, more than $750 million belonging to Osama bin Laden is still in short-term accounts in several financial markets. In August 1998 the banker referred to is said to have purchased for bin Laden quantities of shares on the French stock market (in BNP, Usinor, Sacilor, Axa, and Société Générale) that he resold a few weeks later with a profit of 20 million francs. According to several analysts in Europe and America, this kind of one-shot transaction does not draw attention to itself and was one of bin Laden's favored methods for realizing profits on his capital and establishing reserves in several European countries, particularly Belgium, Bulgaria, Italy, and the Netherlands. Through a Singapore real estate agent, he is said to have made property investments in London and Paris and on the Côte d'Azur. Other sources in northern Europe claim that he had also begun to invest in the dairy industry in Denmark, through an Egyptian who once worked as a construction foreman in the bin Laden group in Mecca between 1983 and 1988. Bin Laden and the "dairyman" are also said to be associated with a Swedish convert to Islam who is married to the dairyman's sister. It also appears that bin Laden has invested in the hospital equipment sector in Sweden to the tune of $15 million. He and his Swedish partners have targeted the medical markets of Iraq, Jordan, and Egypt. In Norway as well, bin Laden has diversified his activities; through a Palestinian who has lived in Norway since the 1960s, Samir al-Husseini, he has invested $40 million in the wood and paper industries.

In May 1997 a Saudi financier named Sidi Tayyeb was arrested in Saudi Arabia. He admitted being one of bin Laden's treasurers and having opened accounts for him in Europe, Africa, Pakistan, and even the United States. But, aware of the risks involved in moving such large amounts through transparent industrial and commercial markets in Europe, Osama bin Laden and his financial advisers had also begun using the banking systems of the former Soviet Islamic republics. For these transactions, it seems that bin Laden had called on banking establishments located in the Turkish part of Cyprus, with the cooperation of some businessmen very closely associated with the Turkish Cypriot government, reportedly even including a member of the president's family.

But almost all of these financial manipulations were known to Saudi, American, or European intelligence services. In addition, leaks or disclosures, some of which have come from deserters from or captured agents of the Bin Laden Brotherhood in recent months, have seriously worried bin Laden. His caution in financial matters has increased tenfold, and he has had to give up certain lucrative operations that would have allowed him to position funds in strategic places for the future.

Another episode provides a good illustration of the methods of Osama bin Laden's group. In 1991 the scandal of the BCCI (Bank of Credit and

Commerce International), a bank run by Pakistanis, erupted. The establishment was accused of laundering money linked to drug and arms trafficking. British investigators discovered a financial channel that served Islamist terrorists and the Abu Nidal group (Abu Nidal himself had several personal accounts). Following this scandal, funds were transferred from the BCCI to banks in Dubai, Jordan, and Sudan controlled by the Muslim Brotherhood. Some of the money was handed back to organizations such as the FIS. Another portion was transferred by Ayman al-Zawahiri to Switzerland, the Netherlands, London, Antwerp, and Malaysia. When bin Laden's responsibility for the Nairobi and Dar es Salaam attacks was revealed, a senior German judge alerted the Americans and Interpol. "We have testimony from a French national married to a Saudi. When she was arrested for money laundering in 1997, she stated that she had invested funds from Osama bin Laden between 1983 and 1990."

But Osama bin Laden's great strength lies in the fact that he no longer needs to finance his Brotherhood, which is independent, self-sufficient, inexpensive, and particularly proud of contributing to the jihad. The financing of Osama bin Laden's networks relies on a well-oiled mechanism. Just as the Islamist universe cultivates a fragmented political organization, its finances are equally fragmented. The various Islamist leaders have learned the sometimes stinging lessons that Libya administered in the past to Palestinian organizations by transforming them into docile mercenaries in return for their subsidies. In fact, although a single source of financing has the certain advantage of providing financial stability, it also has the disadvantage of making the movement dependent on a single sponsor that integrates the movement into its own foreign policy and would not hesitate, should the occasion arise, to sacrifice it as a good-will gesture when confronted by Western pressure or foreign reprisals. This explains why, in the 1970s and 1980s, Abu Nidal, Carlos, and Ahmed Jibril wandered from one Arab capital to the next at the mercy of their successive sponsors, sometimes forced to renounce their ideological positions in order to satisfy their protectors.

Hence, rather than imitating procedures that proved unsatisfactory in the past, Islamists have chosen to have numerous supporters and several financiers able to help them or to shelter their front organizations, instead of a single source of funds. The lucidity and pragmatism of the Islamist organizations, including the Bin Laden Brotherhood, are clear evidence of a common strategy, in the absence of a single military command structure.

Beyond the shared aim of the jihad against the enemies of Islam, the method of financing is the second common denominator of the organizations of the Islamist universe. Financial contributions from the Gulf states are clearly not negligible. In 1993 French minister of the interior Charles Pasqua, on a visit to Saudi Arabia, asked his Saudi counterpart, Nayef bin Abdelaziz, a brother of King Fahd, to try to limit the financial support provided by some Saudi businessmen to Islamists associated with the FIS and armed groups in Algeria. The Saudi government then promised to monitor the financing of fundamentalists, at least in France.

Powerful NGOs established throughout the Arab world and in the West also pump funds to the extremists, making them even more uncontrollable. (Many officials of humanitarian organizations denounce violence but cannot avoid being unwittingly manipulated.) As examples, we may mention Hezb-e-Islami in Afghanistan, the Committee of Charity and Solidarity in France, the Islamic Relief Agency, and Save Bosnia Now, an organization based in the United States and run by Afghan veterans. These charitable organizations are characterized by their collection and unchecked manipulation of large sums of money under cover of humanitarian activities. These organizations, not subject to taxation because of their nonprofit status, are able to distribute their funds to whomever they please. It was a humanitarian organization of this kind, established in Nairobi that provided funds to the Kenyan network of the Bin Laden Brotherhood responsible for the East African attacks.

Most of these NGOs are known and have recently been subjected to increased surveillance. About twenty of these charitable organizations active in the Gulf nations have been identified by the Egyptian intelligence services. Hamas and the networks of North African and European Islamists are generously and discreetly supported through a system of dual accounting set up by creative financiers. Funds often go through Islamic banks, whose mechanisms may be obscure to conventional bankers and investigators. Indeed, the systems for calculating interest and earnings on deposits governed by sharia are completely different. Use of so-called Islamic banks is another essential component of the financing mechanism of the fundamentalist movements.

The system of Islamic banks came into being in 1969 at the first meeting of the OIC, the Organization of the Islamic Conference, on the initiative of

King Feisal. With the increase in the price of crude oil, it had become essential for the oil-producing countries to find the means to inject their petrodollars into the international economy through their own banking system rather than by enriching Western banks. In any event, this was the central idea. Hence, at the recommendation of King Feisal and the then prime minister of Malaysia, the Bank for Islamic Development was established in 1975. Each of the forty-one countries of the Organization of the Islamic Conference held at least one share, but 25 percent of the capital in reality was held by Saudi Arabia, 16 percent by Libya, 14 percent by the United Arab Emirates, and 13 percent by other Gulf countries. The bank was registered in Jedda and had $2 billion in capital.

In accordance with their charters, the role of these Islamic banks, which began to flourish in 1975, was to help in the propagation of Islam and in the development of infrastructure projects benefiting Muslim countries. The promoters no doubt envisaged the establishment of a "new Islamic economic order." A few years later, with the creation of the Islamic Solidarity Bank in Sudan, the militant and ideological dimension of the Islamic banking system gained preponderance over the purely financial aspect. Proof of this lies in the fact that these banks were never used to deposit substantial assets of the oil-producing countries. Although they are quite rich in terms of deposits, these banks have carried out only minor operations on the international level, and none of them is among the ten largest banks in the world. One of the reasons for this relative lethargy of the Islamic banking system on the international level is the fact that the world economy, and the United States first of all, would never have accepted a massive withdrawal of Arab deposits, and Saudi Arabia would never have risked confronting the United States, or even other Western banks, on this delicate ground. Out of this timorous and ambiguous attitude on the part of Saudi Arabia, despite its being the originator of the project, has come the restriction of Islamic banks to their current status as rich and financially powerful banks, but banks that are almost always marginalized in international financial markets.

But far from being a handicap, this status and the relative isolation of Islamic banks are compatible with the aims and interests of the Islamist universe. It is more comfortable with them than with major international banks, which are rule-bound and highly supervised, and most of which have implemented mechanisms for the control and disclosure of transfers of funds generally over fifty thousand francs or the equivalent of seven thousand dollars. Services such as Tracfin in France do not let any banking operation go through unless the sender and receiver are known and the origin of the funds is clear.

The fact that this separate status of Islamic banks was acceptable was demonstrated by the establishment of such banks in more than twenty-three countries in the 1980s, including Switzerland, Luxembourg, and Malaysia, not to mention establishments in Turkey and the Bahamas.

The collapse of the economic dream of some Islamist theoreticians and economists of creating a universal monetary system founded on a mythical golden dinar forced the Islamic banking system to find a new use for itself. In reality, the Islamic banks played a cardinal role and performed exceptionally well in the domestic economy, much more than on the international level. By collecting and converting into hard currency money from informal commerce[3] or the black market in the countries of the Muslim world and some African countries, these establishments—operating more as currency exchanges than as deposit banks—ended up handling large sums of money that had until then been outside the traditional banking system.

Among the establishments dividing up the deposits of the Islamic banking sector, three have recently drawn special attention because of their "nonbanking" activities. In fact, they have contributed to the financing of fundamentalist Islamist organizations, often unwittingly, through intermediaries or institutions acting as fronts for those organizations.

The DMI, Dar al-Maal al-Islami, a subsidiary of the Feisal Islamic Bank Group, which was registered in the Bahamas on July 27, 1981, is now relatively inactive. A fatwa authorized the establishment of the bank, and the conformity of the bank's operations to Islam was rigorously supervised by a strange two-headed board of directors made up half of financiers and half of clerics. At the time, the bank had no competition. It was the first Islamic bank in the world, and its shareholders were all prestigious political leaders, such as the Pakistani president Zia ul-Haq, the Sudanese president Gaffar Nimeiry, and several Saudi princes. A public subscription had raised $35 million. Beginning in 1982 the DMI and its investment companies moved billions through the international financial markets with an initial capital of $315 million. Although it had a Bahamian charter, the DMI had an office at 7 rue des Alpes in Geneva. This office was supposed to become the bank's bridgehead in the Western world. In fact, one of the ambitions of the directors of the bank was to open agencies in the West and to use the bank for international activities of Islamic proselytism. But the DMI came up against the hostility of the authorities in Europe. On the other hand, Africa was broadly welcoming of the DMI, and countries such as Guinea even agreed to modify their banking laws, notably with respect to earnings on deposits and to questions of credit, in order to make them compatible with the rules of Islamic banks, strictly regulated by sharia, which prohibits earning money from lending it. But money must still be earned, and Islamic banks manage to make profits through a complex system of regulation of banking services and investments.

But the project came to a sudden end. In 1984, the DMI posted a $28 million loss, compared to $7 million profit the preceding year. The losses were due to dangerous speculative operations on the gold market. But this was not the end of Islamic banks, far from it, still less the end of the intentions of some figures to draw them discreetly into the financing of radical Islamism.

At the same time that the DMI was in difficulty, another Islamic bank appeared, the Dellah al-Baraka. With capital of a billion dollars, this bank presented itself as a direct rival of the DMI, which no longer enjoyed the confidence of its depositors. The Dellah al-Baraka was established by a group of unknown Arab businessmen, and it had no Saudi princes on its board of directors. From its headquarters in London, the bank established branches in a dozen countries, including Sudan, Mauritania, Bahrain, Tunisia, and even Thailand and Texas. In 1990, it opened an office in Algeria. Also intent on establishing itself in the Western world, the Dellah al-Baraka entered the market through fiduciary companies such as the Islamic Banking System International Holding Company. By advancing behind a mask, the Dellah al-Baraka succeeded where the DMI had failed and ended up controlling the first International Islamic Bank (IIB) in Copenhagen. This bank, which opened in 1984, soon became, because of the discretion—modeled on that of Swiss and Luxembourg banks—with which it conducted its business, the favored bank for Muslims living in Europe. Among the clients of the IIB was the Islamic Group of France, an organization that was one of the sources for the FIS and for the Tunisian Islamic movement en-Nahda. In 1990 the Dellah al-Baraka opened branches wherever it had become necessary to maintain relations with the Islamic community: Djibouti, Johannesburg, and Shanghai.

But the most mysterious of the Islamic banks remains the al-Taqwa. This bank is so discreet, with a single branch in the Bahamas, that several intelligence services have even come to doubt its existence. However, the al-Taqwa does exist and operates in more than thirty countries. It was set up in Nassau in 1987 with $50 million in capital, two-thirds of which were provided by fundamentalist organizations, in particular by the Kuwaiti Muslim Brotherhood al-Islah. The rest came from public subscription. As in the case of all Islamic banks, the compatibility of banking operations with sharia is supervised by a religious council as well as by a member of the Egyptian Muslim Brotherhood.

Egyptian police reports have established that the al-Taqwa on several occasions financed Islamist candidates in Egyptian municipal elections and that the founder and president of the al-Taqwa is Yussuf Nada, an extremely wealthy Egyptian member of the Muslim Brotherhood, who heads more than two thousand commercial enterprises. The bank's vice president, Ali Ghalib Himmat, is also known for his militant Islamist activities; he was one of the leaders of the Islamic community in Germany and of the Islamic Center in Munich. The two men are now Italian citizens, and no investigator has suspected them of being connected to Islamist terrorist networks. Rather than an office in Nassau, the real headquarters of the al-Taqwa bank is said to be in Campione, near Lugano, Switzerland.

The most intransigent fundamentalist leaders have often sought to use banks with a network extending from Nassau to Peshawar and passing through all the tax havens on the planet. They use the banks cynically, realizing that they are able to bypass conventional financial circuits in order to quickly launder funds of any currency not convertible in the usual markets. In fact, a large part of the financial resources devoted to the jihad comes from criminal or informal activities. Since 1995, international cooperation has made it possible to draw the attention of the heads of Islamic banks to the problem. Several questionable transfers of funds to fundamentalist movements have thus been identified and blocked. The hunt for Osama bin Laden by intelligence services, including Interpol, has often concentrated on the strictly financial aspect, leading experts to take measures likely to interfere with his activities by depriving him of his resources.

12 / Drugs and Terrorism

The jihad's new weapons come at a price. And while the international banking system, including the system of Islamic banks, used well or shrewdly manipulated, allows the financiers of terror to launder dirty money, the wealth still has to be created. It has now been established that drug trafficking is one of their favored methods.

In the case of the Afghans, drug production had been a customary source of revenue for centuries. By the time of the Soviet withdrawal, and even during the occupation, what had in the past been only a back-up economic activity for the tribes had become an organized industry, essentially making it possible to buy weapons. After the withdrawal of the Red Army, resistance forces were not the only ones implicated in drug trafficking; several apparatchiks of the pro-Soviet regime in Kabul also acted as drug barons. In 1991, the head of WAD, the Afghan espionage service, was dismissed because of his too open involvement in an international heroin network.

At the end of the war in Afghanistan, opium production had doubled, increasing from two thousand tons in 1991 to more than four thousand tons in 1992—more than Burma, which at the time produced only 2.5 thousand tons. According to American experts, the crops were sold before harvesting, and four-fifths of the heroin consumed in Europe came from this new Golden Triangle, worthy of the name Narcostan given to it by a Soviet official. The situation has not changed very much. Afghanistan produces three-fourths of the opium consumed in the world, with the rest coming from Burma. Afghanistan laid out a new production zone in 1999 with an annual output of 4.6 thousand tons. Figures for drug seizures at the Indian and Pakistani borders alone speak for themselves: 640 kilos of heroin in 1997; 650 in 1998; 750 in 1999.

This increase in production was in large part caused by the interruption of financial aid granted by the Americans to the Afghan resistance movements. By 1991, now forced to find other resources, Gulbuddin Hekmatyar's organization is said to have specialized in the production of heroin with more than eighty-six rural laboratories, some of which were run by "chemists" obligingly sent by the Russian mafia. The marketing of the drugs remained in the hands of Pakistanis located in the border regions not far from Peshawar. The best known of these Pakistani bosses, Haji Ayyub Zaki ul-Afridi, a tribal chief who was also a member of parliament, by himself and with complete impunity, was responsible for the purchase and distribution of several tons of opium from each harvest. His fortified residence in Landi Kotal, a town known for its gunsmith artisans, had even been subject to several fruitless searches. More than a fortress, ul-Afridi's house was a palace with a white marble floor, surrounded by a magnificent rose garden and lawns, in the midst of a gray stony desert. The few visitors who have seen the house report that it contained paintings by Van Gogh and Renoir, furniture imported from Europe, and—the height of luxury in a town with practically no electric power—an air conditioner in every room. Ul-Afridi, under American protection when he was helping them supply weapons to the mujahedeen, was however trapped by American police on a December 1995 trip to New York, in the course of which he thought he would be able to clear himself from drug charges with the Drug Enforcement Administration (DEA). He was arrested and sentenced to five years in an American penitentiary before he could return to Pakistan.

In Pakistan and Afghanistan, as in all countries producing opium or coca, drugs are highly profitable commodities. Chemists have few requirements for transforming the raw materials: a shed and a few laborers paid a pittance or sometimes held captive by their employers. Opium is abundant and the only additive required is acetic anhydride, a chemical product easily imported from Western Europe or the former Soviet Union through Central Asia or Turkey.

From the Afghan mountains, drugs can then be sent to Europe on more or less known routes going through Chechnya, Russia, and the Baltic republics. Several countries, including Turkey, have registered an increase in traffic in their territory since 1995. The former Soviet republics have also been implicated; experts have discovered a route going from Afghanistan through Khorog in Tajikistan and Osh in Kirghizstan, following the only barely passable mountain road for seven hundred kilometers. Carriers know that they will encounter no border inspectors when they cross into the former Soviet empire. The heroin is then transported to Belarus, Estonia, Latvia, Lithuania, the Russian Federation, and Ukraine, where it is broken up into small packages and then exported to Western Europe by other smugglers or networks of "mules."[1] The cartels of Central Asia have clearly avoided the usual but more heavily watched routes passing through Turkey or Nigeria via South Africa. Traffickers have in fact become better and better informed; they are aware that the movement of drugs through airports and ports known as linchpins in the trade has become riskier because of the implementation of new methods of detection perfected in the West.

One American technique developed by a California laboratory, Ancore Corporation, sent a storm of panic through the networks of traffickers. The new system, initially developed for the ONDCP (Office of National Drug Control Policy) is capable of detecting explosives or drugs without opening baggage, boxes, or containers. The system, which has the form of a screening machine, even allows for automatic inspection without human intervention of fully loaded trucks. This explains why one of the promoters of the procedure, which is more reliable than X rays, was the Anglo-French consortium Eurotunnel, which invested more than $20 million in the development of the detector between 1989 and 1998. The procedure, known as PFNA (pulsed fast neutron analysis), subjects given substances, such as cocaine or heroin, and explosives, to a bombardment of neutrons that uncovers the chemical composition and the exact quantity of the products tested. If the PFNA system becomes widespread, traffickers will have the greatest difficulty in introducing their products into countries equipped with the technology. The only relative obstacle at the moment is the high price of the devices, giving the traffickers a reprieve. The U.S. Department of Defense and the Federal Aviation Administration have invested $35 million over the last several years in this project, taking into account the stakes involved in security matters and the amount of money taken in by the South American and new Asian cartels, including the Taliban. In 1992, according to DEA experts, the flow of money between Afghanistan and the Russian mafia amounted to several billion dollars, some of which clearly went directly to the jihad.

The drug industry has since then grown enormously and until recently served the interests of the new masters of Afghanistan and their fundamentalist and terrorist friends, even though the regime of "theology students" officially condemned drug use. The Taliban claimed—and this was partly true—that they had inherited an established situation. They even organized public destruction of poppy fields or provided broad media coverage of their closing of established laboratories in order to satisfy U.N. representatives. A few dozen kilos of opium would go up in smoke, and the United Nations could prepare a report giving satisfaction to everyone, especially because the Taliban were eager to recover the Afghan seat at the United Nations still held by the Northern Alliance.

On July 27, 2000, the supreme leader of the Taliban, Mullah Omar, banned the growing of opium poppies, declaring it contrary to Islam, and even adding to this very unpopular measure severe punishments for violators. Soon after the prohibition, several dozen farmers were arrested and their poppy fields were destroyed by the militia forces. The decree did not please very many people in Afghanistan, where opium is practically the only source of revenue in rural areas. We must therefore conclude that the decision was aimed primarily at calming world opinion rather than blocking the flow of drugs to the West. By taking this step, the Taliban shrewdly placed the international community in an embarrassing position; while taking a first step, it simultaneously did not fail to raise the question of the future of farmers doomed to poverty. But beyond this fuss targeted at international opinion, the fact remained that satellite surveillance carried out for the United Nations revealed that the surface area devoted to growing opium poppies was greater than 90 thousand hectares, and that it had increased by 50 percent in one year. Afghanistan had overtaken Burma, which was producing "only" 1.2 thousand tons a year.

In the late 1980s Pakistan as well, in campaigns given wide media coverage, had gone to great lengths to destroy crops or poppy fields of Pashtun peasants, going so far as to use highly toxic defoliants in the same family as Agent Orange. These powerful herbicides killed not only poppies, but all other crops, and had devastating effects on cattle, provoking violent conflicts between ordinary peasants and those who grew only opium poppies.

But the eradication of poppy cultivation and opium production in Afghanistan and Pakistan was a daydream. Opium consumption in the region is two centuries old, going back to the period of English colonization. Under the rule of General Zia, the trucks of the National Logistics Cell (the national organization in charge of official transport for the Pakistani government) seldom left the resistance camps in Afghanistan empty after delivering weapons to the mujahedeen on behalf of the Americans. Pakistani officers then had the opium bought from the mujahedeen processed in secret laboratories set up in the so-called tribal zones of Afghanistan, regions outside the rule of law and therefore not subject to any control, and then exported it to Europe through Iran. The huge profits generated by this traffic made it possible for certain officers of the Pakistani secret services to underwrite the war against India in Kashmir or even to acquire military equipment. According to several Western intelligence services, the Pakistani atomic bomb was in large part financed by drug revenues.[2]

Until recently, an analogous situation existed in the Afghanistan of the Taliban. They too needed a good deal of money to fight against Massoud's resistance forces, to buy weapons, and to pay their soldier-monks, and drugs provided several hundred million dollars a year, a decisive argument in favor of taking some liberties with morality and Islam.

One must assume that despite his public stance, cultivation of opium poppies did not ideologically trouble Mullah Omar, who unashamedly tolerated the *zakat*,[3] the religious tax levied on opium, which went into the Taliban's pockets. In New York, Abdel Hakeem Mujahid, Taliban representative to the United States, declared: "We are opposed to growing opium poppies and to the production of drugs and narcotics, but we cannot fight against our own people, which is the source of our legitimacy."

Mullah Omar went even further when he stated that the Taliban would never allow opium to be sold in Afghanistan, but that if non-Muslims, on the other hand, wanted to buy drugs and intoxicate themselves, it was not up to the Taliban to protect them. This helps explain why the traffic showed no signs of drying up. In political terms, the Taliban regime was using drugs as a lever to obtain recognition, and it was not unusual to hear dignitaries claim that only the West could resolve the problem by contributing millions of dollars to foster substitute crops. A form of blackmail, this strategy embarrassed the Western powers, who refused to pay ransom in exchange for the eradication of opium poppy cultivation. Moreover, it was far from certain that the Taliban would be able to curb this age-old production.

It is thus certain that the Islamist universe draws large benefits from drug bosses in exchange for expeditious laundering of money in certain networks of Islamic banks. This was true for the Taliban, who controlled 90 percent of the area in which opium poppies were grown in Afghanistan and who, after collecting a fixed fee of 20,000 rupees (about $5,000) from the cultivator and a tax of 1,000 rupees per kilogram of opium, began to establish a system of taxation more in keeping with sharia.

The scale of basic taxation collected at the point of production in the eastern province of Nangarhar on the Pakistani border was double what it was in the Kandahar region. In the so-called tribal zones, prices could go as high as 5,000 rupees, a fortune compared to average local earnings. The relatively high prices in the province of Nangarhar were explained by the presence of at least fifteen laboratories producing heroin, adding substantially to the value of the opium poppies. Some of these laboratories produced as much as one hundred kilos of morphine base used for heroin production. The Taliban's official collectors would even deliver formal receipts to peasants enabling them to pass through inspection stations.

According to a lab assistant who entered a Pakistani hospital for drug treatment, morphine base was processed in the laboratory where he worked into packages of about six kilos. The Taliban collected $55 in taxes on each package, or about $6,000 in "tax" revenue a day. According to the same technician, there were at least thirty production facilities of the same size in the region, which would have yielded $180,000 in daily receipts. And these laboratories would never lack for Western purchasers, with so many intermediaries profiting from the "brown sugar," the base powder. The price of heroin in New York or Paris told the story: if an Afghan peasant collected $600 for ten kilos of opium, which would produce a kilo of morphine and in turn a kilo of heroin, a wholesaler in Turkey would receive $12,000, his retailer in Holland $50,000, and the original $600 would generate revenues from addicts in the street of $1.5 million.[4] A user would pay as much as two and a half thousand times, or even six thousand times in cases of shortage, the price paid to the Afghan producer, thereby contributing unknowingly to the jihad of the Afghan theocrats.[5]

In general, young Islamists trained in Taliban facilities were used as smugglers or carriers, and mullahs would even bless the loading of trucks. Opium was also sold raw in certain special markets. According to the representative of the United Nation's antinarcotics program, one of the largest centers of the opium trade was the bazaar of the town of Sangin, in the province of Helmand, three hours by road from Kandahar. More than three hundred traders equipped with simple scales sold opium in still humid balls or compressed into large dry cakes. It was not unusual to see one or another of these modest bazaar tradesmen, from a miserable wooden stall, from an old rusty container, or under a shabby parasol, sell several dozen tons of opium per year for a profit approaching $200,000, an amount not possible in any other trade in a country that had been devastated by war for more than twenty years. The bazaar in Sangin sold more than half of Afghan production. The markets were obviously controlled by the local mafias, which also ran an extortion racket on street sellers.

From Afghan bazaars and some of Osama bin Laden's camps, opium followed dozens of routes toward Europe and neighboring countries, where it was sometimes processed. With three million junkies in Iran and more than five million in Pakistan, including nearly eighty thousand children in Karachi alone, the Taliban's local market was far from negligible, but the heralds of Afghan morality did not lose any sleep over the matter. In December 1999 a group of Afghan smugglers transporting seventy-seven kilos of heroin was arrested in India; the drugs bore the label of a Pakistani laboratory that was well known to the police.

Bin Laden has attempted to infiltrate networks in Morocco by backing drug traffickers sought by the Rabat security services. For example, the network recruited a smuggler operating between Morocco and Spain, who was also entrusted with surveillance of Saudi dignitaries owning vacation homes in southern Spain and Morocco.

Money is always the sinews of war, and the fundamentalist Islamists of the world certainly know it. Unlike other terrorist organizations of previous decades, which sometimes found themselves unable to finance their actions or even the survival of their networks, the extremist Islamists have never lacked money. According to *Newsweek,* the FBI recently tracked transfers through Minneapolis of millions of dollars to Somalia and to an organization in bin Laden's sphere of influence.

13 / Jihad's New Weapons

Intelligence and antiterrorism experts are now certain that fundamentalist militants do not intend to limit themselves to attacks against American barracks or embassies, killing a few hundred victims. Their next targets could be entire cities or countries. This escalation relies on the mastery of new technologies and on the financial capacity of subversive networks to purchase these lethal technologies or to corrupt those who understand them. We know that the terrorists are not short of money. Bin Laden is on record as saying, "Acquiring arms for the defense of Muslims is a duty. If it is true that I have acquired [chemical or nuclear] weapons, I thank God who has made it possible. And if I seek to procure such weapons, this is a duty. It would be a sin for Muslims not to try to possess the weapons that could prevent the infidels from harming Muslims."

This statement, ambiguous and troubling like so many of bin Laden's, alarmed many Western foreign offices. It confirmed their suspicions that one of bin Laden's goals was to destabilize Pakistan in order to get hold of Islamabad's atomic bomb. Bin Laden has purportedly spent more than $60 million since 1997 to buy the expertise of Pakistani nuclear engineers and the collaboration of generals and members of the Pakistani secret service.

In September 1998 an official American document described "presumed steps by Osama bin Laden to procure nuclear weapons." The document, a complaint filed against a bin Laden associate, Mandouh Mahmoud Salem, arrested in Germany in 1998 on suspicion of preparing an attack against the American consulate in Hamburg, asserted that there was a direct link between Osama bin Laden and Iran, a nation on Washington's notorious blacklist of states supporting terrorism. According to the federal prosecutor in New York who was handling the case, in the early 1990s, Osama bin Laden formed an anti-American alliance with Iran and Sudan, another country on the State Department's blacklist, and sent emissaries around the world seeking to buy nuclear weapons. According to the eight-page indictment, Salem had secretly met Iranian officials in Khartoum and Teheran to arrange for them to provide Osama bin Laden's militia forces with intensive training that was supposed to be given in Hezbollah camps in southern Lebanon that were controlled and financed by Iran.

The indictment presented Salem as an Islamist eager to unite Shiis and Sunnis for the greater glory of Islam and especially in order to unify forces against the United States and Israel. Salem was also identified as an influential founding member of the armed wing of the Bin Laden Brotherhood, al-Qaeda. According to the federal prosecutor, Salem had belonged to at least two al-Qaeda committees, the Majlis al-Choura—the superior council, whose mission is to authorize military actions—and the fatwa committee, responsible for promulgating edicts and verdicts against the Americans. Again according to the federal prosecutor in New York, Salem was responsible for several al-Qaeda missions in Afghanistan, Malaysia, and the Philippines. He was said to have for a time given training to new recruits and to have headed an al-Qaeda reception center in Pakistan, but above all, he was supposed to procure transmission equipment and electronic material for making detonators. In 1993, the indictment continued, Salem was the author of an internal al-Qaeda memorandum describing the intent to acquire enriched uranium for the purpose of making nuclear weapons. But the prosecutor had to admit that he did not know how far Salem had succeeded, or even whether he had begun.

According to Afghan and Egyptian deserters and informers, Osama bin Laden already possessed several "rudimentary" nuclear bombs stored in suitcases and protected by a secret code. Is this truth or disinformation? Logically, as for most nuclear weapons, detonation requires several levels of authorization, and there is no proof that the terrorists have all the keys. If these suitcases are operational, which has not been verified (bin Laden's buyers may have been cheated by swindlers), the terrorists will not know for certain until they try to set them off, with all the imaginable consequences if they succeed. In any event, the risk must be taken seriously.

According to other reports, notably from the Russian secret services, Osama bin Laden suffered a stinging defeat in his search for nuclear weapons. In 1993, according to these reports, his networks tried to procure a missile warhead on the black market, but finding it impossible to locate one, they turned to illegal suppliers of enriched uranium operating in the former Soviet republics and in Asian countries. The market for fissile material is in fact almost as flourishing as the market for drugs, although the networks and methods are different. In March 1999 an Indian smuggler was caught in Bengal carrying 1.8 kilos of uranium and 350 grams of heroin. He had been paid seven hundred dollars by a gang of smugglers who exchanged heroin produced in Afghanistan or Pakistan for uranium 238 from the Indian mine at Jadugda in Bihar.

Unfortunately for Osama bin Laden and fortunately for his possible victims, his emissaries, with few qualifications in nuclear physics, did not have the right contacts and are even said to have been taken in by Russian traffickers presenting themselves as atomic engineers, from whom they bought, first, uranium not usable for a nuclear weapon and then waste presented as Red Mercury, a radioactive product supposedly used in the manufacture of a secret weapon. It seems that bin Laden's buyers were not the first to have been gulled by the Red Mercury scam; after the dismantling of the South African nuclear arsenal in the 1980s and 1990s, stocks of this mysterious Red Mercury had already been sold at extravagant prices to some ingenuous representatives of Iraqi interests.

The Taliban themselves were said to be in possession of fissile material. On May 25, 1998, one of their representatives presented to the press in Kabul a metal container filled with powdery material said to be uranium. According to the Taliban, this came from stocks buried during the Soviet occupation of Afghanistan. According to a report transmitted at the time by the French embassy to the Ministry of Defense in Paris, another metallic container of the same kind had also been found by the Taliban. If this powder was usable, it is entirely possible that Osama bin Laden would have had no objection to financing a plan for an Islamic bomb for his Taliban hosts.

There was thus no ground for thinking that bin Laden had definitively given up acquiring or manufacturing his atomic bomb. In June 1998 leaks informed Western secret services that bin Laden had approached young Pakistani nuclear physics researchers. Whether the reports were accurate or not, it was of great importance to learn the truth. Osama bin Laden was perhaps simply attempting to dissuade the Americans from striking again against one of his hiding places, an attack that might unleash a process of terrorist nuclear retaliation by militants of the Brotherhood.

Information in this area is difficult to obtain. However, in April 2000, Uzbek security services discovered a truck containing fissile material on the Kirghiz border. It is likely that this shipment was intended for Pakistan or for Osama bin Laden. Another trail leads to a trafficker known as Antonov Botov. This Ukrainian arms dealer, a former Red Army officer who had fought in Afghanistan, was approached on several occasions by emissaries from the Bin Laden Brotherhood wishing to acquire sophisticated nuclear material.

The obstacles to obtaining a nuclear weapon were therefore daunting: subverting Pakistani nuclear capabilities or putting together an atomic bomb from scratch, for which bin Laden's network lacked the technology and the competence. It would make sense for bin Laden's envoys to turn toward the manufacture and purchase of less chimerical chemical weapons. Bin Laden is reported to have several distributed in secret storage facilities in Afghanistan, but perhaps also elsewhere in Asia, in Europe, and in the United States. This information was the subject of special meetings of Western security services in December 1999 and May 2000 in Washington and Paris and at NATO headquarters in Brussels.

These suspicions of Western intelligence services were confirmed by the statement of Ahmed Salama Mabruk, an upper-level Islamist leader of Egyptian Islamic Jihad, at his trial before a military tribunal in Cairo, which ended on April 17, 1999, in a verdict of hard labor for life.[1] According to Mabruk, in a statement made to the Saudi daily *Al-Hayat*, Osama bin Laden had chemical and bacteriological weapons that he intended to use against American targets. According to other disclosures at this trial, Osama bin Laden had purchased substances necessary for the manufacture of chemical weapons from a laboratory situated in a former East-bloc country that simply sent his order through the mail for a payment of $11,185. Mabruk's statement must be taken seriously, because before his extradition from Azerbaijan in September 1998, he was an assistant to Dr. Ayman al-Zawahiri, head of the armed wing of Islamic Jihad and right-hand man of Osama bin Laden, with whom he had joined forces since they shared refuge in Afghanistan. Mabruk asserted that more than one hundred terrorist operations had been planned by the Bin Laden Brotherhood and that the

Egyptian secret services had learned of them when they confiscated one of his computer disks. Although the Egyptian authorities refused to confirm this, the threat is plausible.

This information corresponds to information provided by the Russian secret services. It seems that two former instructors of the East German Stasi (secret police) recently spent eight months in a camp in Afghanistan to initiate Bin Laden Brotherhood recruits in the handling of individual chemical and bacteriological weapons, probably grenades containing poison. According to Yumad Bodansky, former members of Spetsnaz, elite troops of the Red Army, had also been recruited; they were specialists in sabotage and in chemical and biological weapons. According to bin Laden supporters whom we met in London, human guinea pigs—Chechens, Yemenis, Uzbeks—volunteered to test toxic gases in bin Laden camps, notably in Kandahar. Several of them died in the Tora Bora camp near Jalalabad.

Finally, it appears that fighters in Bosnia associated with bin Laden had drawn the attention of the fundamentalist leader to the possibility of recruiting some engineers who had worked in the Zica chemical weapons factory located in a Sarajevo suburb, whose production had been halted by IFOR, NATO's multinational implementation force.

Worldwide investigations following the September 11 attacks on the World Trade Center and the Pentagon revealed that since 1999, bin Laden and his chief lieutenant, Ayman al-Zawahiri, had regularly ordered books on chemical contamination dealing with incidents like the Bhopal catastrophe in India or the sarin gas attacks by the Aum Shinri Kyo sect in Japan. We also know that al-Qaeda bought, through intermediaries, three thousand nuclear-biological-chemical protective suits from the United States and Germany. One of these suits was found with an Islamist suspect arrested in Frankfurt on October 19, 2001. Another troubling discovery in the course of the investigations was a CD-ROM of 5,800 pages on the deployment of bacteriological and chemical weapons. Certain informers who had gone over to the West had already mentioned this CD, revealing that during the training in the Afghan camps it was entrusted only to the fighters considered "strong links," as opposed to the "weak links," who only had access to the so-called encyclopedia of terrorism.

Bacteriological and chemical weapons are, in theory, easier to assemble than nuclear ones because their components are accessible in the markets of the chemical and pharmaceutical industries. European and American military leaders have long made preparations for the risk of this apocalyptic war of the poor. Bacteriological weapons also have an unquestionable superiority over conventional weapons such as grenades or explosives: they are practically undetectable by metal detectors, X rays, or even systems of particle bombardment, which makes them, in theory at least, an offensive device perfectly adapted to the terrorist arsenal. The production costs of bacteriological weapons, finally, is very low compared to the cost of nuclear fission weapons.

As early as 1969 a study by a team of European and American researchers testifying before a U.N. commission had reached the conclusion that a military action aimed at civilians in a given area of one square kilometer would cost two thousand dollars with conventional weapons, eight hundred dollars with nuclear warheads, six hundred dollars with neurotoxic gases, and one dollar with biological weapons. Although costs have increased to some degree, the proportions have remained the same; according to more recent studies carried out since 1995 by Canadian intelligence services that were the subject of a secret and rather alarming report, the investment necessary to prepare an act of biological terrorism would not exceed one million dollars, with, for example, a cost of four hundred dollars for the production of a kilo of botulism toxin A, a substance that is more dangerous than the neurotoxic gases now banned by most of the armed forces in the world.

Similarly, according to the same report, it seems that the production of toxins is disconcertingly easy, compared to the difficulty of making a nuclear weapon. With a minimum of precautions, a small team with college-level scientific knowledge, in a rudimentary laboratory, could handle pathogenic biological agents. Even more disturbing, the formulas and culturing methods are available in any university science library accessible to the public. In short, the manufacture of a bacteriological weapon is not much more complicated than the production of heroin, routinely carried out in clandestine laboratories in South America and the Golden Triangle by people with a rudimentary education, or than the distillation of cheap brandy in a still. Producing pathogenic agents in large quantities amounts to doing what most pharmaceutical laboratories have been routinely doing since Pasteur's discovery; among other things, culturing strains of viruses to make vaccines. It is thus clear that it is not impossible, with a few connections and a little money, to procure the necessary raw materials.

One of the first agents known for this purpose was the anthrax bacterium, causing a disease that most doctors know only from medical textbooks. The *Bacillus anthracis* is not difficult to produce, nor is it very hard to transform it into a weapon. It is reported that the Iraqis for a time considered using anthrax against American forces during the Gulf War, but they probably recognized the reactive capacity of the American military, which had a vaccine, and Baghdad finally gave up the idea. Indeed, in 1997, two and a half million American soldiers were vaccinated, at a cost of $30 million, to be sure, but neutralizing a possible Iraqi initiative. This vaccine has been authorized by American health authorities since the 1970s, but for certain veterans' associations—particularly vigilant about the long-term effects of American weapons since the Vietnam War, such as the notorious Agent Orange, the defoliant used for a while as a replacement for napalm—it is not out of the question that with its six basic injections, the vaccine against anthrax may be as dangerous as the disease itself, which the authorities of course deny.

Botulin toxin, mentioned earlier, is not a novelty in the biological arsenal of apprentice terrorists. In reality, it is an old agent well known to scientists. It is sometimes present in improperly prepared or improperly sterilized canned goods, particularly vegetables, and it was long an illness feared by ocean-going sailors. The illness is also known among Eskimos, who have on several occasions been poisoned by salted meat contaminated by the toxin. In its so-called militarized version, botulin toxin has effects similar to those of food contamination; it provokes neuromuscular paralysis between twenty-four and thirty-six hours after contact with the infecting agent. The outcome is fatal if the toxin reaches nerve endings and if the victim does not receive immediate intensive care. The first clinical signs are a sagging of the eyelids, a dilation of the pupils, and a general paralysis that finally halts respiratory function and causes death by strangulation.

In its military, or potentially terrorist, applications, botulin toxin is not ingested with food but rather inhaled, which makes it, in theory, easier to disperse. But the first effects of the spray on victims are notably different: drying of the mucous membranes and difficulties in speech and swallowing, followed by general paralysis. A serum has been developed in the United States, but it is not available in sufficient quantity to handle an attack of this kind. Moreover, this serum is derived from a veterinary product, and it has numerous side effects when injected into people. During the

Desert Shield and Desert Storm operations, the American army developed an antitoxin produced in the body of a horse and then treated by enzymes to remove the characteristics allowing the human body to identify it and reject it as an animal product. It is not certain that this substance, conceived for military purposes and in an emergency, would receive authorization to be marketed. Followers of bin Laden have asserted that stocks of toxic products are already spread throughout Arab and Western capitals.

An incident that occurred in New York in August 1999, and which has continued through the present, is a good indication of what a terrorist threat of this kind might be like. It was the episode of the West Nile virus, which began to create panic in New York health services after five deaths had occurred. Amplified by the media, the epidemic was even characterized on several occasions as a terrorist attack, on the basis of information from several security services. According to researchers, the symptoms of infection by the West Nile virus are a slight fever and nausea lasting for three to six days, and the infecting agents are mosquitoes. In children and people with a weakened immune system, such as those who are HIV positive, the West Nile virus can cause fatal encephalitis. This virus is not a newcomer either. It has a place in the history of virology; it was discovered in 1937 in the West Nile district of Uganda. Carried by mosquitoes and birds, the virus is a great traveler, following the seasonal migration of birds to Europe—some strains have been found in Volgograd and Rostov-on-Don.

The virus made its first appearance in New York in August 1999, but no one knows what vehicle it used to cross the Atlantic. Considering the date at which the first infected patients appeared, experts think that the infecting agent, perhaps a bird traveling on a freighter, arrived in late June or early July in northern Queens and southern Bronx. In support of this hypothesis, a curious phenomenon occurred in the area around the Bronx Zoo. Around the middle of August, dozens of crows clearly suffering from neurological disturbances and the loss of spatial orientation could no longer fly and crashed to the ground. Autopsies led experts to conclude that they had died from encephalitis. In the following days, the epidemic struck cormorants, flamingos, and eagles in and around the Bronx. And at the same time, two elderly people died from a strange encephalitis caused by a still unknown virus in a Queens hospital a few miles away. The brain samples from the two victims analyzed by the experts of the Centers for Disease Control in Atlanta demonstrated, after a first misidentification as Saint

Louis virus, that it was in reality a virus close to the West Nile virus that had caused the carnage among birds.

Mayor Rudolph Giuliani then had helicopters spray tons of insecticide over Queens. According to municipal authorities, almost all American stocks of insecticides were used up by the city of New York in a few days, more than a million containers. The New York epidemic again raised the question of the ability of the health services to respond to a bacteriological threat. In this particular case, the reaction was satisfactory, but the threat was on a small scale.

Several American intelligence agents had already informed the White House of a plan by Saddam Hussein that they had learned of a few months earlier from a renegade in direct contact with the dictator. According to the source, Saddam Hussein had triumphantly announced to him in one of his secret offices in Baghdad that he had given orders to develop a biological weapon using strain SV1417 of the West Nile virus in April 1999, and that he planned to use it against a target known to himself alone.

Although biological weapons are qualitatively potentially very lethal—they are extremely deadly and terrifying for public opinion—and although their low cost makes them very affordable for terrorists, the problem for this category of weapons is their weakness in quantitative terms. Dispersion of toxic agents over the target requires knowledge of physics, meteorology, and hydrology. A group of terrorists would have the greatest difficulty in carrying out a large-scale deadly operation unless it included a physicist with a mastery of aerosol techniques.

A terrorist commando who was very determined to use this kind of weapon would theoretically have several vehicles available, including contamination of food products at the source, in a dairy or a bottling or canning factory, or pollution of urban water sources. Other vehicles much less subject to control, such as insects or infected animals (rats or cattle), could also theoretically be used, but they would be very hard to handle. However, most studies have concluded that a terrorist action of this kind is improbable, because in almost all developed countries it would be blocked by very strict quality controls in food production industries. But, once again, no risk can be ruled out.

Many scenarios of mass contamination have been worked out by antiterrorism task forces in most Western countries. The American specialists Douglass, Livingstone, and Berkowitz conducted an extremely realistic simulation of a bacteriological attack on Manhattan, using only 90 liters of a pathogenic agent diffused by a powerful aerosol: "On a day with favorable weather conditions, with a light southeasterly breeze (7 MPH), a small boat travelling at a speed of six knots could cover the twenty miles from Battery Park to City Island. . . . If only half the people targeted were exposed and only half those exposed were infected with pulmonary anthrax, and finally if only half those infected were to die (all these estimates are cautious), there would be more than 600 thousand deaths."

The simulation was probably too pessimistic, since mechanical weakening of the contaminating agents can considerably reduce the risks of massive contamination. Fog, atmospheric humidity, changes in temperature, ultraviolet radiation, or a contrary or rising air current could considerably change the virulence of a bacteriological weapon disseminated in the air or water. It is thus not so easy to reach the target, and bacteriological or biological attacks might in fact be of only low intensity, creating a panic but not a cataclysm. But the threat is not thereby negligible, because the creation of panic is in general the aim pursued by terrorists, usually for purposes of blackmail or to create an insurrectionary climate.

Compared to biological weapons, chemical weapons are, according to experts, easier to handle, store, and disperse for inexperienced users, but they are much less deadly than biological agents. According to a North American report, to kill someone who had drunk half a glass of water coming from a reservoir containing five million liters, it would take at least ten tons of potassium cyanide, while only five hundred grams of a biological agent, such as *Salmonella typhi*, would work just as well. The best known toxic chemical agents are battlefield gases such as tabun and sarin, often called mustard gas.[2] These gases were already in use on the European battlefields of World War I. The production of sarin poses no particular problems and its cost is very low compared to that of other weapons. The production of 140 grams of sarin would cost less than ten dollars and would require the investment of less than a thousand dollars in laboratory materials. The ingredients are commercially available, but production requires knowledge of chemistry, particularly for the manipulation of one of the components, hydrofluoric acid.

An effective method of dispersion of sarin gas has already been successfully used by the Japanese terrorists of the Aum Shinri Kyo sect in the Tokyo subway system,[3] who found a way to disseminate toxic vapors in an enclosed space, increasing the effects of the contamination by outbreaks of violence caused by panic. The investigation of the Tokyo subway attack discovered that the terrorists had developed very elaborate methods of dispersion. They had, for example, purchased two scale models of remote control helicopters, each of which could carry several pounds of toxic substances. Shortly after the attack, the arrest of one of the members of the sect carrying a booby-trapped metal suitcase revealed that other similar attacks had been planned. The suitcase contained an automatic aerosol system using a ventilator, a vibrator, and a tube filled with liquid that was to be vaporized by the vibration apparatus. The machine was controlled by ultrasound, a small jewel of high technology. This weapon is certainly available on the terror market, and bin Laden emissaries from Malaysia may have tried to get hold of one.

Secret service specialists are particularly worried that a sarin gas attack by Islamist suicide terrorists, ready to die during the course of contaminating, would be considerably more devastating than the Tokyo attacks, which were carried out by terrorists who placed plastic bags of the chemicals and ran away.

Before the United States launched its war in Afghanistan, a terrorist camp near Jalalabad served as a base for remote-controlled helicopters that could drop containers full of gas, as well as mortars and grenades with the capacity of disseminating fatal gases. One specialist in chemical warfare who was known to be in Afghanistan was Mersa Omar, who went by the name of Abou Khakab, an Egyptian scientist who was the target of a highly confidential investigation by Western intelligence. On September 19, eight days after the attacks on the United States, the French Antiterrorist Coordination Unit (UCLAT) issued a secret memorandum on Abou Khakab, which said that Khakab had most recently visited Duranta, near Jalalabad, where a chemical warfare brigade composed of Yemenis, Chechens, and Uzbeks was training to plan attacks against cities—for example, by polluting water resources or attacking with sarin gas. This camp was one of the first targets of the American raids.

A more recently developed incapacitating agent is VX gas, ten times more toxic than sarin. But its production cost is just as low: a few gallons would cost less than ten dollars, and assembly could be carried out in a kitchen or a garage, provided one had solid knowledge of chemistry. A list of highly toxic products drawn up by the United States government in September

1999 classifies these substances according to their effectiveness and outlines emergency measures for possible victims. The agent VX is presented as the most dangerous, followed by GF, another nerve gas. Next, at the same level, are soman, sarin, and tabun, classic "mustard gases," which, the report acknowledges, are rather easy to make. Considering bacteriological agents, the list states that anthrax and the plague are the most toxic, but that strains are very difficult to obtain and to turn into weapons of mass destruction. Bin Laden hosted former Stasi agents for a period of eight months, during which time they provided instruction in the handling of chemical and bacteriological weapons. Al-Qaeda is said to possess grenades containing deadly poison.

Other studies have considered the risk of terrorists using psychoactive or psychotropic drugs causing personality disorders: apathy, lethargy, or depression. Some substances might even interfere with the reasoning capacity of victims, supporting the notion that it is not necessary to kill a population in order to terrorize it.

In these cases as well, the problem of how to disperse the toxic substance arises. Precise studies have concluded that it would take on average one million times the fatal dose in order to reach a given population because of the limited effectiveness of such an attack. Very small attacks, like the one on the Tokyo subway, or the contamination of a public place with a crop-dusting plane are plausible but improbable scenarios for massive attacks. Of more concern are scenarios envisaging raids of limited size against public establishments housing high-level political decision makers. American experts at Fort Detrick, Maryland, successfully simulated an attack against the White House and the Capitol by "contaminating" the air conditioning systems and "infecting" the water pipes. If the attack had taken place, it would not have had many victims, but they would have included the president of the United States, members of his staff, and some senators and congressmen.

Historically, terrorist groups have never gone very far in this area. In the 1980s the German far-left Baader-Meinhof terrorist gang threatened to spread anthrax bacteria through the mail in West Germany, but the threat was never carried out. American and European police archives are full of more or less imaginary cases of bacteriological threats, from contamination of baby food or granola bars, for which responsibility is frequently claimed by organizations demanding the end of animal experimentation, to the arrests of maniacs growing toxic mushrooms or castor beans[4] in their gardens, intending to place their poisons at the service of some great planetary cause.

Bacteriological and chemical agents have never been used on a large scale by a terrorist organization, essentially because their use is not so simple. It should also be considered that terrorists have ambitions other than causing terror to reign. Recourse to such uncontrollable weapons of extermination would have the immediate effect of mobilizing world opinion against them, turning them from victims into executioners, which is not what they are seeking.

However, whatever the terrorists' position on the question, Western antiterrorism services have been especially vigilant since the attack on the Dahran base in Saudi Arabia on June 25, 1996. In the aftermath of the attack, Secretary of Defense William Perry stated: "We know that even larger attacks are possible. We want to anticipate them and make plans accordingly. In the Gulf and in countries such as Turkey and Bosnia, we should prepare for an attack with a chemical weapon, a biological weapon, bombs of more than 1,500 kilos or on the order of five to ten tons, and mortar attacks."

More concretely, the Bin Laden Brotherhood also forged its new weapons with the modern means of everyday information technology. On December 16, 1999, the expulsion from Pakistan and the arrest in Jordan of Khalil Deek and thirteen other militants implicated in the preparation of an attack planned to coincide with the millennium shed new light on the methods of Islamist activists.

In 1997 Khalil Deek, a naturalized American computer technician who was born in the Occupied Territories, had gone to Pakistan to preserve the writings of a great Muslim cleric for posterity on CD-ROM. In California, where he was living at the time, Deek was a specialist in Web site design. The CD-ROM that the police seized in his Pakistani residence near the Afghan border after his arrest in Jordan was not a theology text or a mere collection of Surats. To the great surprise of investigators, it contained several thousand pages that had been digitized by a scanner making up a veritable encyclopedia of guerrilla warfare and subversion written in Arabic. Several articles were concerned with the maintenance of small arms and assault rifles and their use in street battles. Others were devoted to first aid for men wounded by bullets or antipersonnel mines. Others presented detailed instructions for the making of automatic machine rifles, from the butt to the tip of the barrel.

The encyclopedia was made up of eleven volumes dealing with the art of war in every form. One volume of the compilation was devoted to armaments, from handguns to wire-guided antiaircraft guns. In these documents of more than five hundred pages, apprentice mujahedeen could learn how to disassemble a Russian Makarov pistol, a 12.7 DH-SK heavy machine gun, an 82-mm mortar, and an antiaircraft battery. One entire section dealt with tanks, detailing types, motors, various cannons carried, as well as the weak points that could be attacked in a guerrilla action.

Various models of antitank mines and grenades were also presented in one of the volumes devoted to explosives, along with the method for laying them on a battlefield. The laying of charges of TNT and Semtex, one of the terrorists' favorite explosives, was the subject of another very detailed manual. Trainees learned the rudiments of terrorism through an abundance of illustrations. Some pages that I have refrained from reproducing (in order not to inform aspiring terrorists) explained very precisely how to booby-trap a cigarette package, an envelope with a thin leaf of C4 explosive, a door into a building, a radio, a television, and a couch. One chapter of this manual presented several formulas for the manufacture of explosives, from the age-old black powder to nitroglycerine. Detonation systems, from a slightly modified kitchen timer to an improvised detonator cobbled together from a jerry can filled with water armed with a float or a rat trap, were described with the same detail. Another chapter featured drawings of suspension and arch bridges. Care for the wounded, topography, strategy, street fighting, and even the manufacture from scratch of an assault weapon in a country forge were all treated in the encyclopedia of the jihad. The advantage of this CD-ROM to the terrorists is obvious; concentrated on a disk weighing less than ten grams were more than six thousand pages of terror and subversion. (See appendix, document 33.)

The use of computers has extended well beyond the collection of known or confidential information. The Internet and its countless websites provide a platform for the propaganda of Islamist fundamentalist movements. The Muslim separatists of Daghestan, for example, who like the Chechens are now challenging Moscow, won the battle of the Internet by posting their communiqués in Russian and English on dozens of sites. Internet sites such as "Center of the Caucasus" and "Free Chechnya" are firing virtual bullets into the heart of Moscow. Some sites are electronic mausoleums in memory of the heroes of the separatist struggle such as General Jokhar Dudayev, killed by the Russians in 1996. These sites engage in intense propaganda, claiming, for example, that drugs have been found on the corpses of Russian soldiers in Chechnya. But the Russians have responded in kind.

Electronic message services on the Internet can also contribute to the jihad and allow a subversive network to communicate in real time, to exchange documents, photos, videos, and graphics, with absolute anonymity. Respect for a few basic security measures makes the circulation of information almost impossible to tap into even for the most effective secret services. Dozens of electronic message service providers, such as Hotmail and Yahoo! in the United States and Libertysurf in Europe make it possible to set up an Internet address in a few minutes, without revealing one's identity, or by using a false name, and to stop using it after one message has been sent or received. It is not even necessary to have one's own phone line or even a computer in order to communicate. The flourishing of Internet cafés throughout the world, especially in developing countries, makes tracking Internet users even more difficult. Cities like Cairo and Peshawar already have dozens of Internet cafés, and electronic message services are accessible there by cellular telephone, as they are in Uganda and Thailand. Terrorists, in fact, no longer need to meet face to face. For a dollar each, from Internet cafés or business centers in hotels in Jakarta, San Francisco, and Johannesburg, the members of an "action cell" can communicate person to person for fifteen minutes, using pseudonyms in an anonymous forum, and exchange information about an attack before disappearing into their respective hiding places. If they consider it useful, they could confirm their decisions with encrypted messages sent through message services in private, in order to outwit the webmasters in charge of supervising websites, who are supposed to keep a vigilant eye on the content of public conversations, although they seem principally concerned with eliminating pedophile matters.

Using the Internet, a terrorist armed with topographical details about a public place in Rabat or Riyadh gathered in preparation for an attack, could send to the terrorist entrusted with setting the bomb, who might still be in hiding in Manila or Toronto, a short video recorded with an amateur camera setting out precisely the path to follow to avoid the security services and surveillance cameras and where to place the explosive charge. Three-dimensional imaging software could make it possible to have a relief view of the site of an attack in order to organize the commando's retreat. Commercially available cameras connected to the telephone network and the Internet, adopting the concept of webcam sites, could allow terrorists to maintain continuous surveillance of their target with no human intervention other than the original setting up of a camera hooked up to a portable computer and a modem in an apartment facing the target.

Jihad's new weapons, already held by Osama bin Laden, are not only offensive weapons. They also belong to the panoply of means of communication and the surveillance of private life evoked in George Orwell's *1984*: "Big Brother is watching you."

Epilogue

The defeat of al-Qaeda, the end of bin Laden, and the fall of the Taliban should not make us forget that this brand of terrorism still has networks around the world, mysterious financial power, and no doubt new leaders lurking in the shadows. The threat remains intact. If the Islamist fanatics were one day to gain mastery of biological, chemical, or nuclear weapons of mass destruction, all of humanity would be in grave danger.

Bin Laden had envisaged sarin gas attacks after the attacks on the World Trade Center and the Pentagon. Chemical weapons had been tested in the Tora Bora camp near Jalalabad, and methods of delivery prepared. This camp was one of the major targets of American bombing from the beginning of the war in Afghanistan. Another of al-Qaeda's strategies was to destabilize Pakistan in order to get hold of the nuclear weapons of Islamabad. Bin Laden had spent more than $60 million since 1997 to subvert Pakistani nuclear scientists and to ensure the collusion of Pakistani generals and members of the secret services. A secret operation code-named Sword of God was planned three weeks after the September 2001 attacks. But the Pakistani generals got cold feet, and the Taliban were very ambivalent about this strategy of a "nuclear hold-up," which carried the risk of cutting them off from the rest of the world once and for all.

The failure of these plots disrupted al-Qaeda's strategy and forced bin Laden to flee. According to a Pakistani source with close ties to the organization, the terrorist leader had attempted to cross the Pakistani frontier in a Red Crescent ambulance, but at the last minute he changed his mind.

Whatever happens to bin Laden, al-Qaeda does not wish to die. The terrorist organization believes that it is entrusted with an eternal mission: to lead the world into the apocalypse by making use of conflicts between religions and civilizations. They have made every preparation to pass on the torch of hatred to their successors, even if it takes a decade. For example, in mid-October, the brains of al-Qaeda, Dr. Ayman al-Zawahiri, smuggled into Egypt and Europe a book in which he justifies his battle and calls for eternal jihad. The title of the book, which I have been able to look at, is *Knights under the Banner of the Prophet.* He calls for holy war to the finish, using, if necessary, thousands of martyrs prepared to commit suicide. (See appendix, document 38.)

This is also, most importantly, the aim expressed in Osama bin Laden's will. In October 2001, after the American air attacks, a bin Laden emissary went to Beirut and London, carrying a document from bin Laden to be distributed in writing and by videocassette after his death. This document, a part of which I have been able to read, is very troubling for the future. In it, Osama bin Laden refers to the legend of Hassan al-Sabbah, known to the Crusaders as "the old man of the mountain," who was the head of a Persian sect of fanatics in the early eleventh century. From his mysterious, mythic fortress in the mountainous region of the Caspian Sea, he spread a reign of terror through assassinations by his followers, members of the sect of "Hashasheen," the origin of the word "assassin."

The reference to this sect is not innocent. Bin Laden included it in his will because he wants to make the point that, almost a millennium later, in 2002, the myth must continue to survive. And bin Laden warns, "After me, the world of the infidels will never again live in peace."

Afterword / *Samia Serageldin*

On the eve of the new millennium, the world collectively held its breath; doomsday scenarios ranged from a global computer meltdown to the auguries of Nostradamus to terrorist attacks on an apocalyptic scale. The New Year came and went, and millennial fever gradually abated. But Armageddon, as it turns out, was delayed, not averted. On September 11, 2001, when the world least expected it, the unimaginable happened.

In the wake of that terrible day, a new world order has been proclaimed: all the cards are reshuffled, all alliances redrawn. The enemies of yesterday—the Soviets—are now allies, the allies of yesteryear—the Taliban—are the enemy. Bin Laden's vision of a divided world is echoed by the rhetoric, coming from the West, that declares "a clash of civilizations." The term was first used by Harvard professor and Clinton administration adviser Samuel Huntington, in a much-quoted article that he later developed into a book.[1] Huntington argued that in the post–cold war world, the central and most dangerous dimension of emerging global politics would be between groups of different civilizations. Since ideologies such as communism no longer operated as unifying paradigms, people would now identify themselves in cultural and religious opposition to others. Clashes of civilization, he said, were the greatest threat to world peace; in particular, Islamic resurgence and Chinese self-assertion were on a collision course with Western universalism.

But this grim scenario is not inevitable. Even Huntington, in a speech in Dubai on November 12, 2001, warned against letting bin Laden succeed by turning this conflict into a clash between Islam and the West. A global war of civilizations can be avoided if world leaders accept the multicivilizational character of world politics and work together to maintain it. Huntington proposed attacking grievances on cultural, political, and economic fronts in the post–September 11 world. He suggested that the United States could begin by reexamining the assumption of the universal appeal of American culture, limiting foreign policy interventions, revising Israeli-Palestinian policy, and promoting economic development in Muslim countries. These initiatives should be met by cooperation on the part of Muslim regimes, which should choose modernization over religious extremism, promote a less ambivalent attitude toward the West in their public education, and reduce repression within their borders.

Huntington is not alone in advocating a broad-based change in policy approach rather than subscribing to a narrow Manichaean view of evil. Wiping out al-Qaeda is not enough to bring about a lasting end to terrorism. The logic that terrorism exists because terrorists exist, as one commentator puts it, is misleading.[2] Terrorists are created, not born, and they are not created in a vacuum. They are the product of a culture of violence arising out of complex political and social circumstances in their own societies, on the one hand, and an even wider global context of conflict, on the other. As such, the root causes of these conflicts must be addressed if the cycle of despair, hatred, and revenge is to be broken.

Thoughtful essayists on the crisis stress the need to address parallel grievances: poverty, injustice, and the sense of lost dignity. Poverty in many Muslim societies is partly attributable to global factors that favor the industrialized North against the South and partly to economic mismanagement by corrupt and repressive domestic regimes. Fighting global poverty and promoting economic development in the Third World are future priorities stressed by many leading policy makers, notably the international financier and public policy advocate George Soros.[3]

The paradox, however, is undeniable: Osama bin Laden and Ayman al-Zawahiri, like other violent revolutionaries before them, are not themselves the products of poverty and despair, though their followers and silent supporters might be. But among the foot soldiers of jihad, the sense of injustice and the need for dignity are paramount. "The only way for [the United States] to feel safe is to deal with these [Islamic] peoples with their long history of civilization" reads a proclamation by an Islamist group after the attack on the destroyer *U.S.S. Cole*. (See appendix, document 25.) "We must make [the U.S.] feel that our souls can no longer tolerate the prison walls of our bodies and that they long for the freedom to fly like birds."

The revolt against a modern age that leaves the excluded behind is a common feature of religious fundamentalism. But violence in the name of religion does not necessarily reject the tools of modernity. We saw that the perpetrators of the attacks of September 11 made effective use of capital transfers, aviation technology, and Internet messaging.

Paradoxically, globalization—as much as the West perceives it as a force for modernization, and as much as religious extremists mistrust it—is equally a force for pan-Islamic solidarity and radicalization. Through the broadcasts of CNN, but even more through the Arabic television station, al-Jazeera, Muslims from Morocco to Indonesia feel they are daily witnesses to the victimization of their co-religionists in Palestine or Chechnya.

For the first time, with the launching of the war in Afghanistan in the fall of 2001, the American public became aware of al-Jazeera, a station based in Qatar, which broke news stories ahead of American television and had privileged access to the Taliban front during the early days of the war. Arabic speakers across the Middle East, however, have been avid watchers of al-Jazeera since its inception five years ago. In a political climate where freedom of opinion and of the media is illusory, al-Jazeera offered the only outlet for uncensored opinion and criticism of the regimes in the region. Its host, the tiny Qatari emirate, remains off-bounds to such criticism, understandably. Today the station claims some thirty-five million viewers worldwide. The numbers understate al-Jazeera's influence, since its views are recycled to a much larger audience through the print media. Moreover, since the Afghan war, the station has been providing other stations with much of its material.

Al-Jazeera truly hit its stride with the Palestinian Intifada in September 2000.[4] Al-Jazeera's daily coverage of scenes of brutality against the Palestinians inflamed Arab viewers and embarrassed pro-Western regimes such as Hosni Mubarak's in Egypt, when it exposed Egypt's role in blocking meaningful sanctions against Israel at an Arab summit.

Bin Laden's venue of choice for his proclamations has been Al-Jazeera. When he said, "America and those who live in America cannot dream of security before it becomes a reality in Palestine," his words were calibrated to appeal to the general sympathy for the Palestinians. Whereas many in the Arab world would respond indifferently or negatively to radical calls for an ideological war against infidels, domestic or foreign, the disapproval of U.S. Middle East policy is ubiquitous.

The United States criticized al-Jazeera's airing of a tape of bin Laden on the first day of the bombing campaign. The tape was banned from American television on the grounds that the message might conceal some hidden code. American viewers were unable to watch bin Laden's message on television, but al-Jazeera viewers or Internet users worldwide had access to the tape in Arabic. The station responded to the criticism by attempting to demonstrate its objectivity, inviting Western officials to express their opinions; British prime minister Tony Blair and U.S. national security adviser Condoleeza Rice were among the more notable figures who took advantage of the air time.

In the war for public opinion, independent stations like al-Jazeera and the increasingly available Internet represent a new factor in the traditional paradigm of state-controlled media in the Middle East. Regimes in the region must increasingly take into consideration popular reaction to their often unpopular policies. Moreover, the glimpses of al-Jazeera reports, rebroadcast on Western television, might open a window to the view of the world from the other side of the cultural divide.

No doubt, Osama bin Laden's final will and testament will be broadcast by al-Jazeera. Once he and his lieutenants are removed from the scene, his organization disrupted and his base destroyed, will that spell the closing of a book or only the end of a chapter? Only time will tell whether bin Laden and his al-Qaeda will go down in history as a fanatic cult, not unlike that of Hassan al-Sabbah and his assassins, cited by bin Laden in a testament he wanted distributed after his death—or whether he will prove to have been only a highly charismatic leader of one phase in an ongoing battle for the minds and souls of Muslims.

Bin Laden has come to play a role in world history out of proportion to his individual significance or genius. Some analysts see the Bin Laden Brotherhood in an even larger context, not as an expression of a specifically Islamic rage but as the spearhead of the uprising of South against North, the disenfranchised and dispossessed against the prosperous and powerful—the barbarians storming the gates. The problem for much of the "West" is that the barbarians are already within the gates: five million French citizens are Muslim, and there are sizeable and growing Muslim populations elsewhere in Europe, creating tension between xenophobia and accommodation.

Islam is neither monolithic nor immutable. "Islam is [not] the victim of history, the prisoner of texts, or a circus of languages and peoples. . . . Islam is Muslims and Muslims are persons shaped by contexts both global and local."[5] There are well over one billion Muslims in the world, Asians, Africans, and Europeans, with only a minority of Arabs. Wherever Islam is found, the native culture, language, and customs of the region transpire through Islamic practice as in a palimpsest. Roughly one-fifth of humanity is Muslim. There are larger Muslim populations in non-Muslim majority India and China than there are in Muslim countries such as Pakistan and Bangladesh.

Muslims, like people of other faiths the world over, respond to multiple personal, communal, national, and transnational agendas, in which the Islamic plays a lesser or greater role, fashioned by infinite variables, geopolitical, economic, and cultural. In that plurality and diversity of interests lies the hope for escaping the doomed scenarios of false amalgamations and dichotomies that are beginning to dominate much of the discourse after September 11.

Of all the multiple faces of Islam, Osama bin Laden's has come to represent Islam for Americans. Yet it would be a serious mistake to imagine that he speaks for a majority, or even a representative minority, of Muslims. Muslim clerics the world over have condemned the attacks of September 11, even the most intransigent among them: anti-American Iranian Ayatollah Khamenei, Hezbollah's Sheikh Fadlallah, and the radical Sheikh Qaradawi.

In Islam, more than in other religions, popular discourse and debate play a vital role in evolving religious beliefs and practices because Islam has no institutionalized church hierarchy. New means of communication and information technology facilitate the dissemination of these discourses across national boundaries. The plurality of voices is instructive. Respected Pakistani writer and activist Eqbal Ahmad, for instance, urges Muslims to reject the absolutist interpretations of Islam that would create "an Islamic order reduced to a penal code, stripped of its humanism, aesthetics, intellectual quests, and spiritual devotion." He analyzes the complex, essentially spiritual meaning of the word "jihad" and its reduction by the Islamist extremists to war against presumed enemies.[6]

The image of the woman in the blue burka has come to represent Muslim women everywhere. This stereotype should be complicated by the fact that women have been elected to rule some of the largest Muslim countries in the world: Benazir Bhutto in Pakistan, Khaleda Zia in Bangladesh, and Tansu Ciller in Turkey.

Today the theory of a new paradigm and a new world order has gained currency, with Islam in the role that communism once held. But the speed with which the old world order collapsed and was turned on its head in one decade should remind us that the new order may be no more permanent.

Appendix

Note. The following documents are translations of originals that are reproduced in their entirety, except where indicated.

Document 1

The following excerpts are from first-hand sources that have lived in close proximity with bin Laden, such as companions, scientists, family members and followers; from the sheikh's own pronouncements or those of his associates; from articles in the Arabic and foreign presses and from television interviews by CNN, ABC, and others.

[p. 24] "The Saudi royal family did not reject bin Laden because he is a terrorist but because he is more important and more famous than it is. There are many Saudi terrorists, but they have not lost their citizenship. . . . The Saudi princes could not humble bin Laden, because he is not under their control, and this explains the hateful language of Princes Nayef and Sultan. Further evidence: al-Khattab, a Saudi mujahed in Chechnya did not lose his citizenship."

[p 25] "Bin Laden grew up in a very healthy and very religious atmosphere; he learned a sense of responsibility and how to have confidence in himself while remaining generous and humble, which is a very rare combination. Shy, laconic, always serious, he avoids raising his voice and laughing aloud. He gives unstintingly, he is patient, he has a sense of sacrifice. . . . He is very popular among his men who love him deeply, because his charisma is not domineering. He does not inspire terror. He participates with the young men in all their activities, shares their meals, dresses like them, and lives in the same kind of place. Although married to several wives, he lives mostly with his disciples.

"Bin Laden is very intelligent. Very observant, he is always ready with an answer. He takes his time before making decisions. He insists on consult-

من يمت من الضحايا حتى لو كانوا أبرياء بل حتى لو كانوا مسلمين و لا مانع أن يقتل المئات مادام هناك ضحايا أمريكان. و الميدان هنا ليس الأراضي المقدسة ولا حتى أمريكا نفسها وبذلك يمكن تجريد بن لادن من التعاطف الإسلامي و العالمي من خلال إظهاره كشخص متعطش للدماء بلا مبرر ديني ولا منطق سياسي مقبول.

من هنا جاء الحماس الأمريكي لمواجهة بن لادن بعد قضية إعلان الجبهة و الانفجارين لكن هذا الحماس الأمريكي تزامن بقدر الله مع قضية فضيحة كلينتون مع لوينسكي مما أدى إلى تخبط مضحك في السياسة الأمريكية تبعه رد الفعل الإسلامي وهو ما نناقشه في المحور الثاني.

المحور الثاني: وهو لماذا حظي بن لادن بكل تلك الشعبية العارمة بين عامة المسلمين ؟ هذه القضية فرع عن الأولى.

في نظري فإن أهم عامل في ذلك لم يكن بيانات بن لادن و لا تفجيري كينيا وتنزانيا و لا تفجيرات الرياض و الخبر. العامل الرئيسي —والله أعلم— هو ردة الفعل الأمريكية المتمثلة في ضرب أفغانستان و السودان وتصريح كلينتون بأنه اتخذ قرار الضرب ردا على بن لادن. من أجل تصور هذه النتيجة ينبغي فهم العقلية الإسلامية الحالية التي تشعر بعداء أمريكا بسبب مواقفها ضد المسلمين و في المقابل ترى انبطاح حكام المسلمين لأمريكا و استعدادهم لتنفيذ خططها و برامجها، و لهذا فهم متعطشون و متلهفون و بقوة لمن يقف بوجه أمريكا و يثبت أنه أوجعها، وأي إثبات بأن بن لادن أوجع أمريكا و شفى صدور المسلمين أكثر من أن يقف كلينتون بنفسه و يردد اسم بن لادن ثلاث مرات و هو يعلن عن ضرب السودان و أفغانستان كرد على بن لادن و ينفجر بعدها الأعلام الأمريكي و تبعا له الأعلام العالمي و العربي بوصف الحرب الدائرة بين بن لادن و أمريكا. و أنني أعتقد —و أرجو أن لا يساء فهمي— أنه لو لم تعمد أمريكا إلى الرد بهذه الصورة لربما لم يتحول بن لادن إلى ذلك البطل الأسطوري، بل انه لو تمهلت أمريكا و حاولت استغلال الثغرات الشرعية في بيان الجبهة العالمية مستعينة بمن ترشحهم الحكومة السعودية و المصرية من علماء السلطة وركزت على الدماء و الأشلاء في كينيا و تنزانيا حيث قتل عدد كبير من المسلمين، لو عملت ذلك لم يحصل ما حصل من الشعبية لابن لادن و الله أعلم، و لعل الله أراد أن يربك الأمريكان حين قدر أن يتورط رئيسهم بتلك الفضيحة فانقلبت المعادلة بالكامل.

المحور الثالث: وهو لماذا يعلق آل سعود على بن لادن بهذا الأسلوب؟ و كما قلنا فهو فرع عن المحور الأول كذلك، آل سعود لم يتبرأوا من بن لادن لأنه "إرهابي"، بل تبرأوا منه لأنه اشتهر و أصبح أعظم منهم شأنا، فالإرهابيين "السعوديين" كثير و مع ذلك لم يتبرأ آل معود إلا من بن لادن. و السبب له علاقة بتركيبة آل سعود النفسية أكثر من علاقته بابن لادن فآل سعود لا يريدون لأحد ينتمي للبلد المسمى باسمهم أن يكون أعظم شأنا منهم. وعادة ما يتعامل آل سعود مع هذه المشكلة بتحجيم الشخص الذي كبر حجمه مثل ما عملوا مع القصيبي و عايض القرني وسلمان العودة وسفر الحوالي، أما بن لادن فليس لهم سبيل لتحجيمه لأنه بعيد عن نفوذهم وكان الحل الوحيد هو نزع صفة الانتماء للمملكة، و لذلك كانت رائحة الانزعاج من شهرة بن لادن و التايق من علو شأنه تفوح من التعبير والأسلوب الذي استخدمه الأمير نايف والأمير سلطان في التعليق على قضية بن لادن. وقياسا على هذه القاعدة لن أستغرب إذا صدر أمر بسحب جنسية الخطاب الذي يجاهد في الشيشان إذا استمرت شهرته في التنامي وانتظروا تصريحات لنايف عن الخطاب تشبه بصريحاته عن بن لادن.

ing the ulemas even if they are difficult to reach, and even if consulting them may cause delays. . . .

"Friends and enemies all recognize his courage. 'He came within an ace of death more than forty times under heavy arms fire. Three times he was covered with fragments of the bodies of men who had been torn to pieces around him; he mourned those deaths but was unmoved by the events.' He was saved by the hand of God when a Scud exploded seventeen meters from him. Another time he barely missed death from the fumes of chemical weapons surrounding him. Bin Laden has always dreamed of *shahada* [dying for God] and believes that he is living a second life, since he has seen so much death. All that gives him strength and faith to lead the jihad."

المصادر هي إما معلومات مباشرة شخصية بمعنى معايشة مباشرة. أو رواية من عدد كبير ممن عايش بن لادن مباشرة من علماء او مرافقين أو أتباع أو حتى من عائلة بن لان. أو بيانات الشيخ باسمه أو باسم الهيئات أو الجهات التي ارتبط بها. أو المقالات التي صدرت عنه بالصحافة باللغتين العربية والانجليزية. أو تسجيلات لمقابلات تلفزيونية لعدة محطات مثل وغيرهما. ABCو CNN

قضايا و تحليلات عن أسامة بن لادن

شخصية بن لادن

نشأ بن لادن نشأة صالحة سواء من حيث الالتزام بفروض الإسلام أو من حيث الأخلاق والأدب العام. تعود بن لادن في ظلال تربية والده على المسؤولية والثقة بالنفس والكرم والتواضع و هي صفات قلما تجمع في شخص واحد. ويعرف عنه كذلك الحياء وقلة الكلام ويبدوا عليه ملامح الجدية معظم الأحيان و يحاول مع ذلك أن يبدو بشوشا لكنه يتجنب رفع الصوت عموما أو المبالغة بالضحك. هذا كله عرف عنه حتى قبل أن ينخرط في الجهاد.

بعد أن انخرط في الجهاد تجلت فيه صفات أخرى من بينها البذل والتضحية و الصبر و التحمل، و ترجمت ثقته بنفسه و قدرته على تحمل المسؤولية إلى قدرة قيادية سواء من حيث المفهوم الميداني أو من حيث مفهوم قيادة الجماعة. و لابن لادن شعبية قوية عند أتباعه فهم يحبونه حبا جما، لكن يقول العارفون به عن قرب أنه لسبب أو لآخر فإن "الكاريزما" عنده ليست طاغية ربما لأنه يتجنب التميز عن أتباعه ويتبسط أكثر من اللازم فتزول آثار الهيبة. و يحرص بن لادن على مشاركة الشباب المرافقين له في كل نشاطاتهم وحياتهم اليومية ويتجنب أن يتميز عنهم بأكل أو شرب أو ملبس أو سكن. ورغم أنه متزوج من عدة نساء ألا أنه يقضي مع أتباعه وقتا أكثر مما يقضي مع أسرته.

القدرات القيادية والذهنية

من حيث المستوى العقلي و القدرات الذهنية يوصف بن لادن بأنه على درجة جيدة من الذكاء و الثقة بالنفس ودقة الملاحظة والبديهة. لكن من حيث ربط هذه القدرات الذهنية بقدرته القيادية و التخطيطية يشير العارفون بشخصيته أن لديه شيء من التردد في اتخاذ القرارات والحكم على الأمور إلى درجة تؤدي إلى الضرر بعض الأحيان. لكن هناك من يبرر تردده بأنه يفضل التريث في اتخاذ القرارات و استشارة العلماء و المشايخ و ليس بسبب عدم ثقة بالنفس. و يحرص بن لادن فعلا على استشارة العلماء حتى مع الظروف الأمنية الصعبة ولعل هذا كان من أسباب تأخر القرارات من قبله. وفي حين يعتبر بعضهم ذلك دليلا على الرشد والتروي فإن آخرين ينظرون إلى توسيع دائرة الاستشارة وتضمنها للقضايا الحركية بتفاصيلها و انتظار الرأي من عدد من العلماء الذين يصعب الاتصال بهم تكلفا زائدا يتعارض مع طبيعة الحسم و العزيمة في القيادة.

الشجاعة والحذر

من الصفات الصارخة التي يتحلى بها والتي يجمع عليها أنصاره و أعداؤه صفة الشجاعة، و يقول القريبون منه أنه بالإمكان أن تنفجر قنبلة ضخمة على مسافة قريبة و لا تتحرك منه شعرة. و لقد تعرض خلال أحداث أفغانستان إلى أكثر من أربعين مرة لحوادث قصف ثقيل وفي ثلاث حالات منها كان اللحم يتطاير عن يمينه وشماله ولم يظهر عليه ما يدل على تأثر يذكر

Document 2

Communiqué no. 17, August 3, 1995.
"Open letter from Osama bin Laden to King Fahd
concerning the latest cabinet shuffle."

[Extract 1] "I would like to speak frankly to you about everything you and your entourage have done against God and religion."

[Extract 2] "The cabinet shuffle was disappointing because it did not touch the source of the disease or the basis for the catastrophe: you, your defense minister, and your interior minister."

[Extract 3] "[You have given] millions and millions of dollars to the infidel Syria, to reward it for having slaughtered thousands of Muslims in Hama in 1982. . . . Your regime supported the Maronites of the Kataeb [the Phalange] in Lebanon. You support the despotic regime that is crushing Islam and the Muslims in Algeria. You support, with weapons and money, the Christian insurgents of southern Sudan."

[Not illustrated] The communiqué goes on to accuse King Fahd of not applying the rules of the Koran, nor sharia, of behaving in an atheistic manner, for example by accepting impious religious practices (usury).

Fahd's foreign policy is "tied to the Crusaders [Christians] and to despotic Muslim countries." He is criticized for supporting the communists in Yemen (p. 8) and for having supported the mujahedeen in Afghanistan not for love of Islam but to protect Western interests threatened by Soviet vic-

هيئة النصيحة و الإصلاح
البيان رقم (١٧) ١-١٠
التاريخ ١٤١٦/٣/٥هـ الموافق ١٩٩٥/٨/٣م

بسم الله الرحمن الرحيم

رسالة مفتوحة إلى الملك فهد
بمناسبة التعديل الوزاري الأخير

[Extract 1]

الحمد لله والصلاة والسلام على رسول الله وعلى آله وصحبه ومن اهتدى بهداه .

إلى ملك نجد والحجاز فهد بن عبد العزيز، السلام على من اتبع الهدى، وبعد، فهذه رسالة مفتوحة نبعث بها إليك بعيداً عن ألقاب المجاملات الملكية وألقاب التفخيم، وهي مصارحة لك ببعض ما يمكن التصريح به مما ارتكبته أنت ومن حولك من أمور عظام في حق الله ودينه، وحق عباده وبلاده، وحق حرمه

[Extract 2]

الشورى الذي انتظرته الأمة طويلاً وخيّب آمالها بعد أن وُلد ميتاً، وما قمتم به أخيراً من تعديل وزاري هامشي لم يمسّ رأس الداء وأساس البلاء الذي هو أنت ووزير دفاعك ووزير داخليتك وأمير الرياض ومن على شاكلتكم.

[Extract 3]

أعلن عن دفع أربعة مليارات من الدولارات مساعدة للإتحاد السوفيتي السابق الذي لم يغسل بعد يديه الملطخة بدماء الشعب المسلم في أفغانستان، وذلك سنة ١٩٩١م ،ونظام حكمكم حارس العقيدة الصحيحة فهو الذي دفع قبل ذلك آلاف ملايين من الدولارات للنظام النصيري السوري سنة ١٩٨٢م، مكافأة له على ذبح عشرات الآلاف من المسلمين في مدينة حماة، وهو كان يدعم الموارنة النصارى من حزب الكتائب اللبناني ضد المسلمين هناك، ونظام حكمكم (الرشيد!) هو الذي دفع مليارات الدولارات للنظام الطاغوتي الذي يطحن الإسلام والمسلمين في الجزائر، ونفس النظام هو الذي دعم بالمال والسلاح المتمردين

[Extract 4]

وآخر دعوانا أن الحمد لله رب العالمين

عنهم / أسامة بن محمد بن عوض بن لادن
(التوقيع)

التاريخ : ٥ / ٣ / ١٤١٦ هـ
الموافق : ٣ / ٨ / ١٩٩٥ م

tory. The communiqué condemns his pro-American attitude in Somalia (p. 9) and in Palestine, for having advocated submission and capitulation.

[p. 9, not illustrated] "You financially support Arafat so that he can impose what the Jewish occupiers have not succeeded in doing (win the repression, conquer Jihad and Hamas). . . . Your kingdom is nothing but an American protectorate, and you are under Washington's heel."

[p. 12, not illustrated] Fahd is criticized for the country's indebtedness; for the educational and health situation—hospitals are badly maintained—and unemployment, especially among graduates; for his fairytale royal palace and sumptuous residences in all the cities of the country and in Western capitals and seaside resorts. He is also blamed for his role in the collapse of the price of oil.

[p. 13, not illustrated] Fahd is criticized for the expenses caused by the Gulf War, with the purchase of British Tornado jets, while the number of pilots was insufficient.

[p. 14, not illustrated] Bin Laden reminds Fahd of the fate of the shah of Iran, of Marcos in the Philippines, of Ceaucescu in Romania, and even of King Saud who had been forced to abdicate, and complains of the inadequacy of Saudi troops on land, at sea, and in the air, which wastes of hundreds of billions of dollars.

[p. 17, not illustrated] Bin Laden attacks General Sultan [head of Saudi forces during the Gulf War] for his "blazing failure" and blasts kickbacks on arms sales.

[p. 18, not illustrated] "To protect your tottering throne, you require the presence of troops of the Crusaders and the Jews who are profaning the holy places."

[p. 20, not illustrated] "For your own good and the good of your family, abdicate. You who demanded the removal of King Saud who was tens of times less corrupt than you, dismiss your defense minister who brought about a border dispute with Qatar and almost caused a war with Yemen."

[Extract 4] From Osama bin Mohamed bin Awadh bin Laden [signature]

[Date] 5/3/1416 [of the Hegira, i.e., August 3, 1995]

Document 3

Excerpt from the transcript of the interrogation of Ahmed al-Sayed al-Najar, September 13, 1998

This document shows that al-Najar has been connected since 1979 to the Tanzim al-Jihad, which was under the command of Ayman al-Zawahiri (Osama's future right-hand man). Al-Najar was in charge of the Daawa (Islamic preaching) branch of the Tanzim of the Interior (Egypt). Using a false passport in 1993, he was able to reach Yemen via Jordan, where he lived with Marjan Salem and Mohammed al-Zawahiri (Ayman's brother). Short of money, they committed robberies, notably of tools and electrical equipment from the German consulate in the capital of Yemen. Al-Najar met Ayman al-Zawahiri in Khartoum, and al-Zawahiri appointed him head of the civilian branch of the Tanzim in Egypt.

The Umra, a religious ceremony that takes place in Mecca during Ramadan, served as a cover for him to meet militants in 1995. In October of the same year, Ayman al-Zawahiri also appointed him head of the Tanzim in Yemen.

In January 1996, he found work in Albania first in a charitable association, Al Haramaïn, then in an association called Resurrection of the Islamic Heritage, in Tirana, from which he had telephone contact with London. In case of difficulties in Albania, he learned that Osama bin Laden was prepared to take care of any member of the Tanzim going to Afghanistan and to offer them one hundred dollars a month for each family, although he pointed out that life was very primitive and opportunities to educate sons were infrequent. The Tanzim found welcome in Sudan, Yemen, Azerbaijan, Afghanistan, Saudi Arabia, and Southeast Asia, but also in Austria, Germany, and London.

Sources of finance were the following:

1. The support of bin Laden

2. Ten percent deducted from the pay of Tanzim members

3. Economic activities involving the sugar trade and trading in Southeast Asia, as well as sheep-raising in Albania

4. Renovation of old buildings in London

Statement of September 15, 1998

Al-Najar reveals that Ayman al-Zawahiri was responsible for the explosion at the Egyptian embassy in Islamabad (late 1994). After the attack on Khan el-Khalili (a bazaar for antiquities, gold, and carpets, heavily frequented by tourists), al-Zawahiri suspended operations in Egypt and reorganized the Tanzim of the Interior because of lack of money, which forced the leaders to look for work.

"I broke off all contact with the members who remained in Egypt," says al-Najar. Through the Resurrection of the Islamic Heritage association in Albania, which was also in charge of aid to orphans, he was offered a position teaching sharia and Arabic in Al Haramaïn.

"I gave up my duties at the head of the Tanzim of the Interior," he goes on, "when I left for Tirana."

He flew to Damascus in January 1996, where he took a bus to Istanbul; in Istanbul he bought plane tickets for Tirana. An Albanian immigration officer sent him back to Turkey "because I did not want to give him a bribe." He continues: "But I had only one visa for a single entry into the country. The Turks wanted to deport me to Egypt. But the representative of the Egyptian airline refused to board me because I did not have enough money. I was able to contact a Syrian or a Lebanese, who gave me an airline ticket to Damascus. The organization would send me a new ticket for Tirana, provided I only went through Turkey in transit. The head of the association, a Saudi, was interested in my contacts with other organizations, my criminal charges, and my stays in Afghanistan.

"Our association is financed by donations and has offices in Azerbaijan and Bosnia, and I believe in Kenya, Tanzania, America, and Bangladesh. One of the members of the Tanzim in Albania was denounced by the Albanian press. He had to leave for the Netherlands and then went to England. Another settled in Bulgaria where he was arrested; a third left for Azerbaijan, after he was arrested carrying counterfeit passports for Ireland.

"I remained in charge of the civilian branch of the Tanzim of the Interior during the first eight months of my stay in Albania, until Doctor Ayman al-Zawahiri had me replaced.

"The sharia committee published a journal entitled *Nida al Jihad* [Call to Jihad], but I don't know where it was published."

Statement of September 16, 1998

This transcript reveals that Osama bin Laden offered the necessary financial support and participated in several actions of the Egyptian group Islamic Jihad. We also learn that he built a reception center for Arab mujahedeen and that his relations with the other organizations were excellent. He offered leaders the opportunity to participate in profitable commercial speculations and provided jobs in his businesses in Sudan.

The Taliban required bin Laden to bear the whole responsibility for the Afghan Arabs on his own, not only in Afghanistan but also in Yemen and Sudan. Islamic Jihad and Gamaa Islamiya disagreed on the emirate of Omar Abdul Rahman: Islamic Jihad objected to him because they believed that his blindness made him ineligible to be emir. In addition, Gamaa Islamiya insisted that their leaders, who were in prison, have the last word. Attempts at conciliation by the Sudanese failed. Thanks to his good reputation, bin Laden succeeded in resolving the disagreements, and Mustapha Hamza and Rifaï Taha were able to name Omar Abdul Rahman as emir. According to bin Laden, the weakening of Muslim peoples and governments was caused by the Jewish lobby that governed America: emancipation from that hegemony was the principal objective. For this purpose, worldwide guerrilla war should target American and Israeli interests, which would oblige America and its collaborators to reconsider their Arab and Islamic policies. Its success, despite the insufficiency of forces and resources compared to those of Arab and Muslim states, would prove the degree of weakness of the leaders of those states.

Bin Laden's declaration in March 1998 calling for the resources of the Front to be devoted to striking at American interests, as well as the attacks on the American embassies in Tanzania and Kenya, would also demonstrate to Arab and Muslim countries the fragility of America. In fact, in spite of warnings, it was unable to protect its embassies.

"I confirm that al-Zawahiri is Osama bin Laden's adjutant. Bin Laden is in charge of the greater part of the financing. Our ideology is based on the preaching of the Daawa and the application of sharia, with the establishment of the caliphate that will take charge of carrying out the commandments of Allah."

The fusion of some groups in Southeast Asia will spread confusion within the Front, because Arab presence there will be ambiguous, but the activity of the Front is a source of attraction for all the Muslims in the world.

In Egypt, the organizations had become so weak that they were unable to carry out operations, which could only encourage them to merge. "For me, this Front is the one and only hope; it symbolizes a new orientation for the Islamic movements in the world."

Because of the animosity directed against the interests of Muslims, their culture, and their holy places, non-Muslim political parties in the Arab world, such as socialists and leftists, support this objective.

Al-Najar also hopes for the realization of a single *umma* (a state encompassing all Muslims).

Statement of September 20, 1998

The transcript tells us that preachers of the Tanzim use mosques inside schools and universities and take advantage of various school activities. Gamaa Islamiya had tried to infiltrate the police and the army in order to force the government to resign. But by the early 1980s, this tactic had become unreliable, because of a lack of resources and the impossibility of carrying out a coup d'état. Gamaa Islamiya then turned toward guerrilla-style actions. Because of the unfavorable context, these operations suffered failure after failure. In early 1990, Gamaa Islamiya carried out jihad operations, such as the attack against the interior minister Hassan al-Elfi and prime minister Atef Sedki, as well as the attack against American and Israeli tourists at Khan el-Khalili.

Al-Najar confirms that the principal financing for operations comes from bin Laden, other sources being provided by commercial activities.

The Tanzim relies on two councils: the Shoura, the more important, headed by al-Zawahiri after 1991, and the Institutional Council.

Document 4

Communiqué of the Popular Arab and Islamic Conference

The communiqué calls for Palestinian national union, despite the proliferation of organizations (*tanzim*), and for the establishment of committees for weapons supplies and for propaganda.

Gamaa Islamiya met in order to make contact with Abu Amar [Yasser Arafat].

Dated January 4, 1993, the communiqué is signed by Salim Zaamur, president of the Committee of Fatah (bottom right of the document; see illustration), but most important, by Hassan al-Turabi, general secretary of the Popular Arab and Islamic Conference (bottom center), and by Mussa Abu Marzuk, president of Hamas (bottom left).

بسم الله الرحمن الرحيم

المؤتمر الشعبي العربي والإسلامي

POPULAR ARAB AND ISLAMIC CONFERENCE

الأمين العام

الشعب الفلسطيني نحو الوحدة الوطنية، وتتفرع عن اللجنة اللجان التي ترعى شؤون الإمداد والإعلام والتعبئة الجماهيرية والسياسية وتتصل اللجنة بالسيد ياسر عرفات في تحركات العمل الرسمي الدبلوماسي.

وعلى اللجنة أن تجتمع في كل مكان [illegible] خاصة الرئاسية التي أوردها في الاجتماع ومن ذلك في لبنان والأردن وتونس.

٧. اتفق على أن يعود أربعة بمناوبة الوافدين إلى الخرطوم عند تمام أسبوعين ذلك لتسمية أسماء سائر اللجان منهما، والتشاور حول الأمكنة التي تجتمع أو تعمل فيها اللجان وأي تدابير إجرائية بشأن ذلك.

٨. اتفق على أن تستأنف لجنة الجامعة الإسلامية بغزة أعمالها ويجري الاتصال والتشاور مع الأخ أبي عمار والجهات المعنية بشأنها.

٩. اتفق الطرفان على مراجعة المواثيق التي حررت أولياً بينهما لإجازتها ولتأكيدها هادياً للعمل التنسيقي المشترك.

١٠. اتفق الطرفان على أن يلتزما عملاً بأن تجتنب أصوات الإعلام الصادرة عنها أي تهجم على الآخر أو ذكر سلبي مباشر أو غير مباشر وأن ينضبطا أو أحدهما عن أي مظهر للصراع أو فعل للاشتباك أو الكيد والقتال مع الآخر وأن يراعيا عرفهما في اللفظ والتعامل الفلسطيني يحسن الخطاب المتبادل رغم بعض اختلاف الرأي وروح الوحدة الفلسطينية رغم تعدد التنظيمات.

١٩٩٣/١/٤

د. موسى أبو مرزوق
رئيس وفد حركة حماس

سليم الزعنون
رئيس وفد حركة فتح

د. حسن الترابي
الأمين العام للمؤتمر الشعبي العربي الإسلامي

Document 5

Statement believed to be from the Gamaa Islamiya in Egypt

"Your crime will not go unpunished! With missiles and planes, the Americans have carried out the largest terrorist operation in the world. Bombs were dropped yesterday on Sudan and Afghanistan killing women and children and destroying a pharmaceutical factory. These are the same bombs that were dropped on a shelter in Iraq [an American missile pierced through the Amariya shelter in Baghdad on February 13, 1991, incinerating 1,200 people].

"The White House is drowning in a sea of shame and crimes. The Americans are unable to confront the mujahedeen on a battlefield. . . . Muslims must support Sudan and Afghanistan. We must surround American embassies in the Arab countries and force Arab leaders to close them, because they are nests of spies. The Americans must stop applauding their leaders when they kill Muslims."

بسم الله الرحمن الرحيم

<u>لن تمر جريمتكم بدون عقاب</u>

لقد رأى العالم الولايات المتحدة الأمريكية وهي تضرب بصواريخها وطائراتها ما تسميه بالقانون الدولي في أكبر عملية علنية للإرهاب الدولي الذي تمارسه دولة امتلكت كل أسلحة القتل والدمار والإرهاب .

إن القنابل التي ألقيت بالأمس على السودان وأفغانستان لتقتل المدنيين والنساء والأطفال وتحطم مصنعا للأدوية هي نفسها القنابل التي ألقيت على المدنيين العزل في ملجأ العامرية وقانا ومدرسة بحر البقر .

إن هذه الغارات التي شنتها الطائرات الأمريكية بزعم ضرب قواعد المجاهدين لهي عمل إرهابي جبان لم يأبه بأي قواعد وتخطى كل الحدود ، وجاءت لتستر سوءة البيت الأبيض الأمريكي بعد أن تمرغ في وحل الجريمة والعار . ولتغطي عجز القوات الأمريكية عن قدرتها على مواجهة المجاهدين في ميدان القتال ، فذهبت تلقي بالقنابل على المدنيين والأطفال .

إن الجماعة الإسلامية وردا على هذا العمل الهمجي الأحمق لتؤكد على ما يلي :

١- أن المسلمين كافة مدعوون رغم [illegible] على [illegible] وهم مطالبون أمام هذا الصلف الأمريكي برد العدوان والانتباه [illegible] الصهيونية والسيطرة الأمريكية على مقدراتنا وأرضنا .

٢- أن الحركات الإسلامية والجهادية منها على وجه الخصوص مدعوة للقيام بدورها في مواجهة هذه الغطرسة ومخاطبة الولايات المتحدة الأمريكية باللغة التي تفهمها "وكم من فئة قليلة غلبت فئة كثيرة بإذن الله" .

٣- أن الشعوب المسلمة مدعوة للتعبير عن غضبها والوقوف مع شعبيها في السودان وأفغانستان وهي مطالبة بمحاصرة السفارات الأمريكية في بلادنا الإسلامية وإرغام الحكام على إغلاقها وطرد البعثات الدبلوماسية منها .

٤- أنه آن الأوان لإنهاء مهزلة ذبح المسلمين وتقديمهم قرابين على أعتاب البيت الأبيض الأمريكي للتغطية لنزوات حكامه وفضائحهم وإخفاقاتهم الداخلية .

٥- أن الشيطان الأمريكي عليه أن يكف عن التمسح [illegible] كلما أرادوا [illegible] مسلما ، وأنه ينبغي أن يدرك أنه إذا كان كثرة عدد القتلى من المسلمين تعني كثرة المؤيدين في صناديق الاقتراع للرؤساء الأمريكيين ، فإن ذلك لن يكون سهلا ولن يكون بدون ثمن .

Document 6

Communiqué of the World Islamic Front

"Clinton scorns more than a billion Muslims.

"Kill the infidels where they are, drive them out of the places from which they have driven you. America is the leader of the infidel countries. The aggression against Sudan and Afghanistan is an aggression against the Muslims of the entire world. To fight the infidel countries, America and Israel, is a duty for all Muslims. These two aggressions are the height of world terrorism, worthy of pirates or cowboys. . . . This aggression proves the Americans' lack of strategy, which brought Clinton to power. This attack demonstrates American cretinism and its contempt for Muslims. It proves the ineptitude of the CIA, for there was no connection with Sheikh Mujahed Osama bin Laden. . . . These attacks prove the hostility of 'black dogs and swine, vile beings against men full of pride.' Let us fight in the jihad for our pride and our lands. It is a duty imposed by Sharia to answer aggression from America and its allies.

"We must close all their embassies in Muslim countries, boycott their economy, withdraw all our money from their banks and companies, prohibit their use of our air space, and block their means of communication.

"Muslims, awake!

"Return to your religion, stop supporting your corrupt leaders so that they will stop humiliating you, terrorizing you, and making you into a consumer product."

بيان صادر عن الجبهة الإسلامية العالمية

كلينتون يحتقر أكثر من مليار مسلم

(هذا بلاغ للناس ولينذروا به)

إن الحمد لله نحمده ونستعينه ونستغفره، ونعوذ بالله من شرور أنفسنا ومن سيئات أعمالنا، من يهده الله فهو المهتد ومن يضلل فلن تجد له وليا مرشدا، ونشهد أن لا إله إلا الله وحده لا شريك له، ونشهد أن محمداً عبده ورسوله؛

قال الله تبارك وتعالى: (وقاتلوا في سبيل الله الذين يقاتلونكم ولا تعتدوا إن الله لا يحب المعتدين واقتلوهم حيث ثقفتموهم وأخرجوهم من حيث أخرجوكم)

إن ما قامت به أمريكا زعيمة دول الكفر هذا اليوم من اعتداء وحشي على السودان وأفغانستان [illegible] اعتداء على المسلمين [illegible] فمن اعتدى عليكم فاعتدوا عليه بمثل ما اعتدى عليكم [illegible] الاعتداء على أي بلد من بلاد المسلمين، من قبل أية دولة أو قوة كافرة، سواء كانت أمريكا أو إسرائيل، يجعل قتالها فرضا على المسلمين.

إنه اعتداء [illegible] في الإرهاب الدولي [illegible] وقطاع الطرق [illegible] الإبادة والإرهاب [illegible] وهو أسلوب [illegible] الدولة [illegible] الدولة الأولى في العالم.

إنه اعتداء [illegible] على مدى الغطرسة الأمريكية التي أوصلت كلينتون [illegible] التقدير [illegible] على معالجة القضايا كدولة لا كعصابة.

إن ما قامت به أمريكا من قصف [illegible] الخرطوم [illegible] الكثير من المسلمين والأبرياء العزل يدل على مدى استهانة أمريكا واحتقارها للمسلمين.

إن هذا العمل [illegible] من قبل أمريكا يدل على [illegible] لأنها تعرضت [illegible] إن سفارة أمريكا [illegible] القواعد [illegible] في الخليج. لقد تحدت أمريكا جميع المسلمين في العالم [illegible] ولا من أطفال [illegible] ولا من أعزاء [illegible] في سبيل [illegible] أيها المسلمون [illegible] دياركم [illegible].

أيها المسلمون: يجب علينا جميعا أن نرد على عدوان أمريكا [illegible] من جميع بلاد المسلمين [illegible] أموالنا من مصارفهم وبلادهم وأن نطرد جميع شركاتهم، وأن نزيل كل وجود لهم [illegible] بلاد المسلمين، وأن نحرم أجواءنا [illegible] على طائراتهم [illegible] ووسائل مواصلاتهم.

أيها المسلمون: [illegible] والله أن تستيقظوا من نومكم [illegible] من سباتكم، وأن تعودوا إلى [illegible] من هؤلاء الحكام [illegible] موارد الهلاك [illegible] في إذلالكم والعسف بكم، والتآمر [illegible] والمتاجرة بكم، والتسلط عليكم [illegible].

أيها المسلمون: نعاهد الله عز وجل بأن هذا العمل الوحشي لن يمر من دون عقاب رادع وأن [illegible].

الجبهة الإسلامية العالمية

Document 7

[This is the first publication in English of this document]

"In the name of Merciful God

"Abdallah Azzam has revived the soul of the jihad with his words and his writings.

"He has presented the Afghan jihad to the entire Muslim world.

"He has given his life and that of two of his children for the jihad.

"The communiqué commends his soul to God.

"May he continue to inspire the martyrs in Afghanistan."

[Signed] Office of Services

Command of Camps and Fronts.

[The Bureau of Services coordinated all the actions of bin Laden and his associates.]

بسم الله الرحمن الرحيم

الإهداء الأول

كلمة حق ودمعة وفاء

إلى الأخ الحبيب وشيخنا الفاضل عبد الله عزام (رحمه الله تعالى)

الذي أحيا روح الجهاد في نفوس الشباب بكلماته ؛ وكتابته .

الذي ربى النفوس على الجهاد بصدقه وإخلاصه .

الذي قدم ما تعجز أي جماعة عن عمله .

الذي قدم الجهاد الأفغاني الإسلامي للعالم

الذي صبر ولم يترك الميدان رغم الحجج ورغم الضغوط ورغم الإيذاء من معظم الناس إلا من والديه رحمهم الله .

الذي قدم حياته وحياة ثمرتين من فؤاده من أجل الجهاد .

إلى الله هذا العمل ثم إليك .

أسأل الله أن يجعله في ميزان حسناتك وكل من يستفيد منه إلى يوم القيامة ثم إلى أرواح الشهداء المسلمين في أفغانستان وغيرها

مكتب الخدمات

إدارة المعسكرات والجبهات

Document 8

Extract from an interview with Ibn-ul-Khattab, commander of the mujahedeen in the Caucasus, as published in London by Azzam Publications

"The West and the rest of the world are accusing Usama Bin Ladin of being the prime sponsor and organizer of what they call "International Terrorism" today. But as far as we are concerned, he is our brother in Islam. He is someone of knowledge and a Mujahid fighting with his wealth and himself for the sake of Allah. He is a sincere brother and he is completely the opposite to what the disbelievers are accusing him of. We know that he is well established with the Mujahideen in Afghanistan and other places in the world. But the distance between him and us is very big. As you know, routes and communications between him and us are severed. . . .

"What the Americans are saying is not true. However, it is an obligation for all Muslims to help each other in order to promote the religion of Islam. Usama Bin Laden is one of the major scholars of the Jihad, as well as being a main commander of the Mujahideen worldwide. He fought for many years against the Communists in Afghanistan and now is engaged in a war against American Imperialism. Usama Bin Laden never financed us in the Jihad in Dagestan because the distance between us is too huge and we have no contact whatsoever. Even during the Jihad in Afghanistan, such amounts of money ($25 million) were never spent by the Mujahideen in order to fight the Russian Forces. The Mujahideen have very basic means, with little weapons and money. Million or not, this will not delay or boost our Jihad for the sake of Allah. Our weapon is to believe in Allah (Iman). We just have to rely on Allah for help. Weapons, funds, support from individuals or groups is not everything. Allah will help those who are sincere in their intention of fighting for His Sake."

Military Commander of the Mujahideen in the Caucasus: Ibn-ul-Khattab. This interview was made on 27 September 1999.

Azzam Publications is only a news outlet. We do not have links with Mujahideen anywhere.

Azzam Publications

BCM Ubud, London WCIN 3XX, United Kingdom.

"And with the likes of all these (martyrs), nations are established, convictions are brought to life and ideologies are made victorious." [Shaheed Dr. Sheikh Abdullah Azzam, assassinated 1989]

INTERVIEW WITH IBN-UL-KHATTAB,MILITARY COMMANDER OF THE MUJAHIDEEN IN THE CAUCASUS.

MONDAY 27 SEPTEMBER 1999.

Distributed by: Azzam Publications,

The West and the rest of the world are accusing Usama Bin Ladin of being the prime sponsor and organizer of what they call 'International Terrorism', today. But as far as we are concerned, he is our brother in Islam. He is someone of knowledge and a Mujahid fighting with his wealth and himself for the sake of Allah. He is a sincere brother and he is completely the opposite to what the disbelievers are accusing him of. We know that he is well established with the Mujahideen in Afghanistan and other places in the world. But the distance between him and us is very big. As you know, routes and communication between him and us are severed.

What the Americans are saying is not true. However, it is an obligation for all Muslims to help each other in order to promote the religion of Islam. Usama Bin Laden is one of the major scholars of the Jihad, as well as being a main commander of the Mujahideen worldwide. He fought for many years against the Communists in Afghanistan and now is engaged in a war against American Imperalism.Usama Bin Laden never financed us in the Jihad in Dagestan because the distance between us is too huge and we have no contact whatsoever. Even during the Jihad in Afghanistan, such amounts of money ($25 million) were never spent by the Mujahideen in order to fight the Russian Forces. The Mujahideen have very basic means, with little weapons and money. Million or not, this will not delay or boost our Jihad for the sake of Allah. Our weapon is to believe in Allah (Iman). We just have to rely on Allah for help. Weapons, funds, support from individuals or groups is not everything. Allah will help those who are sincere in their intention of fighting for His Sake.

Military Commander of the Mujahideen in the Caucasus: Ibn-ul-Khattab This interview was made on 27 September 1999

Azzam Publications is only a news outlet. We do not have links with Mujahideen anywhere.

Azzam Publications

BCM Ubud,London WC1N 3XX,UNITED KINGDOM.

"And with the likes of all these (martyrs), nations are established, convictions are brought to life and ideologies are made victorious." [Shaheed Dr. Sheikh Abdullah Azzam, assassinated 1989]

Document 9

From *Al Anssar* (*The Partisans*) ["the weekly of the jihad in Algeria and everywhere"], no. 107 (July 27, 1995)

[p. 1] The front page headlines report that brigades of the GIA have hit the "despots" very hard in the east, the west, the north, and the south. The soldiers of the Islamic groups of Gamaa Islamiya in Egypt are multiplying military operations. In a heroic and rare suicide operation, the Al Kassam brigades [Palestine] have killed a large number of "sons of monkeys and pigs [Jews]." A large explosion has shaken the capital of the Crusaders [Paris], causing many deaths and wounding many others (p. 13 specifies that this was the Saint-Michel Metro station, which is "in one of the most fashionable neighborhoods in the city . . . located to the west of the Élysée palace [*sic*]) .

[p. 2] A Swedish post office box is listed, the only indication of the source of the newsletter. The newsletter explains the meaning of the Daawa and claims that thousands of Muslims have been killed for the sake of this word in Sarajevo, Chechnya, Tajikistan, Kashmir, Eritrea, Palestine, Saudi Arabia, the Philippines, and China.

[p. 3] A report of the assassination by the GIA of a high official in the Ministry of Religious Affairs, because the ministry had called on all Christian countries for assistance. Other reports: ten members of the FLN have been killed by the GIA, because the FLN is a secular party that has destroyed the country and the faithful. An Italian Christian has been machine-gunned: "The pig died in no time."

بسم الله الرحمن الرحيم

الأنصار

عن أبي هريرة رضي الله عنه قيل يا رسول الله ما يعدل الجهاد في سبيل الله ؟ قال لا تستطيعونه فأعادوا عليه مرتين وثلاث كل ذلك يقول لا تستطيعونه ، ثم قال : « مثل المجاهد في سبيل الله كمثل الصائم القائم القانت بآيات الله لا يفتر من صيام ولا صلاة حتى يرجع المجاهد » رواه الخمسة إلا أبو داود

(نشرة أسبوعية تصدر عن أنصار الجهاد في الجزائر وفي كل مكان — الخميس 28 صفر 1416 هـ الموافق لـ 27/07/1995 — العدد 107)

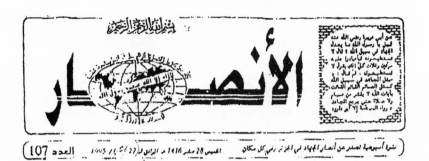

في كل الإتجاهات .. شرقا وغربا ، شمالاً وجنوبا

كتائب الجماعة الإسلاميّة المسلّحة تضرب الطواغيت بقوّة .

رغبة من قيادة الجماعة الإسلامية المسلحة في الحفاظ على ثمرة الجهاد ..

نشرة « الأنصار » تعيد نشر البيان رقم 29 .

في تعهيد عسكري جهادي أرعب العدو المرتد

جنود الجماعة الإسلاميّة بمصر يكثّفون من عملياتهم العسكرية المركّزة ..

في عملية استشهادية بطولية نادرة

« كتائب القسّام » تقتل عددا من أبناء القردة والخنازير .

تتسبّب في مقتل عدد من الأشخاص وجرح عدد آخر .

انفجار عنيف يهزّ العاصمة الفرنسيّة الصّليبيّة باريس .

An armored vehicle of the Algerian army, bought with the aid of the "Saujudi" family [the Judaized Saudi royal family] was destroyed by a mine. A drug seller was kidnapped "before the judgment of God was carried out." Two prostitutes known for their relations with the oppressors [representatives of the government] have been slaughtered. Many roadblocks have been set up; "the most amusing thing is that the cup of the Republic which was to be presented to the winner by the impious Zeroual [Algerian president] was confiscated" at one of these roadblocks.

[p. 5] The newsletter reports that "our" prisoners are rotting in "the jails of the anti-Prophet militants, Fahd, Qadaffi, Saddam, Hassan II, Hussein of Jordan, Zeroual, Mubarak [in Arabic, "blessed," but the text calls him "unblessed"]. It threatens to cut off the finger of a secular writer.

[pp. 6 and 7] Readers are told of a Palestinian sheikh who leans to nonviolence and of Khomeini's having renounced a part of his faithfulness to his people in return for the treatment shown him of the French [who provided refuge during his exile and allowed him to return to Iran]. Gandhi was created by the English to prevent the Muslims from ruling India.

[p. 13] This page contains four reports. The first, after claiming responsibility for the assassination of army and police officers in Upper Egypt, is devoted to Palestine, noting that Hamas has planted a bomb in downtown Tel Aviv, which killed seven "Jewish pigs and wounded thirty-three others. . . . The miscreant Arafat condemned this operation which can only give hope to the hearts of good Muslims."

The second report is devoted to France and says that the GIA glorifies the attack on the Saint-Michel metro station in Paris.

Next, the situation in Tunisia is described, with the repression against the En-Nahda movement (described as a democratic political movement), headed by Rashid Ghannouchi.

The last report gives news from Bosnia, noting battles between the Muslims of Bosnia and the Serbs "heavily armed by Russia, Israel, and miscreant Arabs."

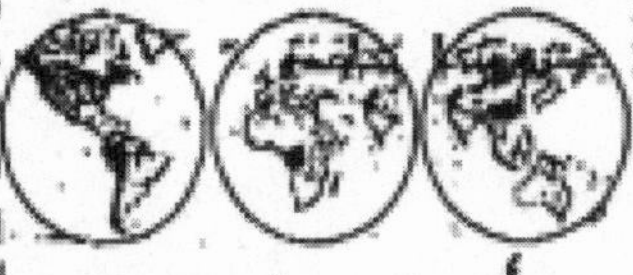

أخبار وتعاليق

مصر : كنا قد ذكرنا في العدد الماضي من نشرة «الأنصار» خبراً مفاده أن مجاهدي الجماعة الإسلامية بمصر اغتالوا ضابطاً رفيعاً، لكن الشائعات أوضحت بعد ذلك أن الهالك لم يكن الوحيد في هذه اللحظة، بل نقل إلى جانبه أيضاً نائباً وملازماً أولاً.

وفي عملية جديدة خلال اليومين الماضيين قامت سرية تابعة للجماعة الإسلامية بصعيد مصر بالهجوم على سيارة تابعة لشرطة الطاغوت : فقتلوا ثلاثة من ركابها وجرحوا آخرين، وقد عاد المجاهدون إلى قواعدهم سالمين بعد تنفيذ هذه العملية الجريئة.

ثم ثلاث من المجاهدين في صعيد مصر بالتحام أحد البنوك وقام بغنيمة كبيرة من الأموال وعادوا إلى قواعدهم سالمين غانمين.

فلسطين : في عملية استشهادية بطولية نادرة نفذها أحد أعضاء حركة حماس الإسلامية تم تفجير قنبلة في أحد الحافلات بأحد شوارع تل أبيب المكتظة باليهود، وعلى إثر هذه العملية قتل 7 خنازير يهود وأصيب 33 آخرا بجراح خطيرة. وقد كان رد فعل المرتد عرفات أن وصف هذه العملية التي تبعث الأمل في النفوس بالعملية (الإرهابية)، أما رد فعل اليهود فقد انتقدوا بشدة حكومة رابين التي لا تزال تصر على عملية السلام في الشرق الأوسط واتهموه أنه سبب في مقتل هؤلاء الستة.

فرنسا : هز انفجار عنيف وضخم باريس يوم الثلاثاء الماضي، وقد أسفر هذا الانفجار الذي وقع في محطة القطار سان ميشال التي تقع في قلب باريس في إحدى أرقى المناطق في العاصمة الفرنسية حيث يكتظ السواح الفرنسيين والأجانب في هذا المكان القريب من قصر الشانزليزي. وقد أسفر هذا الانفجار عن مقتل 7 أشخاص وجرح أكثر من 80 آخرين 30 منهم في حالة خطيرة وتبقى قائمة القتلى مفتوحة نظرا لوقوع إصابات كثيرة. كما ذكرنا في صفوف من كانوا يتواجدون في مكان الحادث.

تونس : بعد حملة الاعتقالات لجماعة الإخوان في مصر والذي أصبح شيئا عاديا ومألوفا، يأتي دور حركة النهضة التونسية التي يرأسها الزنديق راشد الغنوشي. فقد قامت أجهزة الأمن التونسية بتمشيط الأحياء السكنية والبيوت وانتهاك الحرمات والاعتداء على أهالي أعضاء هذه الحركة. للتذكير فإن جماعة الإخوان والنهضة تبنوا الديمقراطية كمبدأ ووسيلة للوصول إلى الحكم وأظهروا ذلك في كثير من المناسبات المحلية والدولية. لكن وبالرغم من هذا فلا تزال الحكومات المرتدة تتعامل معهم على أنهم (أصوليون). أما آن لهؤلاء أن يثوبوا لرشدهم وينزعوا غطاء الذل والصغار والاستسلام ويتركوا المعاقل والمنابر ليلتحقوا بإخوانهم في ساحات الوغى وميدان النزال !!

البوسنة : تدور معارك شرسة بين الصرب الكفار والمسلمين في منطقة جيبا بيهاتش والتي يقاتل المسلمون بأسلحتهم الخفيفة ضد الآلاف من جنود الصرب بأسلحتهم الهائلة المقدمة لهم من قبل روسيا وإسرائيل والصليبيين الغرب. وأكدت الحكومة البوسنية أن جيبا لم تسقط كليا كما تروج الدول الغربية وأنها ما تزال تقاوم رغم حظر الأسلحة المضروب على المسلمين. أما الأمم المتحدة العميلة فبدلا من أن ترسل قواتها لرد هجومات الصرب، فقد أرسلتها لحماية القوات الدولية المحصورة هناك.

الجزيرة العربية : وجه بن باز تحذيرا إلى السعوديين بعدم تنظيم رحلات إلى أوروبا وأمريكا وأكد أن وراء هذه الرحلات خطرا كبيرا على المسلمين. ونحن نسأل : وهل في سفر المسلمين إلى الكيان الصهيوني (كما جاء في فتواه بإجازة الذهاب إلى هناك) خير ونفع للإسلام والمسلمين. ﴿ فإنها لا تعمى الأبصار ولكن تعمى القلوب التي في الصدور ﴾.

الشيشان : بعد توقف المفاوضات بين الروس والشيشان شهدت العاصمة غروزني اشتباكات عنيفة أدت إلى مقتل جندي روسي وجرح آخرين، ويستمر هذا الاشتباك للأسبوع الثاني على التوالي.

ماليزيا : شهدت العاصمة الماليزية كوالالمبور مظاهرات كبيرة تنتقد موقف الأمم المتحدة اتجاه البوسنة وطالبت بإقالة الصليبي الحاقد بطرس غالي من منصبه وحملته استمرار معاناة المسلمين اليومية هناك.

Document 10

Two posters of the mujahedeen movement

[Upper] The poster has an inscription (bottom right) that calls for the jihad for God and for combat against the infidels. It depicts a globe in chains, held by a hand covered in snakeskin, within which is the mosque of the Prophet and the Kabaa. In the upper left is a circular calligraphic text that reads "Fight for God and participate in the Jihad." On the globe is more calligraphy, reading "Expel the infidels from the Arabian Peninsula." The five flags of the United Nations, the United Kingdom, France, the United States, and Israel are depicted in the lower part of the poster, covered with blood. In the background (top center), behind an AK-47, flies the flag of the Harakat ul-Mujahedeen. (The posters of this movement are usually linked to the fight of the mujahedeen in Indian-occupied Kashmir.)

[Lower] This poster represents the logo of Harakat ul-Mujahedeen. In the upper right, an Arabic verse, repeated below in Urdu, reads "Fight for God." In the middle, the word "Allah" is spelled out in letters made of cartridges and underlined by a Pakistani automatic weapon, frequently used by the "Freedom Fighters."

حركة المجاهدين

Document 11

Excerpts from the communiqué of Islamic Jamaa of the mujahedeen

[1.] "The objective: to restore the land to its people despoiled by the West, Morocco."

[2.] "Morocco is Islamic, speaks Arabic and Berber."

[3.] "The Maghreb is divided among Morocco, the Sahara, Mauritania, Algeria, and the parts annexed by Niger and Mali."

[4.] "This division is a conspiracy of the colonialist miscreants: the French, the Spaniards and Portuguese, the Jews, and the international companies. The conspiracy was hatched by world Jewry and the weaklings governing the country, whose leader is Bastard II [*sic*][Hassan II]."

[5.] "Islamic Jamaa does not recognize Algeria, an artificial country. It asks the Arab League and the Organization of the Islamic Conference to suspend its membership until it disappears, or else the members of those two organizations will be punished."

[6.] "Bastard II confesses in his book that he killed his father with the help of the doctor."

[7.] The Jihad threatens the former and present Spanish prime ministers with death, along with their families, as well as the German chancellor, in particular for their anti-Islamic positions in Greater Syria, Bosnia-Herzegovina, and Kosovo.

[8.] Islamic Jamaa speaks out against world Judaism, the IMF (International Monetary Fund), and the World Bank.

[9.] "We must eliminate all the French present in Morocco and kill all those who speak French in public."

[10.] Mohammed Abdul Rauf (alias Abu Amar [Yasser Arafat]) is in-

بسم الله و الحمد لله الذي فطر السماوات والأرض و من فيهن و ما بينهما بالحق و كان هو [illegible]

و على صراط مستقيم والصلاة على رسوله الكريم و آله و صحبه أجمعين.

تعلن الجماعة الاسلامية المجاهدة بأن هدفها هو إعلاء كلمة الله على أرض بلاد المغرب الأقصى، مما يستوجب إسترجاع الأرض التي سلبت من المغاربة ثم إقامة الإسلام عليها [illegible] مساحته بحوالي ثلاثة مليون كيلومتر مربع.

تحديد المغرب الأقصى: هو البلد الإسلامي الناطق أهله بالعربية و اللهجات البربرية والذي يحد غرباً بالمحيط الأطلسي و شرقاً بالحدود التونسية والليبية، و جنوباً بنهر السنغال والنيجر و مالي و شمالاً بالبحر الأبيض المتوسط و المغرب الأوسط، والذي قسم إلى خمسة أجزاء:

- المملكة المغربية (حوالي 16% من مساحته)
- الصحراء المتنازع عليها والتي سميت بالغربية
- موريطانيا الإقليم المنفصل بعد الدعم الخارجي الدولي
- القسم الذي ضم إلى المغرب الأوسط و تقدر مساحته بحوالي مليون و ستمائة ألف كيلومتر مربع ليؤسس به ما يسمى بالجزائر بحدودها الحالية.
- القسم ضم إلى مالي و النيجر و كذلك الجزر الأخرى.

و تعتبر الجماعة بأن التقسيم هدف لإضعاف المسلمين و المؤامرة على الإسلام و بذلك فإن الاعتراف بما صنعه الكافر سواء الإستعمار الصليبي الفرنسي والإسباني والبرتغالي أو [illegible] والشركات الدولية هو كفر مخرج من الملة الإسلامية، والنصوص الدالة على ذلك كثيرة في كتاب الله و منها (ألم تر إلى الذين يزعمون أنهم يؤمنون بالله واليوم الآخر يتحاكمون إلى الطاغوت وقد أمروا أن يكفروا به) وإلى جانب التفكيك فقد أخضع أبناء البلد إلى ثقافات الكافر و سياساته و [illegible]؛

و تذكر الجماعة المؤمنين بكافة أرجاء البلاد بمناسبة ما سمي بذكرى ثورة الملك و الشعب بأن المغاربة يومها طالبوا بإخراج المستعمر من كافة التراب الوطني لكن الأمر انتهى [illegible] formed that "the struggle against the Jews is a sacred duty, even if they leave Greater Syria, until they leave the planet Earth and their possessions are given to the Muslims."

[11.] Islamic Jamaa "will not tolerate one Jew walking on earth without reaching out to deliver punishment, so how can it accept the presence of twenty thousand monkeys and pigs in Morocco?"

[12.] Islamic Jamaa prohibits civilian airlines from France, Britain, Spain, Germany, and the United States from flying over Morocco. It is capable of destroying them if they disobey.

[13.] Great Britain is a mortal enemy because it created the Jewish entity in Greater Syria.

[14.] The Wahhabis [the Saudi dynasty] serve the Jews and the Nazarenes [Christians].

[15.] Islamic Jamaa will pursue "around the world, journalists, writers, artists, filmmakers who attack the Prophet and good people chosen by God, that is, Muslims, including the Virgin Mary."

[18.] "Islam is peace. Hence there can be no peace with the Jews until they are converted."

[20.] "Democracy is a great sin for God and an oppression for the people."

[21.] Islamic Jamaa "gives the Portuguese six months to leave the country [Morocco]."

[23.] "The decisions of Islamic Jamaa will be carried out by an iron hand, whatever the consequences."

[Signed] Emir of the Mujahida Islamic Jamaa, Abu Abdullah al-Sharif.

الجيش والدرك والشرطة الذين عزموا على تحرير البلاد من الكفار و أعوانهم بالداخل.

7 - ملاحقة رئيس الوزراء الإسباني السابق، و خلفه الحالي حتى الاغتيال بما في ذلك [illegible] كذلك المستشار الألماني الحالي نظرا لمواقفه المعادية للإسلام والمسلمين ببلاد [illegible] والهرسك و الثلم كوسوفو إلى غير ذلك و مارتن انديك اليهودي.

8 - جهاد اليهودية العالمية و مؤسساتها و عملائها بما في ذلك صندوق النقد الدولي والبنك الدولي [illegible] العاملين بهما لما ألحقاه من ذل و مهانة للمسلمين عامة، والمغاربة المسلمين خاصة، و كذلك [illegible] العاملين بهذه المؤسسات.

9 - العمل على القضاء على النفوذ الفرنسي بالمغرب الأقصى، و تدمير الشركات الفرنسية و [illegible] الفرنسيين، و كذلك الفرنسيين الموجودين بالمغرب الأقصى، و تنفيذ أحكام الإعدام [illegible] عيون الجماعة من تسول له نفسه التكلم بالفرنسية بالأماكن العامة في البلاد أو أمام [illegible] العائلات التي أصبحت الفرنسية لغتها الرسمية، و تستثني الجماعة من يستعملها من أبطال الهجوم الإعلامي على الفرنسيين، أو لإلحاق الهزيمة النفسية بهم أو الدعوة إلى الإسلام.

10 - تتبنى الجماعة القضايا المصيرية للإسلام، و تخبر محمد عبد الرزاق [illegible] بوعمارو [illegible] منظمة والتزوير وبأن قتال اليهود واجب مقدس حتى وإن [illegible] البلاد التي احتلوها بأرض الشام، بل من الكرة الأرضية و تسليم أموالهم للمسلمين فدية [illegible] آخر، وإن الحرب ستكون، ولن تكون يومها حربا بين الكواكب لكن حربا مقدسة دينية لتطهير البشرية من شعب أنجس من النجاسة.

11 - إن الجماعة الإسلامية المجاهدة تكره أن يكون في هذا العالم يهودي واحد يمشي فوق الأرض دون أن تصله [illegible] جزاءه تكيف بها أن تقبل بوجود حوالي عشرة آلاف [illegible] والخنازير بالمغرب الأقصى.

12 - تمنع الجماعة أن تحلق الطائرات المدنية الفرنسية والإسبانية و البريطانية و الألمانية [illegible]

Document 12

Excerpts from an Islamic Movement document

[title page] "Published by the Islamic Movement, Egypt.
Jihad: The Missing Duty
By [the late] Mohamed Abdel Salam Farag
New edition."

[p. 19] "To take power, studies are not enough."

[p. 21] "Fighting is more important than studying the sciences."

[p. 28] "Call to jihad if the infidels are established in the land of Islam or if an imam prescribes it."

[p. 39] "If, in order to kill infidels, you kill their women and children at the same time, it is of little importance."

من إصدارات الحركة الإسلامية
مصر

الجهاد
الفريضة الغائبة

بقلم

محمد عبد السلام فرج
(رحمه الله)

طبعة جديدة

Document 13

Training of volunteers for the jihad

This document recalls that the Islamist camps grew in size during the Soviet-Afghanistan war [1979–89] and denounces the role of several NGOs,

DOCUMENT DE TRAVAIL

FORMATION DES VOLONTAIRES POUR LE DJIHAD
EN CAMPS D'ENTRAINEMENT

[illegible]

including the Office of Services. Under cover of charitable activities, these Islamist organizations were relays for the FIS and the Egyptian Gamaa Islamiya. Many Frenchmen, Muslim in origin or converts, fought alongside Muslim Bosnians. The Dayton Accords in late 1995 brought about closure of those camps and the departure of armed volunteers, notably to France.

The document also notes that camps have been opened, notably in Kashmir, but also in Malaysia, the Philippines, and a place that may seem unexpected, Angola.

Document 14

Note from the Central Office of the National Police, France

Ministry of the Interior

Paris, May 28, 1993

NOTE ON CURRENT AFFAIRS

No. 18/33

Re: Threat of assembly on French territory of residents of the Maghreb, veterans of Afghanistan now taking refuge in Pakistan

The attention of the Central Service of the Air and Border Police has been drawn to the possible arrival in France of residents of the Maghreb, veterans of Afghanistan now taking refuge in Pakistan.

When checking Algerian passengers' passports showing a stay in Pakistan or Afghanistan, it is recommended that the DST be informed.

Roger LeJeune

MINISTERE DE L'INTERIEUR
ET DE L'AMENAGEMENT DU TERRITOIRE

[illegible]

DIRECTION GENERALE
DE LA POLICE NATIONALE

DIRECTION CENTRALE
DE LA POLICE TERRITORIALE

SERVICE CENTRAL DE LA POLICE
DE L'AIR ET DES FRONTIERES
DCPAF/SCPAF/BRAE/N°

PARIS, le 28 MAI 1993

N O T E D ' A C T U A L I T E

N° 18/93

<u>O B J E T</u> : Menace de regroupement sur le territoire français des ressortissants maghrébins, anciens combattants d'Afghanistan réfugiés actuellement au Pakistan.

L'attention du Service Central de la Police de l'air et des frontières a été appelée sur la possible arrivée en France de ressortissants maghrébins, anciens combattants d'Afghanistan et actuellement réfugiés au Pakistan.

En cas de contrôle de passagers Algériens faisant apparaître un séjour au Pakistan ou en Afghanistan, il convient d'en aviser la D.S.T.

[illegible]

Document 15

Excerpts from a confidential report of the Antiterrorism Task Force, France

Meeting of Antiterrorism Task Force
Paris—October 21 and 22, 1996
REPORT

Welcoming the delegations, M. Claude GUEANT, director general of the National Police, noted that this meeting, requested by the ministers at their meeting last July 30 in Paris, has the particular purpose of implementing points 22 through 25 of the conclusions reached on that occasion, with a view toward improving the means of communication and analysis of the services.

Various threats will be examined from an operational perspective, aiming to define them more clearly and to bring forth the following points:

I.—Evaluation of the terrorist threat
in its various forms and the responses appropriate
in each case in the light of recent events

Terrorism of the extreme left and the extreme right

The threat from the extreme left seems to be in decline in most member states even if there remain centers requiring surveillance in Germany and Italy, where small groups are continuing their activities against NATO and other international organizations. More troubling are references to support for Sunni Islamist terrorism.

In France, we have noted a pause in violent actions while a new genera-

G7/P8

Réunion des responsables de la lutte anti-terroriste
PARIS - 21 et 22 octobre 1996

CONFIDENTIEL

COMPTE RENDU

Accueillant les délégations, Monsieur Claude GUEANT, Directeur Général de Police Nationale rappelle que cette réunion, voulue par les Ministres lors de leur rencontre le 30 juillet dernier à PARIS a notamment pour objet la mise en oeuvre des points 22 à 25 des conclusions relevées à cette occasion, dans le but d'améliorer les moyens de communication et d'analyse des services.

Les diverses menaces seront examinées dans un objectif opérationnel visant à mieux les cerner et à mettre en évidence les points suivants :

I. - Evaluation de la menace terroriste sous ses différentes formes et des ripostes adaptées à chacune, à la lumière des événements récents

Le terrorisme d'extrême-gauche et d'extrême-droite

La menace d'extrême-gauche apparaît en déclin dans la plupart des Etats-membres même s'il subsiste des foyers à surveiller en Allemagne et en Italie où des groupuscules poursuivent leurs activités contre l'OTAN et des organismes internationaux. Plus inquiétantes sont les références à un soutien au terrorisme islamiste sunnite.

En France on constate une pause des actions violentes tandis qu'émerge une nouvelle génération qui investit davantage la sphère politique tout en maintenant des liens avec ses homologues à l'étranger.

La situation est également contrastée en ce qui concerne l'extrême-droite dont les activités sont en hausse aux Etats-Unis (mouvements antigouvernementaux,

---

II. - Terrorisme d'origine islamiste sunnite : rôle des réseaux internationaux

La menace terroriste d'origine sunnite

Pour la délégation française bien qu'aucun centre unique n'ait été détecté à ce jour l'extrémisme sunnite s'apparente à une véritable « internationale » disposant de nombreux réseaux de solidarité. Il est avant tout lié à des contestations locales (Algérie, Egypte) auxquelles s'ajoute un facteur déclenchant, la guerre d'Afghanistan, qui a permis l'émergence de combattants faisant référence au Djihad, disposant de lieux d'accueil (Afghanistan, Pakistan, Soudan mais aussi Malaisie) et de sponsors, souvent des ONG. De nouveaux foyers de confrontation (Bosnie, Tchétchénie, Cachemire) ont favorisé leur action.

Situation intérieure

Les communautés musulmanes et les groupes activistes sont inégalement représentés au sein des Etats membres.

La France accueille près de 4 000 000 de musulmans. Majoritairement sunnite, c'est une communauté inorganisée et peu pratiquante au sein de laquelle la propagande islamique opère essentiellement dans les banlieues auprès d'une jeunesse désoeuvrée qui sert de vivier de recrutement (ainsi que l'ont montré les attentats de l'été 1995 en France mais également des affaires précédentes - attentats de Marrakech

5

au Maroc-), mais également au sein d'associations prétendument culturelles et dans les mosquées où les plus fanatiques sont repérés. Leur endoctrinement théorique achevé ces nouveaux militants sont envoyés en Afghanistan ou au Pakistan pour y parfaire leur formation. A leur retour ils deviennent à leur tour « recruteurs ».

Rompus aux techniques de clandestinité (utilisation de faux documents, « pertes » systématiques de documents authentiques, conversations et adresses codées) dotés de matériels de communication performants les membres de ces réseaux cloisonnés se répartissent hiérarchiquement les tâches.

De plus on relève des connexions entre délinquance de droit commun - souvent des jeunes algériens endoctrinés en prison (tel KELKAL) ou des Français convertis à l'Islam - et l'activisme islamiste (affaire de ROUBAIX)

Connexions internationales

Malgré la fin de la guerre d'Afghanistan (où plusieurs milliers de volontaires arabes, en majorité Saoudiens, Algériens et Egyptiens ont combattu les Soviétiques) la zone pakistano-afghane demeure une aire de trouble qui continue à accueillir et à former de nombreux « Combattants d'Allah ».

On y recense la plupart des camps d'entraînement où les Moudjahidins sont formés au maniement des armes et à la lutte subversive. L'existence de camps a également été signalée au Tadjikistan mais aussi en Somalie, au Yemen, au Soudan, en Iran et en Malaisie.

L'ex-Yougoslavie a constitué, durant un temps, un nouveau pôle d'attraction pour les « Afghans » qui l'ont massivement quitté depuis, nombre d'entre eux pour la Turquie. Quelques centaines se sont fixés sur place constituant le vecteur d'un prosélytisme virulent.

Enfin certains sont signalés en Tchétchénie ou ils pénètrent par des filières d'acheminement s'activant depuis la Turquie.

L'activisme des Moudjahidins est d'autant plus inquiétant qu'il apparaît en expansion et qu'il diffère radicalement de celui des organisations terroristes du passé mieux connues dans leurs modus operandi et leurs structures.

Ce phénomène est perçu comme une internationale diffuse, sans centre directeur, constituée de réseaux personnels de solidarité, où toutes les nationalités se côtoient, disposant de financement d'Etats mais aussi de particuliers et de structures de soutien telles certaines Organisations Non Gouvernementales.

Le Royaume-Uni, où la situation est perçue comme moins critique, accueille une communauté musulmane essentiellement originaire du sous-continent indien mais également une faction dure du Groupe Islamique Armé.

L'Allemagne sert de base de repli aux activités du GIA ainsi qu'à un noyau d'activistes (150 membres, 300 sympathisants) du Hamas et du Djihad Islamique Palestinien.

L'Italie relève une convergence tactique entre diverses organisations sunnites, la plus dangereuse à ses yeux étant la Jamaa Al Islamiya égyptienne bien

tion has emerged that is more engaged in the political sphere, while maintaining contact with its foreign counterparts.

The situation is just as varied with regard to the extreme right, whose activities are on the increase in the United States (anti-government movements). . . .

III.—Terrorism of Sunni Islamist origin:
Role of international networks

The terrorist threat of Sunni origin

According to the French delegation, although no single center has been yet detected, Sunni extremism is connected to a veritable "international force" with many networks of solidarity at its disposal. It is principally tied to local disputes (Algeria, Egypt), supplemented by a precipitating factor, the war in Afghanistan, which has permitted the emergence of combatants referring to the jihad, with access to host sites (Afghanistan, Pakistan, Sudan, but also Malaysia) and to sponsors, often NGOs. New centers of confrontation (Bosnia, Chechnya, Kashmir) have fostered their action.

---

implantée à Milan où des tracts revendiquant des actions terroristes en Egypte ont été envoyés. Le GIA est également présent en Italie. La mobilité de ses militants, vers d'autres pays européens (transit de Milan vers Dublin d'individus munis de faux papiers) et l'Amérique du Nord a été remarquée

---

Filières de financement à caractère chiite et sunnite

Le Hezbollah dont les informations concernant les finances sont rares dispose de diverses sources de financement : aide mensuelle de la République d'Iran, impôts et dons religieux émanant des communautés chiites du Liban mais également de la diaspora, bénéfices réalisés par les sociétés et commerces contrôlés par le Parti, taxes prélevées sur les activités illégales de certains de ses membres.

Pour les sunnites et notamment les « arabes afghans » une partie du financement transite par les Organisations Non Gouvernementales, elles-mêmes alimentées par l'Arabie Séoudite. De généreux mécènes tel Oussama BIN LADEN apportent également leur contribution.

D'autres mouvement, tel le Hamas se financent via des collectes de fonds auprès des populations musulmanes effectuées par des associations de soutien à but officiellement humanitaire.

Internal situation

Muslim communities and activist groups are of different sizes in the various member states.

France is home to nearly four million Muslims. Mostly Sunni, it is an unorganized and not very observant community, within which Islamic propaganda operates principally in working-class suburbs among unemployed young men, who serve as a source of recruitment (as was shown by the summer 1995 attacks in France, but also by earlier episodes—Marrakech attacks) but also in purportedly cultural associations and in mosques, where the most fanatical have been detected. Once their theoretical indoctrination has been completed, these new militants are sent to Afghanistan or Pakistan to complete their training. On their return, they become "recruiters" in turn.

Experienced in techniques of secrecy (use of fake documents, systematic "losses" of authentic documents, coded conversations and addresses) and possessing sophisticated communications equipment, the members of these compartmentalized networks distribute tasks hierarchically.

Moreover, connections have been established between petty criminals—often young Algerians indoctrinated in prison (like KELKAL) or Frenchmen converted to Islam—and Islamist activism (the ROUBAIX affair).

International connections

Despite the end of the Afghanistan war (where several thousand Arab volunteers, mostly Saudis, Algerians, and Egyptians, fought the Soviets), the Afghan-Pakistani region remains a trouble spot that continues to receive and train many "Combatants of Allah."

This is where most of the training camps are located in which the mujahedeen are trained in the use of arms and subversive combat. The existence of camps has also been reported in Tajikistan, but also in Somalia, Yemen, Sudan, Iran, and Malaysia.

For a time, the former Yugoslavia was a new center of attraction for the "Afghans," who have since left it in large numbers, many of them for Turkey. Several hundred have remained in place and are the vehicle for virulent proselytism.

Finally, some have been reported in Chechnya, which they enter through transport networks operating from Turkey.

The activism of the mujahedeen is all the more troubling because it appears to be expanding and it differs radically from that of terrorist organizations of the past, whose modus operandi and structures are better known.

This phenomenon is seen as a loose international force, with no governing center, made up of personal networks of solidarity, in which all nationalities are blended, with access to financing from states, but also from individuals and from support structures such as certain NGOs.

The United Kingdom, where the situation is seen as less critical, has a Muslim community mostly from the Indian subcontinent, but it is also home to a hard-line faction of the GIA.

Germany serves as a rear base for GIA activities, as well as for a core of activists (150 members, 300 sympathizers) of Hamas and the Palestinian Islamic Jihad.

Italy has noted a tactical convergence among various Sunni organizations, the most dangerous in its view being the Egyptian Gamaa Islamiya, well established in Milan, where leaflets claiming credit for terrorist actions in Egypt have been sent. The GIA is also present in Italy. The mobility of its militants traveling to other European countries (transit from Milan to Dublin of individuals with counterfeit papers) and to North America has been noted.

Shii and Sunni funding channels

Hezbollah, information about whose finances is scanty, has various sources of funds: monthly aid from the Republic of Iran, taxes and religious gifts from Shii communities in Lebanon, but also from the diaspora, profits from companies and stores controlled by the party, fees levied on the illegal activities of some of its members.

For the Sunnis, and notably the Afghan Arabs, part of the funding goes through NGOs, themselves funded by Saudi Arabia. Generous donors, such as Osama BIN LADEN, also make contributions.

Other movements, such as Hamas, finance themselves through collections of funds among Muslim populations carried out by support associations, officially set up for humanitarian purposes.

Document 16

Two pages of a notebook belonging to a Pakistani fighter

The notebook was found on the corpse of a Pakistani member of an organization fighting against the presence of Indians in Kashmir. In it, we find, in Urdu, the names of martyrs of the jihad, members of suicide commandos, with the programmed date of their deaths in 1998–99. They were trained in bin Laden's special camp for these suicide fighters: the Khalid bin Walid camp, in Khost, Afghanistan.

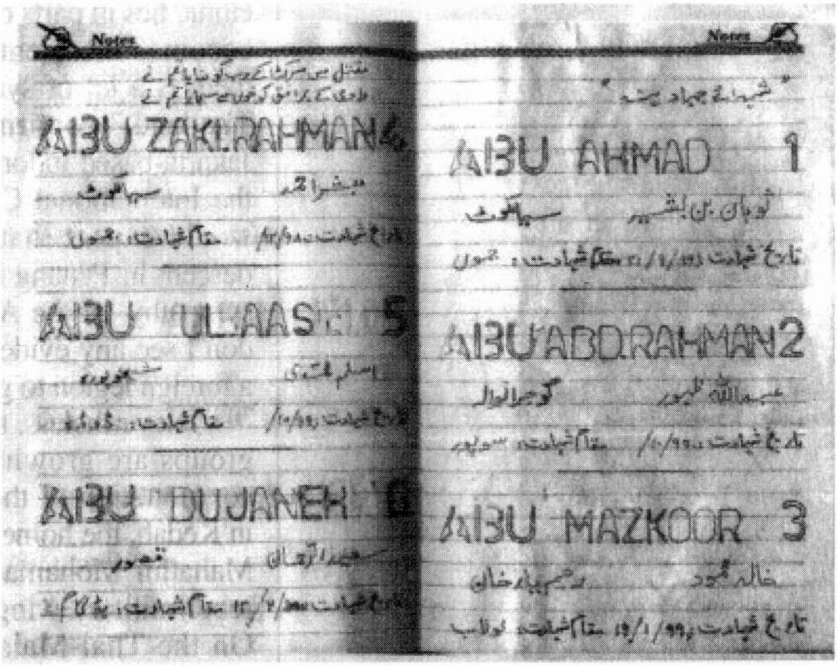
Notes
ABU AHMAD 1
ABU ABD.RAHMAN 2
ABU MAZKOOR 3
Notes
ABU ZAKI.RAHMAN 4
ABU UL-AAS 5
ABU DUJANEH 6

Document 17

Gamaa Islamiya in Egypt

On November 17, 1997, fifteen mujahedeen of one of the Talaat Yassin companies took a group of foreign tourists as hostages in Luxor, with the aim of securing the release of the supreme emir of Gamaa Islamiya, Dr. Omar Abdul Rahman, as well as members of the Historic Command of Gamaa Islamiya and other prisoners held by the Egyptians and the Americans.

Gamaa Islamiya accuses the Egyptian government of having provoked the death of a great number of hostages and "natives" by its armed reaction.

لاإله إلا الله — الجماعة الإسلامية

محمد رسول الله — بمصر

هذا بيان للناس وأول السيل قطرة

في عملية جريئة نفذتها صباح الإثنين ١٧-١١-١٩٩٧ إحدى سرايا كتائب الشهيد طلعت ياسين حاولت فيها إحتجاز أكبر عدد ممكن من السائحين الأجانب بأحد المعابد السياحية بالأقصر بغرض الإفراج عن أمير عام الجماعة الإسلامية الدكتور عمر عبد الرحمن والقيادات التاريخية للجماعة وأبنائها وغيرهم من السجناء المعتقلين في السجون الأمريكية والمصريه ولكن تعامل القوات الحكومية برعونة واستخفاف بأرواح السائحين والمواطنين أدى إلى سقوط هذا العدد الكبير من القتلى ..

والجماعة الإسلامية في هذه المناسبة إذ تحتسب شهدائها عند الله تعالى فإنها توضح مايلي :-

(١) أن خمسة عشر (١٥) من مجاهدينا عملوا إلى إحتجاز عدد من السائحين وأن تسعة منهم تمكنوا من العودة إلى قواعدهم سالمين وقد أفاد أحدهم أن إثنين من بين مجاهدينا وقعا في الأسر وقد ادعى النظام إستشهادهم مع أربعة آخرين من إخوانهم .

(٢) أن الجماعة الإسلامية تحمل النظام المصري المسئولية الكاملة لتزايد عدد القتلى والجرحى من السائحين الأجانب وذلك لإستعمال قواتهم للذخيرة الحية في محاولة منهم لمنع عملية الإحتجاز .

[illegible] قد أكدت في بيانها الصادر في ٣٠-٩-١٩٩٧ م والذي نشرت [illegible] الحياة اللندنية فقرات منه في ٤-٧-[illegible] دعت فيه العالم للتدخل لدى [illegible] المصري لوقف عملياته الوحشية ضد أبناء شعبنا وطالبت الجماعة من أبناء [illegible] وقد حذرت في حينه من مواجهة أشد [illegible] مالم يستجب النظام لمطالبها المشروعة .

Document 18

Communiqué of November 17, 1997, from the Movement, Units of Islamic Fatah

The communiqué states that, since the Egyptian government has refused reconciliation and the cessation of violence, the taking of hostages in Luxor—which will not be the last such incident—is the movement's response to the execution of Islamists, as long as Egypt tortures and executes militants. Foreigners are not targeted, but they support the regime by coming as tourists; their money is used to buy instruments of torture in the West.

The movement demands the release of more than thirty thousand Islamist prisoners and accuses the government of being illegal, since it rigs elections.

بسم الله الرحمن الرحيم

بيان إلى حكومات وشعوب العالم

• إن ما حدث في مدينة الأقصر اليوم ضد الأجانب الذين جاءوا لزيارة مصر على الرغم من تحذيرنا لهم الدائم والمتكرر ليعبر بشكل لا لبس فيه عن فشل السياسات التي ينتهجها النظام المصري المجرم الذي قام بإعدام خيرة شباب مصر بعد محاكمات هزلية يسميها بالمحاكم العسكرية والذي تبنى جلاديه في وزارة الداخلية سياسة التصفية الجسدية والاعتقالات الجماعية والتعذيب البشع، الذي لم تعرف مصر مثيلاً له في تاريخها الطويل .

• والحركة الإسلامية الجهادية في مصر تود توضيح الآتي :-

1 - إن النظام المصري رفض في السابق عرضاً من قيادات تاريخية للحركة الإسلامية لوقف مسلسل العنف في مصر وكذلك رفض تبني أساليب المصالحة وحقن الدماء .

2 - إن عملية اليوم في الأقصر لن تكون الأخيرة فالمجاهدون سيواصلون عملهم ما دام النظام المصري مستمراً في التعذيب والقتل لأبناء الحركة الإسلامية .

3 - إن الأجانب ليسوا مستهدفين لذاتهم بالنسبة لنا وإنما نحن حذرناهم من تقديم الدعم المالي للنظام عبر مدخلات السياحة لأن هذه الأموال لا تستخدم لصالح الشعب المصري وإنما تستخدم في شراء أدوات التعذيب من الغرب وتوظيف مزيد من الزبانية في وزارة الداخلية .

4 - على الدول الغربية أن ترفع دعمها اللا محدود للنظام المصري، وتطالبه باحترام حقوق الإنسان ووقف المهازل (المحاكم) العسكرية والإفراج عن أكثر من (30) ثلاثين ألف معتقل إسلامي يتعرضون هم وأسرهم بشكل دائم لأشد أنواع القهر والظلم الذي يتعرض له بني البشر

5 - إن دخول مصر ينبغي أن يكون باتفاق أمان من الشعب المصري لا بمواثيق كاذبة عقدت مع حكومة غير شرعية جاءت بتزوير الانتخابات ولا تمثل الشعب المصري المسلم تمثيلاً حقيقياً .

حركة الجهاد
طلائع الفتح الإسلامي
الاثنين :17 رجب 1418 هـ
الموافق :17 نوفمبر 1997 م

Document 19

Excerpts from a communiqué from Abi Hamza Hassan Hattab

Hattab is the emir of the Salafi Groups for Preaching and Combat. In this communiqué he condemns the various sorts of humiliation and torture "suffered by our Muslim brothers in France especially, and in other infidel countries in general."

"We inform all our imprisoned brothers that we support them in every way and that we are for their victory.

"We consider that the French authorities bear the responsibility for everything that will result from the trials carried out against these imprisoned brothers."

بسم الله الرحمن الرحيم

الحمد لله وصلى الله على نبينا محمد وعلى آله وصحبه وسلم

الجماعة السلفية للدعوة والقتال

موقف وبيان

يقول الله في كتابه: ﴿إنما المؤمنون إخوة...﴾

وقال عليه الصلاة والسلام في الحديث الصحيح: "مثل المؤمنين في توادهم وتراحمهم وتعاطفهم مثل الجسد إذا اشتكى منه عضو تداعى له سائر الجسد بالسهر والحمى".

إن [illegible] بسبب الأوضاع التي يعانيها ويعيشها إخواننا المسلمون في فرنسا خاصة وفي غيرها من بلاد الكفر عامة، بخاصة الإخوة المساجين الذين يتعرضون لشتى أنواع الإهانة والتعذيب وهذا إن دل على شيء إنما يدل على حقد هؤلاء للإسلام وأهله.

ومن [illegible] الذي حثنا عليه الإسلام فإننا نعلم كل الإخوة المساجين أننا في نصرتهم ما [illegible] الإسلام والمسلمين [illegible] السلطات الفرنسية مسؤولية ما يترتب من جراء هذه المحاكمات في حق هؤلاء الإخوة المساجين.

قال تعالى: ﴿وإن استنصروكم في الدين فعليكم النصر...﴾

أمير الجماعة السلفية للدعوة والقتال

أبو حمزة حسان حطاب

Document 20

Communiqué from Osama bin Laden

In the name of God the Merciful

Decision: Office of Council and Reforms—London.

Having met on July 11, 1994, by a decision of the Majlis of Shoura, we have decided to open a branch of the Office of Council and Reforms in London, in order to broaden its activities and to facilitate contacts in order to receive correspondence and requests. Mr. Khalid bin Abdhuram el-Fawaz has been appointed its director.

May God help us to succeed.

Representative of the Office of Council and Reforms 2/3/1415

Osama bin Mohamed bin Laden 7/11/1994

[The document is signed in the lower left in Osama bin Laden's hand, which is extremely rare.]

بسم الله الرحمن الرحيم

هيئة النصيحة والإصلاح
مكتب - لندن

قرار

قرار

بناءً على توصية مجلس الشورى لهيئة النصيحة والإصلاح في جلسته المنعقدة في يوم الاثنين ٣ / ٢ / ١٤١٥ هـ الموافق ١١ / ٧ / ١٩٩٤م، فقد تقرر افتتاح مكتب الهيئة في لندن رغبةً في توسعة نشاطاتها، وتيسيراً للاتصال بها لاستقبال المراسلات والتظلمات.

وقد عُيّن السيد/ خالد بن عبدالرحمن الفواز مديراً لهذا المكتب.

والله الموفق...

التاريخ: ٣/٢/١٤١٥هـ
الموافق: ١١/٧/١٩٩٤م

عنهم/ أسامة بن محمد بن لادن

Tel:0044716242462 Fax: 0044713289651/ Address: BM BOX 7666, London,WC1N 3XX,U.K.

Document 21

Communiqué from the Islamic Observation Center

The communiqué, dated October 22, 1997, from an organization that calls itself the International Commission on Human Rights (Islamic Observation Center, London), condemns the hanging of four Egyptians [the names are given], including Fawaz. After a verdict on January 19, 1997, in this trial of nineteen militants, thirteen others were sentenced to hard labor. The commission protests the trial of civilians by military tribunals without the right of appeal and with no possibility of pardon and claims that the confessions were extracted by torture.

International Commission On Human Rights

لجنة حقوق الإنسان الدولية

مصر : استمرار مسلسل الإعدامات التعسفية في ظل المحاكم العسكرية

تدين لجنة حقوق الإنسان الدولية المنبثقة عن المرصد الإعلامي الإسلامي قيام النظام المصري بإعدام أربعة من المدنيين الأبرياء بناءً على حكم صادر عن محكمة عسكرية جائرة غير عادلة ثبت أنها تجاهلت أن الاعترافات المنسوبة إليهم جاءت وليدة الإكراه والتعذيب فضلاً عن أن هذه المحاكم تتسم بالظلم الفادح ، وقد انتهكت عدداً من أهم الحقوق الأساسية التي يوجبها القانون الدولي ، ومنها حق المتهم في المحاكمة أمام قضاة مستقلين ومختصين ، وحقه في أن يُتاح له وقت كافٍ لإعداد الدفاع ، وحقه في الاستئناف أمام محكمة أعلى ، وهؤلاء الأبرياء الذين تم إعدامهم هم :

١- ياسر فتحي محمد عبد المنعم فواز (طبيب)　　٣- علي محمد أحمد فرحات (طالب)

٢- عرفان محمد حسيب الخولي (طالب)　　٤- ياسر عباس سليمان (دبلوم فني صناعي)

وكانت المحكمة العسكرية أصدرت حكمها الجائر بتاريخ ١٩٩٧/١/١٩م في القضية التي ضمت ١٩ مواطناً على النحو التالي : الإعدام لـ٤ ، وبالأشغال الشاقة المؤبدة لـ٣متهمين ، وبالأشغال الشاقة ١٥سنة على ٣متهمين ، والأشغال الشاقة ١٠سنوات على ٣متهمين ، والأشغال الشاقة ٥سنوات على ٤متهمين ، والسجن ١٠سنوات على متهم واحد ، وبراءة متهمين .

ولقد أصبح من الواضح الجلي بعد تنفيذ أحكام الاعدام الصادرة من محاكم عسكرية ضد مدنيين ، وإفراط هذه المحاكم في إصدار أحكام الإعدام أن النظام المصري فشل فشلاً ذريعاً في إخضاع شعب مصر الأبي المسلم الذي يدافع عن عقيدته ودينه إلا باستخدام الوسائل غير المشروعة والمحرمة دولياً ، فهو ما زال مستمراً في انتهاك حقوق الإنسان وإحالة المدنيين إلى محاكم عسكرية وممارسة أبشع أنواع التعذيب والقتل داخل السجون وخارجها -خارج نطاق القضاء - ضد أبناء الشعب الصابر .

ومن الجدير بالذكر أنه لا يحق للمتهمين استئناف الأحكام أو العقوبات التي تقضي بها المحاكم العسكرية أو الطعن فيها أمام محكمة أعلى ، إذ لا تخضع جميع أحكام الإعدام التي تصدرها المحاكم العسكرية إلا لتصديق رئيس النظام ، بعد مراجعتها من جانب « مكتب الاستئناف العسكري » وهو هيئة غير قضائية يرأسها رئيس النظام نفسه - مما يدعو للدهشة ألا يعترض المكتب على أي حكم بالإدانة أو على عقوبة صدرت في أي قضية بل تم إقرار جميع أحكام الإعدام - ، ولا يجوز اللجوء إلى الاستئناف القضائي أو المراجعة بالنقض ، وتعد هذه الإجراءات قاصرة عن الوفاء بالمعايير الدولية للمحاكمة العادلة ، بما في ذلك المادة ١٤ (٥) من « **العهد الدولي الخاص بالحقوق المدنية والسياسية** » ، والتي تنص على أنه « **لكل شخص أدين بجريمة حق اللجوء ، وفقاً للقانون ، إلى محكمة أعلى كيما تعيد النظر في قرار إدانته وفي العقاب الذي حكم به عليه** » . ومن العجيب أن رئيس النظام يضطلع بدور مشبوه (الخصم والحكم) باعتباره ينتمي إلى السلطة التنفيذية وإلى النظام القضائي معاً ، ولم يستخدم حق العفو أو استبدال العقوبة لصالح أبناء مصر في الوقت الذي يكشف فيه عن إطلاقه أكثر من ثلاثين جاسوساً من الصهاينة .

وفي الأخير : فإن لجنة حقوق الإنسان الدولية المنبثقة عن المرصد الإعلامي الإسلامي إذ تستنكر وتدين استمرار الإعدامات وإحالة المدنيين إلى محاكم عسكرية تعرب عن قلقها من هذا التصرف الذي ينذر بمزيد من التصعيد والمواجهة بين أبناء الحركة الإسلامية والنظام المصري ، وتطالب اللجنة المجتمع الدولي باستخدام آليات ضغط ضد النظام المصري تلزمه باحترام القوانين والمواثيق الدولية التي صادق عليها والتي منها « **العهد الدولي الخاص بالحقوق المدنية والسياسية** » و« **اتفاقية مناهضة التعذيب** » . كما تطالب اللجنة المجتمع الدولي والمنظمات الحكومية وغير الحكومية التدخل السريع لإلغاء المحاكم العسكرية ووقف هذه الأحكام الجائرة بحق المدنيين .

وحسبنا الله ونعم الوكيل.

المرصد الإعلامي الإسلامي

الخميس : ٢٢ جمادى الآخرة ١٤١٨هـ

الموافق : ٢٣ أكتوبر ١٩٩٧م

Islamic Observation Center, PO Box 13575, London W9 1FG, UK.
E-MAIL : observer @ islamic.netkonect.co.uk　Tel /Fax : 44 171 624 Bag

Document 22

Open letter from the Islamic Liberation Army to the people of Kenya

This communiqué is dated August 11, 1998. It claims that the attack carried out by the company of the martyr Khaled al-Saad on the U.S. Embassy in Nairobi was directed only at the United States. "The Americans humiliate our people, occupy the [Arabian] Peninsula, bleed us of our wealth, and subject us to their blockade. In addition, they support our bitter enemy the Israeli Jews who occupy the al-Aqsa mosque."

It goes on to explain that the attack was justified because the Kenyan government had authorized the Americans to use their country to combat neighboring Muslim countries, notably Somalia. Moreover, Kenya has collaborated with Israel, because it has the most anti-Muslim Hebrew center in all of East Africa.

The document also states that the Americans have used Kenya as a base of support for the secessionist movement in southern Sudan led by John Garang.

بسم الله الرحمن الرحيم

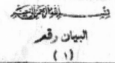

الجيش الإسلامي لتحرير المقدسات

البيان رقم

(١)

رسالة مفتوحة إلى الشعب الكيني

إلى الشعب الكيني ... وإلى رئيسه عرب موي   السلام على من اتبع الهدى .. أما بعد :

لم يكن خافياً عليكم ولا على المنصفين من تابعوا عملية الكعبة المشرفة أن سرية الشهيد خالد السالم كانت تستهدف الرعية الأمريكية فقط. ومن لأجل ذلك اختاروا الموقع وأطلقوا قنابل صوتية قوية لتفريق المشاة الكينيين قبل عملية التفجير بقليل. فليس مقصد جيش إسلامي رباني إصابة المواطنين الكينيين المسالمين، بل كل طاقتهم موجهة للثأر من جبابرة الغصب والنهب من الأمريكيين الذي يذيقون شعوبنا ألوان الإهانة والذلة. فلا أحد يجهل أن الأمريكيين منذ سنين طويلة يحتلون جزيرة العرب ويستنزفون ثروة المسلمين ويحاصرون بأساطيلهم وقواتهم مقدسات رب العالمين في بلاد الحرمين. وهم الذين يدعمون بشكل محموم عدونا من اليهود الإسرائيليين الذين يغتصبون المسجد الأقصى.

وإن المسئولية كاملة فيما جرى تقع على أمريكا فيجب أن تعوض الشعب الكيني حين جلبت لأرضه نار الحرب (500) مليون دولار عن الخسائر المادية و(30) مليون دولار تعويضاً للجرحى الكينيين كل بحسب إصابته و(30) ألف دولار لأسرة كل قتيل مع (500) مليون دولار عن الأضرار العامة اللاحقة بالاقتصاد الكيني.

أيها الشعب الكيني المسالم :

لعل الكثير منكم يتساءلون بعد التسليم بما ذكرناه ... ولكن لماذا تطاردون الأمريكيين وتحسبونهم فوق أرضنا بالصورة التي تعرض مواطنينا للقتل واقتصادنا للتخريب؟! والإجابة على ذلك يحسن أن يتذكر الكينيون أن حكومتهم هي التي جلبت لهم الموت ولبلادهم الدمار حين سمحت للأمريكيين باستخدام أرضها لتقتيل شعوب الإسلام المجاورة لكينيا، وإنهاك دولها ومحاصرة اقتصادها، والحكومة الكينية هي التي تعاونت مع إسرائيل للكيد للأمة الإسلامية في شرق القارة وفي غربها. وللذين غفلت ذاكرتهم من الكينيين نقول :

- في كينيا توجد القواعد الأمريكية التي تحتل بلاد الحرمين الشريفين وتحاصر جزيرة العرب وتستمد قوات أمريكا في جزيرة العرب، وتتمتع أساطيل أمريكا البحرية والجوية وجنودها تسهيلات واسعة في موانئ، ومطارات كينيا.
- وفي كينيا مركز للكيد الإسرائيلي تنشط ضد المسلمين في القارة وفي الشرق الإسلامي عموماً. ودور إسرائيل في ما يجري للمسلمين من مآسي انطلاقاً من كينيا وتنزانيا وغيرهما من دول شرق إفريقيا غير خاف على أحد. فالتعاون مع الإسرائيليين وهم يحتلون المسجد الأقصى يعتبر إعلاناً للحرب على كل المسلمين في العالم.
- وسفارة أمريكا في كينيا هي التي خططت وأدارت حملة أمريكا الشرسة ضد أقوى دول الإسلام في القرن الإفريقي : الصومال. هذه الحملة التي لا تزال متواصلة، والتي أخذت ذروتها في الهجوم الذي قادته أمريكا مع حلفائها والذي قتل فيه أكثر من (13000) من أبرياء الصومال من الأطفال والنساء والشيوخ. هذا فضلاً عن ألوان التعذيب وصور التمزيق التي باشرها المحتلون الغربيون في الصومال.
- ومن كينيا خططت وأديرت منذ الثمانينات حرب متواصلة دنيئة ضد الشعب السوداني المسلم المسالم، وقامت أوكار التآمر الغربية وعلى رأسها سفارة أمريكا في نيروبي باصطناع عصابة المجرم قرنق، وسعت من خلال ذلك لتشطير السودان بفصل جنوبه عن شماله، وتعطيل السعي إلى تطبيق شريعة الله في بلاد المسلمين وتقتيلهم وتهجيرهم، مما شكل نزيفاً قتل فيه عشرات الآلاف من النساء والأطفال والشيوخ. ولقد أوشك التمرد في السودان أن يوصل الغربيين إلى السيطرة على السودان بحيث تصبح قواتهم على بعد أقل من (280) كلم من مكة المكرمة.

أيها الشعب الكيني المسالم :

هذا الذي ذكرناه غيض من فيض يتضح به أن كينيا -مثلها في ذلك مثل تنزانيا- غدت أكبر قواعد الأمريكيين المستخدمة ضد المسلمين في إفريقيا والشرق الإسلامي. ولهذه الأسباب كانت السفارة الأمريكية في كينيا هدفاً لضربات جيش تحرير المقدسات الإسلامي المرجحة. بل إن الأمريكيين غدوا في نيروبي يتحركون كساسة وقادة لبلد دون أن يعيروا لشعبها أو رئيسها أو حكومتها أي اعتبار. فعلى الكينيين -إن كانوا صادقين في تجنيب بلادهم ويلات الحرب- أن يمتنعوا عن تسخير أرضهم وبيع بلادهم للطغمة الأمريكيين والإسرائيليين، وليسحقوا حرماتهم أن تستخدم كقاعدة لضرب أي شعب مسلم، وليغلقوا مكتب المجرم قرنق، وليوقفوا أي مدد لتمرده، فكل الدعم الواصل إليه كان ولا يزال يمر عبر الأراضي الكينية. وإن لم يفعلوا ذلك فليكن في يقينهم أن دماء المسلمين لا يمكن أن تذهب هدراً طال الزمن أم قصر، وسنكون مضطرين لاستخدام الأرض التي ينطلق منها عدونا. ﴿ قل يا أهل الكتاب تعالوا إلى كلمة سواء بيننا وبينكم ألا نعبد إلا الله، ولا نشرك به شيئاً ولا يتخذ بعضنا بعضاً أرباباً من دون الله فإن تولوا فقولوا اشهدوا بأنا مسلمون ﴾ .

التاريخ : ١٤١٩/٤/١٨هـ
الموافق : ١٩٩٨/٨/١١م

(مكتبه الإعلام)

Document 23

Communiqué no. 4, August 12, 1998, of the
Islamic Army for the Liberation of the Holy Places

"Given the American Crusader and Jewish Israeli occupation of the environs of the al-Aqsa mosque, given what the Jews are doing in Palestine by killing our children and women and . . . destroying the houses of our innocent brethren, . . . given that more than a million Iraqis have died; given the imprisonment of ulemas in America and in the countries dominated by the United States, and given the theft of Muslim fortunes through oil development, we are compelled to wage the jihad throughout the world and at all times.

"Combating the United States and their allies the Jews of Israel is a life and death struggle. Before Nairobi, we had warned Muslims to avoid contact with everything American, and we repeat that warning."

بسم الله الرحمن الرحيم

الجيش الإسلامي لتحرير المقدسات

البلاغ رقم (٤)

بلاغ للناس

أيها الناس:

إن الجيش الإسلامي لتحرير المقدسات،

- نظراً إلى احتلال الصليبيين الأمريكيين واليهود الإسرائيليين لأرض الله المقدسة [illegible] في بلاد الحرمين وحول المسجد الأقصى،
- ونظراً إلى واقع الاحتلال والمهانة المفروضة على أمتنا المسلمة منذ أكثر من [illegible]،
- ونظراً إلى ما يمارسه اليهود في فلسطين من تقتيل لأبنائنا ونسائنا، ومن [illegible] ومن نسف لمساكن الآمنين من إخواننا،
- ونظراً إلى ما تفرضه أمريكا على شعوبنا المسلمة من ألوان الحصار وفنون القتل [illegible] التي ذهب ضحيتها أكثر من مليون (1.000.000) من أطفالنا ونسائنا في العراق [illegible]،
- ونظراً للحملة الأمريكية الشرسة لاستئصال جذور الإسلام في أرضنا والقضاء على [illegible] وجودنا.. مستخدمة في ذلك أنظمة الحكم العميلة التي ملأت السجون بعشرات الآلاف من إخواننا، وأشرعت سكاكينها في رقابنا،
- ونظراً إلى سجن علمائنا وقادتنا في أمريكا وفي كل بلد تكون لها فيه هيمنة [illegible]،
- ونظراً لنهب أمريكا وحلفائها لثروات المسلمين وخصوصاً الثروات الحيوية كالنفط و[illegible]،

نظراً إلى ذلك كله فإن الجيش الإسلامي لتحرير المقدسات مضطر إلى مواصلة الجهاد [illegible] الأمريكيين في كل مكان وفي أي وقت. فمعركتنا مع هؤلاء المجرمين المتكبرين الأمريكيين [illegible] الإسرائيليين هي بالنسبة لنا معركة حياة أو موت، ووسيلتنا المعتمدة حتى الآن [illegible] شحن مزيد من جثث الأمريكيين إلى حكومتهم الظالمة حتى تكسر شوكة أمريكا [illegible] كرامتها في أوحال الهزيمة بإذن الله.

ولقد كنا أنذرنا كل المسلمين في بياننا الأول قبل عملية [illegible] كل ما هو أمريكي. ونحن نعيد ذلك التحذير اليوم، فرجاؤنا لكل الناس أن يبتعدوا عن كل شيء [illegible] بأمريكا من أي وجه كان، حتى لا يتكرر ما جرى في نيروبي وحتى لا [illegible] المسلمون.

والله من وراء القصد وهو الهادي إلى سواء السبيل

التاريخ: ١٩/٤/١٤١٩هـ
الموافق: [illegible]/٨/١٩٩٨م

Document 24

Communiqué no. 4, August 12, 1998, of the
World Islamic Front against Jews and Crusaders

"On Friday, we learned that two huge explosions in the capitals of Kenya and Tanzania targeted the American embassies [and succeeded] thanks to the clear plans and the determination of the militants. . . . Operations in Riyadh and Khobar [in Saudi Arabia] killed thirty American occupiers. Young Muslims, particularly Saudis, must get revenge for the unholy pollution of the Holy Land and al-Aqsa. The Americans are eating away our wealth and humiliating our peoples. . . . The Americans believed the lies of the Jews to the extent of bringing about war between the mujahedeen and the American occupiers. . . . Muslim blood was shed in Bosnia in the sight of the Americans (mass graves, rapes, tortures, the work of infidels) . . . .These two embassies that the Islamic Army for the Liberation of the Holy Places blew up had supervised the killing of thirteen thousand Somali civilians at least in the treacherous attack led by the United States against this Muslim country in the year 1412 of the Hegira. . . . America has forgotten Nagasaki and Hiroshima and wrongly accuses young Muslims of terrorism. . . . The Americans encouraged the Jews to occupy Jerusalem, and then they occupied Saudi Arabia. They have supported the corrupt rulers of the region. The coming days will prove that America will share the fate of the USSR: it will be struck from all sides.

"August 12, 1998."

الجبهة الإسلامية العالمية
لجهاد اليهود والصليبيين

بيان رقم
(٤)

ولمن انتصر بعد ظلمه فأولئك ما عليهم من سبيل ..

الحمد لله الذي بنعمته وجلاله تتم الصالحات وتستمر والصلاة والسلام على رسول الله ﷺ الذي [illegible] الناس أيام [illegible] .. أما بعد :

لقد طالعتنا الإذاعات في مساء الجمعة الماضية بأنباء انفجارين كبيرين هزا عاصمتي كينيا وتنزانيا واستهدفا السفارتين الأمريكيتين في البلدين الإفريقيين المذكورين. ولقد ذكرتنا قوة هذه الأحداث الهائلة وتخطيطها [illegible] الدقيق وتصميم منفذيها العجيب بالأحداث التي وقعت في جزيرة العرب ضد القوات الأمريكية المتمركزة في الرياض والخبر تلك الأحداث التي ذهب ضحيتها ما يناهز ثلاثين جندياً من جنود الاحتلال الأمريكي.

وحين أعلن من قيام جيش تحرير المقدسات الإسلامية من خلال هذه العمليات ذات الدلالة [illegible] الجميع -بما فيهم الشعب الأمريكي- أننا لم نكذب عليه حين حذرناه من مغبة الاحتلال التي تمارسه [illegible] أمريكا في بلاد المسلمين، والإذلال والتدنيس الذي تروجه في مقدساتهم. فقد كنا على يقين أن شباب [illegible] في بلاد الحرمين لا بد أن يثأر لبيت الله الحرام وللمسجد الأقصى من أمريكا التي أهانت [illegible] واستنزفت ثرواتنا وأذلت شعوبنا وقاهرت عمرنا. وحين صدّق الشعب الأمريكي قيادته الكاذبة المفضوحة .. [illegible] والدمار توالت عليه الضربات ... ولقد تلهى الشعب الأمريكي بحديث شرائم اليهود عن المصالح [illegible] حرب مقدسة ثلاثية بين الإسلام المجاهد وبين أمريكا المحتلة الغاصبة.

وغني عن القول أن شعب أمريكا وحلفاءها هذه العمليات لن يغني شيئاً كما لم يغن [illegible] من قبل هذا أي شيء، ولا معنى لهذا الشجب لأنه يأتي في الوقت الذي تراق فيه دماء المسلمين [illegible] على يد سفاح الصرب، كما أريقت من قبل ذلك في البوسنة تحت إشراف أمريكا وحلفائها، [illegible] الجماعية التي تضم الآلاف من القتلى وانتشرت معسكرات التعذيب والنهب والاغتصاب، ولقد أشرفت [illegible] جيش تحرير المقدسات الإسلامي على قتل (13000) مدني صومالي على الأقل في [illegible] التي قادته أمريكا ضد هذا البلد المسلم في عام ١٤١٢هـ. وهل نسيت أمريكا -وهي اليوم تذرف دموع التماسيح على الأمن والسلام العالميين- ما فعلته بسكان هيروشيما وناجازاكي وكيف حصدتهم بقنابلها الذرية في [illegible] وهل يعرف [illegible] القادة الأمريكيين قيمة غير نزواتهم الهابطة وأحقادهم الحانقة؟

فالإدارة الأمريكية تعمد إلى اتهام الشباب المسلم المجاهد بالإرهاب كي تخادع شعبها عن [illegible] الأحداث الخطيرة وتقوم بإثارة زوبعة إعلامية وسياسية خادعة لامتصاص غضب شعبها [illegible] في تحريض أبناء شعبها للقتل والحق. فالسبب الوحيد الذي يدفع شباب الإسلام الأطهار لتحريض [illegible] يسعون لضرب الأهداف الأمريكية ليس إلا الظلم الذي مارسته الحكومة الأمريكية على شعوب الإسلام، [illegible] اليهود على احتلال بيت المقدس، ثم قامت بعد ذلك باحتلال جزيرة العرب بما فيها [illegible] المسلمة، ومكنت لحكام الجور والفساد من عملائها في المنطقة، فكيف تنتظر من شباب الإسلام [illegible]

والأيام القادمة كفيلة بإذن الله بأن تُري أمريكا مصيراً أسوداً كالذي حلّ بالاتحاد [illegible] الضربات من كل مكان وستظهر جماعات إسلامية تلو جماعات كلها تحارب المصالح الأمريكية التي [illegible] على السرقة والنهب، وستنطلق جيوش إسلامية إثر جيوش تقاتل القوات الأمريكية المجرمة الغاصبة [illegible] ﴿ولا يزال الذين كفروا تصيبهم بما صنعوا قارعة أو تحل قريباً من دارهم حتى يأتي وعد الله إن الله لا يخلف الميعاد﴾.

وآخر دعوانا أن الحمد لله رب العالمين

[illegible]

التاريخ : ١٩/٤/١٤١٩هـ
الموافق : ١٢/٨/١٩٩٨م

Document 25

Excerpts from a document by Rifaï Ahmed Taha, November 12, 2000

Rifaï Taha is the Egyptian fundamentalist leader who instigated the attack on American tourists at Luxor. This document, on the destruction of the American destroyer *U.S.S. Cole,* was written on November 12, 2000, one month after the attack.

He writes that despite the massacres of women and children in Palestine by the Jews, Aden welcomed the *Cole* on October 12. The *Cole* was very well protected. The operation cost between five and ten thousand dollars. Journalists in the pay of the West claim that "our strength cannot compare to that of the Zionists. Moreover, the Americans have made Iraq an example in order to terrorize the opposition. The Americans demolished a pharmaceutical factory in Sudan, perhaps the only one in the country. They attacked training camps in Afghanistan where there were only rocket launchers and submachine guns. The Americans want to try in their courts people whom they have decreed are terrorists. . . . They can stuff us with alcohol and cosmetics . . . with what they call fashion, but nothing will stop us. Those who have experienced pleasure will not have the strength of character to withstand a long world war. . . . The infidels will not be able to bear a life of terror with the sword of Damocles hanging over them.

"Western propaganda has blamed attacks on civilian targets, but the West does not care when Muslims are killed in Palestine or Chechnya.

"Hitting targets that are called civilian has been portrayed as heinous by the gigantic Western media machine, whereas targeting the destroyer is more painful to the United States; at the same time no one, not even the

بسم الله الرحمن الرحيم

ضرب المدمرة كول

الدروس والعبر

شهر كامل مضى منذ أن اتجه قارب صغير صناعة محلية نحو مدمرة أمريكية ليصارعها فيصرعها ..

ففي الثاني عشر من شهر أكتوبر الماضي وبينما كانت شواطئ عدن تفتح ذراعيها لاستقبال المدمرة الأمريكية " كول " غير عابئة بما يُقدم عليه اليهود وبدعم من الولايات المتحدة الأمريكية من ذبح لأطفالنا ونسائنا أمام كاميرات التليفزيون في فلسطين ، بينما كانت ترسو هذه المدمرة الأمريكية في الميناء البحري تتزود بالوقود وبعض الخدمات ، انطلق نحوها قارب بسيط من صنع محلي ربما زود بموتور سيارة أو جرار زراعي أو حتى دراجة بخارية ..

والقارب لم يكن متجها نحو المدمرة ليؤدي التحية العسكرية أو يبتهج لاستقبال المدمرة الأمريكية أو ليتسول أصحابه بعض النقود من راكبي المدمرة حيث الفقر الشديد في اليمن وفي مدينة عدن

إن ضرب المدمرة كول بوصفه هدفا عسكريا حصينا أضاف بعدا آخر ، فضرب الأهداف التي اصطلح على أنها مدنية استطاعت الآلة الإعلامية الضخمة للغرب أن تجعله عملا مدانا عند البعض في حين أن استهداف المدمرة هو عمل أكثر إيلاما بالنسبة للولايات المتحدة وهو في نفس الوقت لا يستطيع أحد حتى من القوى الكفرية نفسها إدانته واستعمال ذريعة مهاجمة المدنيين ، وهم يعنون بالطبع المدنيين من غير المسلمين أما المسلمون فلا بأس أن يقتل أطفالهم ونساؤهم وشيوخهم في فلسطين والشيشان وغيرهما !!! ..

كما أن أصحاب مقولات الإعتدال والعقلانية وضرورة صون حياة المدنيين من غير المسلمين لن يستطيعوا أن يدينوا هذا الحدث بشيء حيث أن الهدف هدف عسكري وأنه لدولة كافرة محاربة ومعادية تدعم الكيان الصهيوني في احتلال أرضنا وتشريد شعبنا ..

infidel powers, can condemn this action or claim that it is attacking civilians. By which, of course, they mean non-Muslim civilians; as for Muslims, there is no objection to killing their children and women and old men, in Palestine and Chechnya and elsewhere!

"America supports the Zionists, occupies our lands, drives our peoples to emigration. . . . We, the Islamic movements, are paying a heavy price to resist censure. . . . The Jews dictate American decisions. Muslims must understand that the Americans can change policies if they are struck directly.

"The only way for [the United States] to feel safe is to deal with these [Islamic] peoples with their history of civilization and struggle. . . .

"In the face of American nuclear power, we have our faith. America cannot live in peace and out of range of attack by the Muslim peoples, because a nation cannot be vanquished as long as its young men are willing to die, while their young enemies live in shame and sin, even if they have weapons of mass destruction.

"We must make [the United States] feel that our souls can no longer tolerate the prison walls of our bodies and that they long for the freedom to circle like green birds, and that (our souls) have the will and determination to push our bodies to destroy shields and tanks."

ولقد كان توقيت توجيه الضربة للمدمرة كول في ظل العدوان الهمجي والبربري الذي يقوم به اليهود في مواجهة شعبنا في فلسطين توقيتا موفقا ، وقد دفع الكثير من أبناء الحركات الإسلامية لأن تحذو حذوه في صمت ، مما يدعو لتوقع المزيد من العمليات على هذا النحو ، وفي عمل تصعيدي مدروس في مواجهة الولايات المتحدة الأمريكية في ظل تنامي الشعور عند الكثيرين من أن الشعب الأمريكي لن يكف عن دعم الكيان الصهيوني بل ودفع قيادته السياسية في قراراتها ضد المسلمين على غرار ما تم في الكونجرس الأمريكي لمواجهة شعبنا في فلسطين لن يكف عن هذه الأعمال إلا إذا شعر هذا الشعب عمليا بخطر هذه السياسة عليه وتعريض أمنه للخطر سواء كان مدنيا أو عسكريا ، وإذا كانت الجالية اليهودية يعتبرها متخذ القرار الأمريكي مصدر ضغط ينصاع له في ظاهر الأمر ، فإن الشعوب المسلمة عليها أن توقن أن الشعب الأمريكي يمكن أن يغير سياسته إذا ما أضير ضررا مباشرا من جراء هذه السياسة ، وإذا ظلت الولايات الأمريكية حريصة على أن تجعلنا نعيش تحت مظلة رعبها

الرغبة في نيل الشهادة وبلوغ الدرجات العلى ما يجعلها تضع أسلحتها هذه في المتاحف ليتندر عليها الناس ..

علينا أن نشعرها أن أرواحنا قد ضاقت بسجنها داخل أسوار أجسادنا وإنها ترغب في حرية تحلق من خلالها بحواصل طير خضر ، وأنها تملك من الإرادة والعزيمة ما يجعلها تدفع بهذه الأجساد لتحطم بها الدروع والمدرعات ..

لقد جاء ضرب المدمرة كول ليؤكد للولايات المتحدة الأمريكية أن قوة عتادها وبطشها لن يجعلها في مأمن من أيدي الشعوب الإسلامية ، وأن دعم الحكام لها لن يحميها من رعايا هؤلاء الحكام وأن السبيل الوحيد ليشعروا بالأمن هو أن يتعاملوا مع هذه الشعوب بما لها من تاريخ حضاري وجهادي لن يستطيعوا طمسه مهما امتلكوا من آلة عسكرية أو وظفوا حكاما لهم يحرصون على معاونتهم في ضرب شعوبهم ..

إن أمتنا الإسلامية ذاخرة برجالاتها وقادرة في أحلك الظروف على تقديم التضحيات ، ولن تُهزم أمة يحرص شبابها على الموت بأكثر مما يحرص شباب أعدائها على الخنا والفسوق ، وإن امتلكوا كل أدوات القهر والدمار ..

Document 26

From a French-language newspaper

This front page of the June 1998 issue of *Les Partisans de Shariah* includes the headline "The First Islamic Nuclear Sword?"

LES PARTISANS DE SHARIAH

NEWS ...NEWS ...NEWS ...NEWS...

Juin 1998 - Safar 1419 Fichier 1 Edite 3

LE ROI FAHAD CACHE DEUX INFIRMIERES DE ALLAH'S PUNITION

Dans Mai tard les deux infirmières Britanniques' accusé de meurtre leur collègue Australien étaient acquittées. La révision entrait l'imprimé d'un pardon par le " - Gardien des Deux Mosquées Sacrées " -, Roi Fahad. Cette intervention royale est, et probablement sera un phenomène unique. Il est invraisemblable qui avait l'accusé été soeurs Musulmanes un tel répit n'aurait pas été accordé. Dans le contraste ils auraient été traités avec dans une humiliant et embarrassant la façon, leur honneur cabossait et exécutait ultimement à titre d'exemple du - " Islamique Sharia " - prédominant dans Saudia Arabie. Le système de justice dans Saoudienne Arabie est évidemment imparfait, comme telle couverture et faveurs n'étaient pas aimées par les Musulmans arretées et exécutées dans une cour très discréte et rapide case dans 1996 suivant le bombardement d'un USA base militaire à Riyad. Bien que pas De musulmans n'étaient supprimés dans cette attaque sur la base vies Musulmanes étaient prises dans l'egalisation et beaucoup souffraient plus de torture et humiliation. Cet exemple surintensifie le manque de suivre la Qu'ran et Sunna comme la SCIE De prophète rapportait que " - **Pas de vies Musulmanes Ne devraient être prises comme un recompense pour les vies de** Kaffirs " -. Un exemple de davantage de la justice du Saudian pouvoirs est où 40 fréres

Document 27

Excerpts from a communiqué from the Egyptian Gamaa Islamiya, October 22, 1997

"This morning, four of our members were hung."

[1.] "These executions will not break our determination. We will pursue our jihad to establish sharia."

[5.] Gamaa Islamiya will avenge the martyrs "before the ink with which we are writing this communiqué is dry."

لا إله إلا الله — الجماعة الإسلامية

محمد رسول الله — بمصر

لن تفلح مشانقهم وإنهم لهم المقهورون

وإن جندنا لهم الغالبون

في صباح اليوم قامت السلطات المصرية بقتل أربعة من أبطالنا شنقا وصبّرا بعد وقوعهم في الأسر وتقديمهم لأحد المجازر العسكرية..

إن الجماعة الإسلامية إذ تحتسب شهداءها عند الله تعالي وتسأله أن يسكنهم فسيح جناته فإنها وأمام هذه المجازر التي يقوم بها النظام في حق شعبنا ومجاهدينا تؤكد علي ما يلي :

1- إن المجازر العسكرية والمشانق لن تستطيع بحول الله وقوته أن تهز صمودنا وستواصل جهادنا لهذه الطائفة المبدلة لشرع الله تعالي إقامة لشرعه وثأرا لأوليائه ..

2- إن هذه المشانق لن تجلب لهذا النظام أمنا ولن تجلب له استقرارا ولكنها ستجلب له هزيمة واندحارا ، وما كان الله ليذر أولياءه دون أن ينتصر لهم من عدوهم ..

3- إن النظام قد أخطأ حساباته عندما ظن أنه يستطيع أن يؤثر في إرادة صمودنا واستمرارنا وكان عليه أن يدرك أن همجيته وجبروته وبطشه لن تستطيع أن تصمد أمام عزيمة شعبنا وطليعته المجاهدة من أبناء الجماعة الإسلامية ..

4- إن قيام النظام المصري بقتل أربعة من أسرانا صبّرا ليقدم دليلا جديدا على همجية هذا النظام وأنه لن يتخلي عن سياسة القبضة الحديدية وسياسته القمعية ..

5- إن الجماعة الإسلامية ستثأر بإذن الله تعالي لشهدائنا قبل أن يجف مداد بياننا هذا ، وإننا سنستمر بإذن الله تعالي أوفياء لديننا ولشهدائنا ما بقي فينا عرق ينبض أو عين تطرف ..

إن نظاما يقتل أبناءنا ويرهب شعبنا ويستحيي نساءنا ويقوم بأسرهن ولا يعرف إلا لغة الجبناء ولا يجيد إلا منازلة العزّل والنساء ، ليس له منا إلا السيف ، ولن يفلّ الحديد إلا الحديد ..

ولن تفلح مشانقهم في كسر إرادتنا والنيل من صمودنا ، وإنهم لهم المقهورون ، وإن جندنا لهم الغالبون ..

والله غالب علي أمره ولكن أكثر الناس لا يعلمون ..

الجماعة الإسلامية

الأربعاء

1997/10/22

Document 28

Communiqué from the Egyptian Gamaa Islamiya,
October 14, 1997

This communiqué claims responsibility for the death of fifteen police officers in retaliation for the sentences handed down by the Egyptian military tribunals.

It asserts that operations will continue as long as "our women are imprisoned and being raped." It will not accept the continued incarceration of "our women" behind bars while "monkey and pig spies" [Jews] have been released. It urges soldiers and officers to desert and join them, and Arab and Muslim governments not to support the Egyptian government, because "it is neither democratic nor based on sharia."

It also urges tourists not to come to the country, in order to preserve their lives and property, all the more because this is a conflict in which they have no part.

"The jihad will go on," it concludes, "until Egypt is freed from the Jewish and American stain and all freedoms are restored."

لا إله إلا الله — الجماعة الإسلامية

محمد رسول الله — بمصر

<u>الله أكبر وجهادنا لن يتوقف</u>

في صباح الاثنين 1997\10\11 م وفي عملية مباركة قامت كتيبة الرعب أحد كتائب الشهيد طلعت يس همام بقتل مايناهز خمسة عشر من القوات الحكومية في ثاني عملياتها الجريئة الرد على أحكام المجازر العسكرية والصادرة في حق مجاهدينا وأخواتنا في منتصف شهر سبتمبر الماضي ..

إن الجماعة الإسلامية وهي تعلن مسئوليتها عن هاتين العمليتين تؤكد على مايلي :

1-إن عملياتها ستتواصل مالم يفرج عن نسائنا وتتوقف انتهاك أعراضنا، وهي تؤكد أنها لن تقبل أن يستمر تغييب نسائنا خلف الأسوار في الوقت الذي يُفرج فيه عن الجواسيس من القرود والخنازير..

2-إن كتائب الشهيد طلعت يس قد رصدت ردا على أحكام المحكمة العسكرية السابقة عددا من العمليات لن تتوقف قبل الإفراج عن الحرائر العفيفات ..

3-إن الجماعة تعلن أن عملياتها الموجهة ضد القوات الحكومية توجه ضد عناصر منتقاة من هذه القوات معروفة بعدائها للإسلام والمسلمين، والجماعة تنتهز هذه المناسبة لتدعو ضباط وجنود القوات الحكومية بصفة عامة إلى سرعة ترك العمل في القوات النظامية الحكومية والانضمام إلى صفوف المجاهدين ..

4-إن الجماعة الإسلامية إيمانا منها بمصلحة ديننا ووطننا فإنها ترحب بكل جهود حميدة تقوم على أساس الشرع والدين للإفراج عن كل المغيبين خلف الأسوار ..

5- إن الجماعة الإسلامية تكرر دعوتها للحكومات العربية والإسلامية بعدم دعم النظام المصري على اعتبار أنه نظام جاء على غير أساس من شرع أو إختيار شعبي صحيح ، بل هو نظام متجبر تسلط على البلاد والعباد بقوة الحديد والنار .. إن أي دعم لهذا النظام إنما يصب في خانة العداء لشعبنا المسلم في مصرنا الحبيبة ..

6- إن الجماعة الإسلامية تدعوا كل زائري مصرنا من سائحين وغيرهم إلى الامتناع عن زيارة مصرنا في هذه الآونة حفاظاً على أموالهم وخشية أن يصابوا في معركة هم ليسوا طرفا فيها ..

7- إن الجماعة الإسلامية تؤكد أنها ماضية في جهادها لهذا النظام ما بقي فيها عرق ينبض أو عين تطرف حتى يقام شرعنا على أرضنا وتحرر مصرنا من دنس اليهود والأمريكان ويحرر كل أسرانا وتعاد مساجدنا وتطلق الحريات فلا تكمم أفواه ولا يحجر على رأي ويعم الأمن البلاد والعباد ..

والله أكبر وجهادنا لن يتوقف ..

والله غالب على أمره ولكن أكثر الناس لا يعلمون ..

الجماعة الإسلامية

الثلاثاء

1997/10/14

Document 29

Open letter from Gamaa Islamiya

This communiqué claims to be the final warning from the "company of destruction and annihilation," directed to tourists from America and the West and to infidels, "as long as Dr. Omar Abdul Rahman has not been released." The men of Mustapha Hamza [Gamaa Islamiya] are carrying on the jihad to put an end to those who are "sold to foreigners and set up gallows." "The best young men are ours. Not an infidel on our soil while the governments, agents of foreign powers, destroy our religion.

"We will purify our land and avenge our martyrs."

[Signed] For the Muslims of Egypt.

التحذير الأخير

كتيبة الخراب والدمار

الخراب والدمار

كتيبة الخراب والدمار

Document 30

From the transcript of the interrogation of Ahmed Ibrahim al-Sayed al-Najar, September 1998

In this excerpt we read that the two al-Zawahiri brothers left for Afghanistan in 1997 after the Taliban had opened their borders to the Arabs. Al-Najar's signature is found in the bottom center of each hand-written page.

The statement tells us that Islamic Jihad found the Taliban movement to be a proper religious movement. It considered it normal that women were denied all education and that men were required to wear beards.

As soon as they had taken power, Osama bin Laden was able to make an agreement with the Taliban allowing him to take up residence in the country and to take charge of the Arab mujahedeen, on whom they imposed unification under the sole leadership of bin Laden. Those who settled in Afghanistan would receive a monthly stipend of one hundred dollars from bin Laden. The leaders of Islamic Jihad, as well as those of Gamaa Islamiya, like Mustapha Hamza and Rifaï Taha, began to come to Afghanistan, along with Islamists from Pakistan and Bangladesh.

In March 1998, al-Najar learned through London that a new group named the Liberation Front for the Islamic Holy Places had been established under the leadership of Osama bin Laden, and that Ayman al-Zawahiri had joined it. Its goal was to liberate the Islamic Holy Places and to strike at Jewish and American interests throughout the world in order to eradicate the Israeli and American "poison."

"We had a slight disagreement with Osama bin Laden about the way of conducting the jihad in Egypt. Bin Laden claimed that our actions in

Egypt were too costly and the expenses required for militants to survive were too high because of the vigilance of Egyptian security services. I proposed moving the funds and the militants of the Tanzim, as well as its members, to countries such as Bosnia and Kosovo, for the military training that that would contribute. Several leaders of the Tanzim asked me to think

of the possibility of becoming a political refugee in Great Britain, whereas others had reservations about the massacres carried out by Islamists in Algeria.

"Since the time I left Egypt in 1993, Gamaa Islamiya has suffered heavy losses and serious funding problems, after Islamists attempted to assassi-

nate Prime Minister Atef Sedki, an attempt that was carried out despite the lack of preparation and in disobedience of orders. That drove Dr. al-Zawahiri to strike the Egyptian government in late 1994 by attacking on the same day the Egyptian embassy in Pakistan, and Khan el-Khalili (bazaar in Cairo). After these two operations, al-Zawahiri had to reorganize the

Tanzim of the interior and he compelled the leaders of the organization to earn their livings.

"As for me, for a year and a half I was unable to carry out what was asked of me.

"Afghanistan is our best solution along with the establishment of the

Front for the Salvation of Islamic Holy Places under the leadership of Osama bin Laden. I think that al-Zawahiri and Gamaa Islamiya will agree to unity under the aegis of Osama bin Laden, even though the principles of the Front imply animosity against America, which is dangerous for Islamists, because of the weak protection we can secure from the Taliban."

Document 31

Communiqué from Rifaï Ahmed Taha, June 8, 2000

Rifaï Ahmed Taha is one of the leaders of Gamaa Islamiya and the man responsible for the Luxor massacre. His communiqué asserts that according to media reports "the engineer Mohamed al-Zawahiri has been turned over to the Egyptian authorities. The Egyptian authorities denied this in one of the papers today . . . which is dangerous for Engineer Zawahiri. It is certain that the Egyptian authorities have taken custody of him. According to his brother, Dr. Ayman al-Zawahiri, he was kidnapped at least five months ago.

"The Egyptians killed Dr. Ala, official spokesman of Gamaa Islamiya. In full daylight and with the support of the Americans, they kidnapped the engineer Talat Fuad Kassem, spokesman of Gamaa Islamiya.

"Mohamed al-Zawahiri is in fact in prison in Egypt, despite the government's denial."

بسم الله الرحمن الرحيم

هذا بيان للناس فاعتبروا يا أولي الأبصار

تناقلت وكالات الأنباء والصحف والقنوات الفضائية أول أمس خبرا يؤكد تسليم المهندس محمد الظواهري إلى السلطات المصرية ، وقد نقلت إحدى الصحف أمس تكذيب السلطات المصرية للخبر .. مما يؤكد خطورة الأمر بالنسبة للمهندس محمد الظواهري .. فمن المقطوع به أن السلطات المصرية قد تسلمت المهندس الظواهري ، وقد أكد الدكتور أيمن الظواهري أن عملية اختطاف أخيه قد تمت منذ خمسة أشهر أو يزيد ..

أما تكذيب السلطات المصرية لوجود المهندس في سجونها فليس مستغربا فقد اعتدنا منهم الكذب ، وعمليات القتل والاختطاف في وضح النهار فقد قتلوا الدكتور علاء المتحدث الرسمي باسم الجماعة الإسلامية في وضح النهار ثم نفوا مسئوليتهم عن الحادث ، وكذلك قاموا بالتواطؤ مع الولايات المتحدة الأمريكية باختطاف المهندس طلعت فؤاد قاسم والذي كان أيضا متحدثا باسم الجماعة الإسلامية ، ورفض وزير الداخلية المصري آنذاك التصريح بشيء حول عملية الاختطاف واعتبرها مما يمس الأمن القومي ..

إننا بهذا نؤكد وجود المهندس الظواهري في السجون المصرية ...

وإننا إذ نؤكد ذلك ، فإننا نؤكد في نفس الوقت أن استمرار هذه العمليات الإجرامية التي يقوم بها النظام في مواجهة أبناء الحركة الإسلامية بالتواطؤ مع الولايات المتحدة الأمريكية ومن يدور في فلكهم ، نؤكد أنها لن تثني أبناء الحركة الإسلامية عن مواصلة دعوتهم وتحريضهم لأمتهم وجهادهم حتى يتم اقتلاع هذا النظام المهترئ ...

إن هؤلاء الذين استباحوا لأنفسهم التحاكم إلى شريعة الغاب وقاموا بعمليات الخطف والاغتيال عليهم أن يدركوا أن ما استباحوه لأنفسهم لابد يوما يصيبهم ..

إن استمرار النظام المصري في تغييب شرع الله تعالى والاجتراء على ديننا ومقدساتنا وتكميم الأفواه ومصادرة الحريات واستمرار عمليات الاعتقال والخطف والاغتيال ومطاردة أبناء الحركة الإسلامية داخل وخارج مصر يؤكد عدم حرص النظام على استقرار البلاد وأمن العباد ...

إن النظام عليه أن يدرك أن هذه العمليات الجبانة والحمقاء لن يجني من ورائها إلا الشوك ، وأنه بهذه العمليات يهدد استقرار البلاد ويعبث بأمن العباد .. { **وظنوا أنهم مانعتهم حصونهم من الله فأتاهم الله من حيث لم يحتسبوا وقذف في قلوبهم الرعب يخربون بيوتهم بأيديهم وأيدي المؤمنين فاعتبروا يا أولي الأبصار** } .

والله غالب على أمره ولكن أكثر الناس لا يعلمون

رفاعي أحمد طه

من قيادات الجماعة الإسلامية بمصر

6 من ربيع الأول 1421 هـ – 8 من يونيو 2000 م

Document 32

Front page of the Urdu weekly *Takbeer*

In its February 25, 1999, issue *Takbeer* (Value God), published in Karachi, analyzes the relations between Pakistan and bin Laden. Among its other offerings is an article by Ali Othman entitled "Saddam has a nationalist vision, bin Laden has a vision of Islam."

INTERNATIONAL URDU WEEKLY
TAKBEER
KARACHI PAKISTAN
تکبیر
25 FEB 1999
8
آزادی اظہار کی فتح
اسامہ کو روپوش کس نے کرایا؟
فوجی عدالتیں فیصلہ کیا ہوگا؟

Document 33

In a report made public on Feb 23, 2000, the International Narcotics Control Board, acting under the aegis of the United Nations, denounces the Taliban's role in the production and trafficking of heroin.

369. En Inde, les autorités de répression continuent de signaler des saisies de comprimés de méthaqualone ainsi que le démantèlement de laboratoires illicites fabriquant cette substance, tandis que l'intensification des activités de répression et l'adoption d'une réglementation sévère se sont traduites par une baisse continue de la fabrication illicite de ce produit. L'Organe invite les autorités indiennes à demeurer vigilantes afin de prévenir toute relance de la fabrication illicite de cette substance. Il est préoccupé par le fait que des comprimés de méthamphétamine fabriqués illicitement dans la région montagneuse de Wa, au Myanmar, ont fait leur apparition sur le marché illicite indien.

Asie occidentale

Principaux faits nouveaux

370. En Afghanistan, la culture illicite à grande échelle du pavot à opium continue de s'étendre à des régions du pays qui n'avaient jusque là pas été touchées. On estime qu'en raison des conditions météorologiques favorables, la production d'opium a augmenté en 1999 par rapport à 1998, pour atteindre le niveau record d'environ 4 600 tonnes. Il est donc probable que l'Afghanistan représente environ 75 % de la production mondiale d'opium.

371. La volonté des autorités talibanes d'interdire la culture du pavot à opium et la fabrication d'héroïne reste douteuse, car elles continuent à percevoir des impôts sur la récolte de cette plante et sur la fabrication d'héroïne. Selon la dernière enquête en date, 97 % des superficies consacrées à la culture du pavot à opium se trouvaient dans des territoires sous contrôle taliban. La fabrication d'héroïne s'est déplacée du Pakistan, où elle a quasiment disparu, vers l'Afghanistan. L'Organe s'inquiète de cette grave situation qui a des incidences préjudiciables non seulement en Asie occidentale, mais aussi en Europe et dans le reste du monde. Il invite instamment la communauté internationale à prendre des mesures appropriées.

372. Les trafiquants utilisent la plupart des pays d'Asie occidentale comme points de transit pour les opiacés en provenance d'Afghanistan et à destination principalement de l'Europe, mais également d'autres régions. Du cannabis provenant de l'Afghanistan et du Pakistan transite également par de nombreux pays de la région de manière clandestine. Les précurseurs utilisés dans la fabrication illicite d'héroïne continuent de faire l'objet d'un trafic en sens inverse.

373. L'Organe s'inquiète de la progression rapide des cultures illicites ainsi que du trafic et de l'abus de drogues, en particulier d'héroïne, dans les pays d'Asie centrale (Kazakhstan, Kirghizistan, Ouzbékistan, Tadjikistan et Turkménistan) et du Caucase (Arménie, Azerbaïdjan et Géorgie). L'augmentation générale de la criminalité en Asie centrale et dans le Caucase ainsi que l'insuffisance des ressources et le manque d'expérience pour lutter contre ces phénomènes font que l'abus et le trafic de drogues risquent d'avoir des conséquences sociales dévastatrices pour les pays concernés si rien n'est fait pour les enrayer.

374. Si des quantités de plus en plus grosses d'opiacés provenant d'Afghanistan transitent clandestinement par l'Asie centrale, la majeure partie continue d'être acheminée par la République islamique d'Iran vers la Turquie, ou depuis le Pakistan vers la République islamique d'Iran et d'autres pays du golfe Persique, avant d'être envoyée vers sa destination finale. La Turquie reste le principal pays de transit de l'héroïne destinée à l'Europe.

375. La République islamique d'Iran a continué de s'employer activement à intercepter les envois illicites d'opiacés en provenance d'Afghanistan et à destination de la Turquie, des États membres de la Communauté d'États indépendants (CEI) et d'autres pays européens. L'Organe félicite la République islamique d'Iran de sa contribution décisive à la réduction des quantités d'opiacés disponibles sur les marchés illicites de ces pays. Plus de 80 % des saisies d'opium dans le monde sont le fait des autorités iraniennes, qui ont subi de lourdes pertes en vies humaines et ont consenti d'énormes sacrifices financiers.

376. La mer Caspienne est de plus en plus fréquemment utilisée pour le transbordement d'importantes quantités d'opiacés et de cannabis provenant d'Afghanistan et transitant par le Turkménistan, à destination de la Fédération de Russie et d'autres pays d'Europe.

377. L'abus d'opiacés a, semble-t-il, continué d'augmenter en Afghanistan et en République islamique d'Iran. Au Pakistan, l'abus d'héroïne semble demeurer très important. Bien que la toxicomanie reste peu répandue dans la plupart des autres pays d'Asie occidentale, une progression a été constatée dans un certain nombre de pays de la région (Azerbaïdjan, Émirats arabes unis, Jordanie, Kazakhstan, Kirghizistan, Liban, Ouzbékistan, Tadjikistan et Turkménistan).

378. Alors que l'Asie occidentale offre maintes possibilités de blanchiment d'argent, nombreux sont les pays de la région qui n'ont pas encore adopté de législation permettant de détecter et de combattre cette pratique.

Document 34

Extracts from a manual for the "perfect terrorist"

"In the name of God the Merciful"

Notes on revolvers and Kalashnikovs and instructions on how to blow up a bridge and shoot down a plane.

بسم الله الرحمن الرحيم

المسدسات

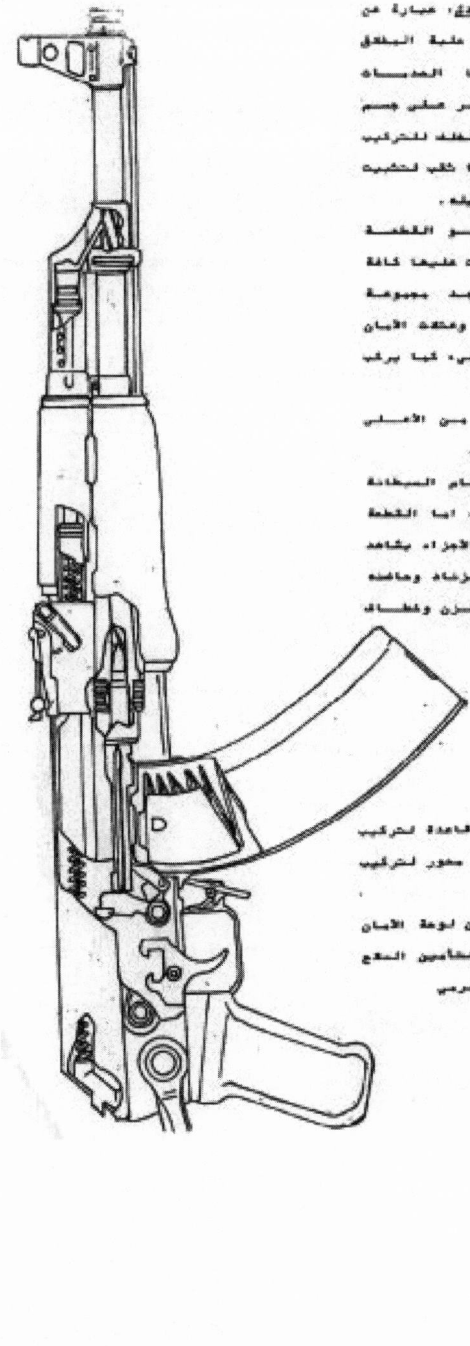

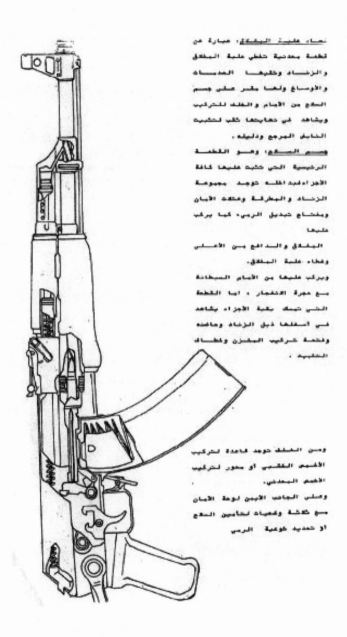

غطاء علبة المغلاق: عبارة عن
قطعة معدنية تغطي علبة المغلاق
والزناد وملحقاتها المعدنيات
والأوساخ ولها مقر على جسم
السلاح من الأمام والخلف للتركيب
ويشاهد في نهايتها ثقب لتثبيت
النابض المرجع ودليله.

جسم السلاح: وهو القطعة
الرئيسية التي تثبت عليها كافة
الأجزاء الداخلية توجد مجموعة
الزناد والمطرقة ومقلقة الأمان
ومفتاح تبديل الرمي، كما يركب
عليها
المغلاق والدافع من الأعلى
وغطاء علبة المغلاق.
ويركب عليها من الأمام السبطانة
مع حجرة الانفجار، أما القطعة
التي تمسك بقية الأجزاء يشاهد
في أسفلها ذيل الزناد وحاضنه
وفتحة تركيب المخزن وغطاء
القبضة.

ومن الخلف توجد قاعدة لتركيب
الأخمص الخشبي أو محور لتركيب
الأخمص المعدني.
وعلى الجانب الأيمن لوحة الأمان
مع ثلاثة وضعيات لتأمين السلاح
أو تحديد نوعية الرمي

تخريب الجسور الحجرية:

الأعمدة: تخرب جميعها بمحاذاة الارض وبشكل بحشوات في ثقوب لا تقل عن نصف السمك .

البلاطات: تخرب بمقطعين في كل فتحة يبعد كل مقطع عن الدعامة (مدى طول الفتحة) عندما تكون الفتحات كبيرة ، ولا تخرب الركائز في هذه الحالة المناسبة شكل (٤٣)

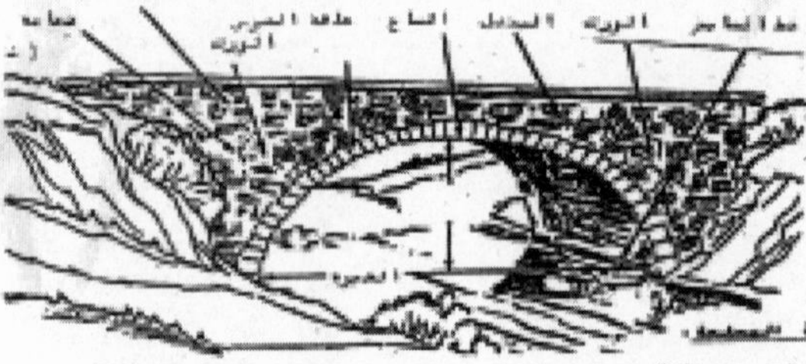

تخريب الجسور الاسمنتية المسلحة:

الأعمدة: تنسف في مقطع واحد بمحاذاة الارض بحشوات مركزة او متطاولة وتنقل الحشوات المثقوبة

البلاطات: تنسف بمقطع واحد في ربع الفتحة

الدعامات: تخرب بحشوات مركزة او متطاولة او ثقوب الجدران عادية

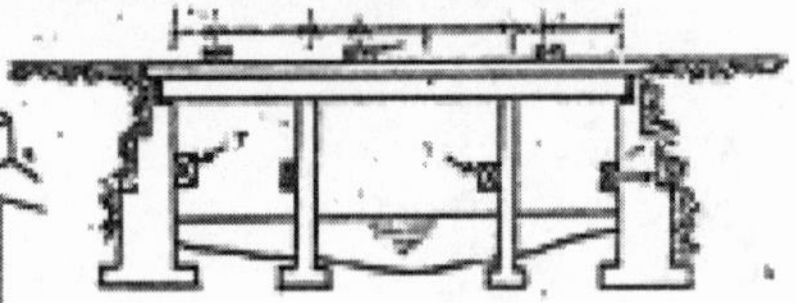

١- عبوات على الاعمدة
٢- عبوات على البلاطات
٣- عبوات على السطح الباطن

شكل (٤٦)

توضيع العبوات على جسر ذي بلاطة

تخريب الجسور المعدنية:

الجسور: تنسف حسب مادتها (معدنية/اسمنتية/مسلحة)

البلاطات: تنسف حسب نوعها

حبال التعليق الرئيسية (القابلات) تقطع في النقط الرئيسية

الجسور العائمة:

تخرب بحشوات (٣) كغ توضع في ثلاث زوارق التجسير وتنسف في وقت واحد

ملاحظات:

تقطع كافة عناصر الجسر في مقاطع التخريب في مستوى واحد (مستوى أفقي)

في حالة التخريب المقاوم بزمن قصير يمكن تخريب الجسور بحشوات غير مقطعة حسب نوع الجسر (خوفا من القوانين)

يمكن استخدام اكثر من حشوة غير مقطعة اذا كانت ابعاد الجسر كبيرة

يمكن حرق الجسور الخشبية

هناك معلومات مفصلة عن تخريب الجسور

شكل (٤٤)

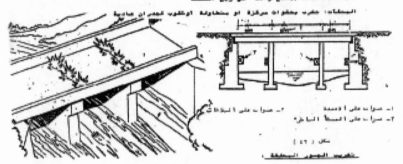

-٢٢٧-

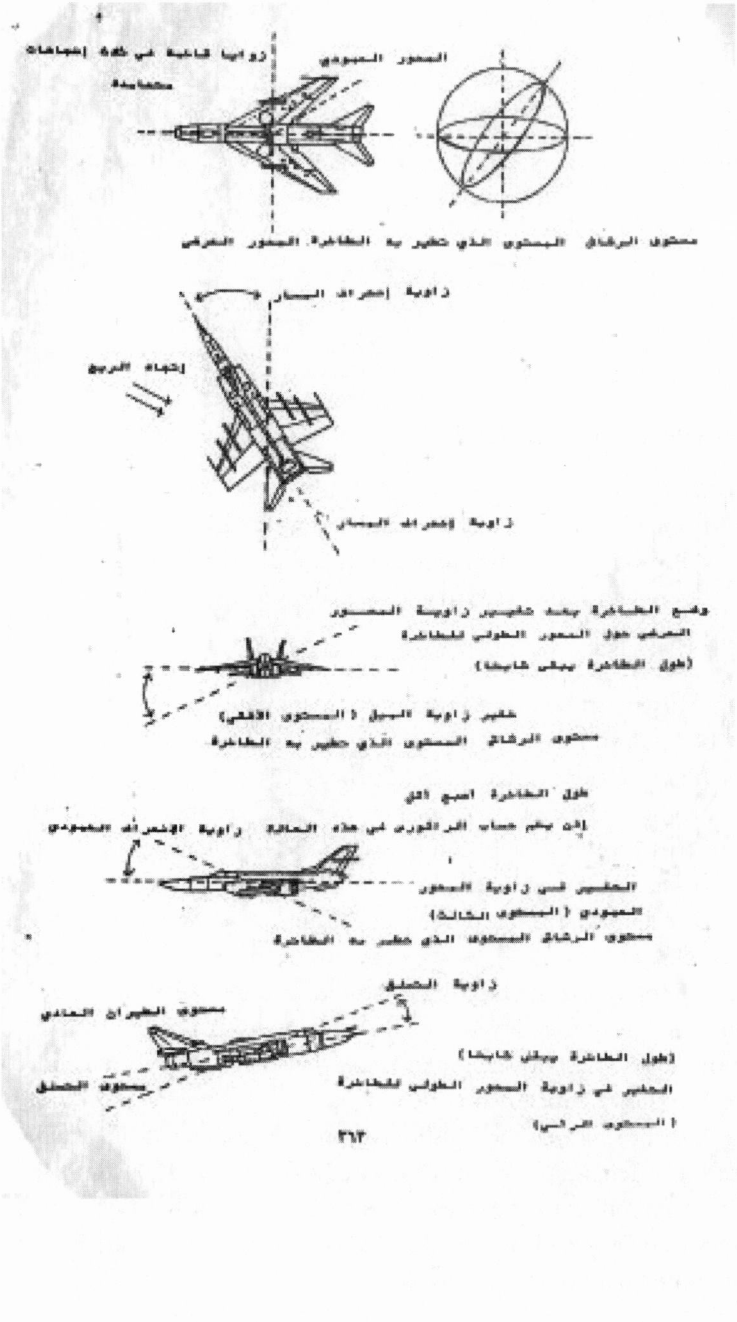
زوايا قائمة في ثلاثة إتجاهات متعامدة
المحور العمودي
مستوى الرشاق المستوى الذي تطير به الطائرة. المحور العرضي
زاوية إنحراف المسار
إتجاه الريح
زاوية إنحراف المسار
وضع الطائرة بعد تغيير زاوية المحور العرضي حول المحور الطولي للطائرة
(طول الطائرة يبقى ثابتة)
تغير زاوية الميل (المستوى الأفقي)
مستوى الرشاق المستوى الذي تطير به الطائرة
طول الطائرة أصبح أقل
زاوية الإنحراف العمودي
التغيير في زاوية المحور العمودي (المستوى الثالث)
مستوى الرشاق المستوى الذي تطير به الطائرة
زاوية التسلق
مستوى الطيران العادي
(طول الطائرة يبقى ثابتا)
مستوى التسلق
التغير في زاوية المحور الطولي للطائرة
(المستوى الرأسي)

٢٦٣

Document 35

An open letter from Osama bin Laden to fellow Muslims in Pakistan

A PROCLAMATION
In the name of Allah the most Merciful and most Gracious
Sunday, Rajab 1, 1422 of the Hegira (September 24, 2001)
(Allah has reserved their reward and their light for the martyrs)
—The Quran

To our Muslim brothers in Pakistan,

Peace be upon you

It is with great sadness that I have learned of the death of some of our Muslim brothers in Karachi when they were demonstrating against the American crusade and its aggression against the Islamic lands of Pakistan and Afghanistan. We beg Allah that he grant them the company of the prophets, the faithful, the martyrs, and the saints, who are the best society for believers.

We also implore that he bless their families and that he enable them to overcome the loss of their loved ones for the glory of Islam.

May those who have lost children know that they are also my children and that I would be their teacher.

It is not surprising that the Muslim nation in Pakistan, which is sacrificing itself for its religion, now finds itself in the front lines of the defense of Islam in the region, in the same way as Afghanistan, which was also in the front lines to defend its land and the land of Pakistan against the Russian invasion more than twenty years ago.

We hope that these deaths will be the first martyrs in the battle that Islam is now waging against the new crusade led by the head of the crusaders and under the banner of the Christians. This battle will be one of the many coming battles of Islam.

We urge our brothers, the Muslims of Pakistan, to use all their resources to combat the American crusader forces and prevent them from invading Pakistan and Afghanistan. The Prophet, may peace and salvation be with him, said: "Whoever does not participate in a battle or does not support a fighter for Allah . . . God will punish before the Day of Judgment."

I remind you, dear brothers, that we are still traveling on the road of jihad, for the glory of Allah, imitating his messenger, with the faithful and heroic Afghan people. [Illegible]

We pray that Allah will help us to vanquish these hegemonic and infidel forces and that he will destroy the Judeo-Christian crusade which is attacking the land of Pakistan and Afghanistan.

(If Allah supports you, no force will conquer you, if he does not give you his support, who else can help you. The faithful know that he is their only support)—The Koran.

Your Brother in Islam

Osama bin Mohamed bin Laden

Document 36

Interview with Osama bin Laden

In April 2001, through a member of the Egyptian Islamist opposition based in London, I sent some questions to Osama bin Laden. In order to reach him, we had to use a telephone connection used by Mullah Omar of the Taliban and bin Laden. The number, listed under the name of Mohamed al-Taheed was 928 18 37 825. What follows are my questions and the answers from the leader of al-Qaeda.

Do you think that American soldiers will one day be able to arrest you or kill you in Afghanistan?

We think that those who waged the jihad in Afghanistan did more than their duty because, with a few mines and a few Kalashnikovs, they destroyed the greatest military legend in the history of humanity. A great military machine was broken, and we no longer believe in the great powers. Our conviction is that America is much weaker than Russia. According to what we have heard from our brothers who fought in Somalia, American soldiers are weak and cowardly. After only eighty of their soldiers died, they ran away, regardless of everything they had said about the new world order. Our way of thinking can accommodate all believers, those who have the means can carry on the jihad, and those who are not yet prepared will have to work to create the necessary conditions.

Can the five-million dollar reward offered by the United States for your capture encourage betrayal?

We have young men, and we pray that God preserve them or accept them as martyrs if they die in this jihad. They have left the world to take refuge in these mountains and in this land. They have left their families and their universities and they have come here to live, to fight, and to suffer. Some of them have died. They are observing and guiding us today.

Are you in good health?

I am in very good health. We withstand the cold of these mountains and the heat of summer. As for the rumors, they could be aimed at weakening the morale of Muslims or at pacifying Americans by insinuating that Osama can't do very much any more. But this cause is not tied to Osama. This umma of 1.2 billion Muslims will never leave the ancient house of God in the hands of Jews and criminal Christians. This umma survives and we are certain that they will not give up the jihad.

The international press has published reports about your attempts to secure nuclear, chemical, and biological weapons, in particular through traffickers in Central Asia and other countries of the former Soviet Union. What is your response?

We claim our rights, we demand the expulsion of the Americans from the Muslim world and the end of their stranglehold on this Muslim world. We believe that that is included among the rights of all men to defend themselves. At a time when Israel is amassing hundreds of nuclear warheads and nuclear bombs, when the West of the Crusaders controls most of those weapons, this is not really an accusation but a right, and this is why we reject any accusation. We congratulated the Pakistani people when it came into possession of a nuclear weapon and we consider that one of our rights.

Document 37

Report from British intelligence on the implantation of al-Qaeda camps in Afghanistan and collusion with elements of the Pakistani ISI.

TRAINING CAMPS FOR MILITANTS IN AFGHANISTAN

Training camps for militants involved in Kashmir, in battlefields around the world and in international terrorism are located in Taliban-controlled Nangarhar, Pakhita, Logar and Kunar provinces of Afghanistan, bordering Pakistan and in several cases it is not clear which side of the Pak-Afghan border they are on. Pakistanis, Kashmiries and Arabs from Saudi Arabia, Algeria, Tunisia, Iraq, Egypt, Jordan and Palestine were among those trained in these camps.

Camps in Khost area

(i) Al Badr-I and Al Badr-II camps in Khost area of Pakhtia province are two major militant training camps in the country. Soon after Taliban captured Kabul, these camps were reported to have been handed over to the Harkat-ul-Ansar (HuA) for its use, after initial reports that Taliban had closed these camps. Al Badr-I was holding among others, about 200 Pakistani recruits being trained to fight against the Indian Forces in Kashmir and for Harkat UI Ansar. Al Badr-II had around 160 trainees, mostly Arabs and Sudanese Muslims for the fight in Chechnya and Bosnia. They were being given lessons in bomb making, use of automatic weapons, rocket launchers and anti aircraft guns. These camps, which were being used by the followers of Osama Bin Laden were however, destroyed in August, 1998 by the US Tomahawk (cruise) missiles fired from the Arabian Sea with the aim of killing Osama, for his alleged involvement in the bomb blasts in the US Missions in Nairobi and Tanzania. These, as well as those camps located in Khost (Paktia province) at Khawaja Mastoon Gundai, Sati Kundo on Pak-Afghan border and Tora-Bora base near Jalalabad (Nangarhar) and Julrez town (Wardak) 30 miles west of Kabul were however, reportedly rebuilt by Osama. A Command and Control Centre for AI Qaida outfit of Osama is also learnt to be under construction in a natural cave system in Kunduz province (near Tajik border).

(ii) Besides Al Badr I & II camps, other camps in Khost area are Omar, Al Khuldan and Farooq camps along the Pak-Afghan border and known to be involved in training of Arab-Afghan mercenaries for fighting in Chechnya. A training centre called Abdullah Azam Training Centre for training of Arabs and Tajiks also exists here. Camps affiliated to Osama Bin Laden for training terrorists for Kashmir operations under the leadership of Egyptians and Algerians are also functioning in Khost area. Mine warfare training is reportedly carried out by the Egyptian militant group Al-Jehad at the Abu Bakr camps on the outskirts of Khost.

(iii) Some of the camps previously located in Peshawar have been shifted to Khost area. Qaida camps is one such example.

(iv) Khost camp - Essentially, Yemeni extremists are trained here, though some Algerian militants have also been trained in the past.

(v) Nearly 700 fundamentalists from Chechenya, Indian Kashmir, Lashkar-e-Toiba, Harkat-ul-Mujahideen, Somalia etc had undergone 9 month military training at a place locally known as Jarangiya in Khost since 15.01.2000. Col Latif of ISI is the Incharge of this training centre. Of the 700 fundamentalists, nearly 90 each belong to Kashmir and POK, which includes activists of Lashkar-e-Toiba. 26 Uighur activists from Xinjiang province of China had also undergone training in this camp.

(vi) Two training camps for Kashmiri militants are currently operating in Khost province. These are at Sarobi village in Nadir Shah district and in the premises of a technical school near the Governor's house in Khost.

<u>Other camps in Pakhtia province</u>

(i) Jaji camp - Known for training Kashmiri militants and earlier linked to Ittehad-e-Isalami (Sayyaf) group. The camp is also known to train Arab mercenaries for the fighting in Kashmir who are linked to Harkat-ul-Ansar. A Syrian is currently believed to be leading the group of Arabs in this camp and was reported to be the main instigator behind the kidnapping of the four western hostages by the Al-Faran group.

(ii) Spin Shaga - A camp for Kashmiri militants.

(iii) Shepuli - A camp for Kashmiri militants located here.

(iv) Al-Jehad - It is near Zambar (Lz-3223). About 650 militants of LeT from J&K and POK under the supervision of Col. Saifullah Akhtar are being trained there.

(v) Khaldoon camp - It is controlled by OBL and is used for training 1800-2000 militants from Egypt, Sudan, Algeria, Saudi Arabia and Philippines. They are prepared to be deployed in Chechenya, J&K, Sudan, and Lebanon etc. This camps had been directed by an Algerian extremist named Kheddar Abden Nasser @ Abu Banane @ Commander Abd-El-Nasser, who died recently following a booby-trap explosion.

(vi) Gurbaz - It is about 4 kms. East of Khaldoon camp. About 150 Uighurs from CAS and Xinjiang province of China are undergoing training there.

<u>Camps in Nangharar Province</u>

(i) Teraki Tangi - Kashmiri militants are known to be trained in a camp located here.

(ii) Nazian Shinwar - Known for training Kashmiri militants and earlier linked to Ittehad-e-Islami (Sayyaf) group. The camp is also known to train Arab mercenaries linked to Harkat-ul-Ansar for fighting in Kashmir.

(iii) Muzaffarabad (Distt. Shinwari) - A camp for Kashmiri militants.

(iv) Dehbala - A camp for Kashmiri militants.

(v) Jalalabad camp - A leader of Egyptian militant group Al Gama'a Al Islamiya Shawki Al-Islambuli, was known to have run a training camp for Arab mercenaries in Jalalabad for the Afghan Jehad. Arabs, especially Egyptians, belonging to the Al Gama'a are known to be undergoing training here for terrorist activities abroad. The area between Jalalabad and Torkham along the Pak-Afghan border is known to be a base of Arabs undergoing training.

(vi) Darunta - It is situated at a distance of 20 kms from Jalalabad close to a dam at its western exit. A camp run by Abu Abdullah, an Egyptian, is located here. Approximately 300 mercenaries from Philippines, Pakistan, POK, Kashmir, Malaysia, Turkey, Egypt, Algeria and Sudan are known to be receiving training in this camp. Militants from here have been involved in fighting in Bosnia and Azerbaijan while a large number are currently in Chechnya and Kashmir. An Algerian here reportedly conducted a training course on explosives for Arab terrorists in early 1996. The camp is financed by Islamic terrorist organisations. Pak ISI officers are learnt to be frequently visiting this camp.

(vii) Moroccans were undergoing training at Darunta camp during early 2000. The training of Moraccans included handling of weapons and preparation of IEDs.

Camps in Logar province

20. Kanjak Camp

Camps in Kunar province

(i) Camps for training of Kashmiri militants exists in Barikot, Pir Qala, Sarkanay and Pench.

(ii) Toshi camp - Located near Asadabad, the camp is a training centre for large numbers of Kashmiri fighters and is under control of Pak ISI.

(iii) A militant Arab group called Khalifa Group, led by Jordanian-Palestinian national Abu Abdullah Al Refaee, is based in Kunar. It recently threatened to raise an Islamic army to wage war against the West. The group is reportedly in league with Takfiris, yet another militant Arab militant group.

(iv) The Ikhwan ul Muslimeen (Muslim Brotherhood) is also active in Kunar province for consolidating their basis in the region bordering the Central Asian States, especailly Tajikistan.

(v) Another Egyptian militant group Al-Jehad led by Islambuli, has training bases in Kunar and Nangarhar province of Afghanistan and also a camp in Jalozai region in NWFP, Pakistan. The group receives financial assistance from private individuals in Saudi Arabia through the `Human Concern International' Organisation registered in Canada. This organisation undertakes social projects in Afghanistan.

(vi) Azad Abbas - It is located in the Taliban - controlled Kunar province. Its armed unit is Hizbul Mujahideen. It prominent leaders are Vaht Zada (Pakistani). It is supported by Pak JI, ISI and is know to be imparting training to Pakistanis and Arabs.

Camps in Kabul province

(i) The Muslim Brotherhood is known to provide training to Kashmiri militants in camps located in Paghman area of Kabul province. There are also reports of camp being run by Taliban some 15 kilometers outside Kabul city.

(ii) Leva Rokig - It is located near Paghman in Kabul province and is under the Taliban control.

(iii) Sarobi - It is located near Kabul. Makab Al Kadam and Pak ISI support it. Its trainees constitute members from Arab, Algerian, Tunisia and Kashmir.

(iv) A Services Bureau, a branch of the Peshawar Services Bureau, is in existence in Kabul and provides support to mercenaries, especially Arabs.

Camps in Jawzjan Province

A training camp for imparting training in light weapons exists in Jawzjan. After training, the mercenaries are sent to Kashmir as well as to the battlefront to fight alongside the Taliban against NA.

Camps in Balkh (Mazar-e-Sharif)

(i) Saidabad - 300 families of Uzbek fighters are housed here. 50 Chechen families have also been accommodated in Mazar-e-Sharif. Further, there is a military training camp at one end of Saidabad, in an area called Dasht-e-shor where 200 Uzbek receive military training.

(ii) Base-E-Sokhta - Located between Mazar town and air base. It is a large place and provides training for Chechens.

Camps in Bamyan province

The Taliban are reported to have established two new militant training camps in Bamyan besides the existing camp in Bagram, run by the Lashkar-e-Jhangvi (military Wing of the Sipah-e-Sahaba). The Bagram (Bamyan) camp, under one ABDUL JABBAR, is currently imparting training to 50 Pak mercenaries.

Camps in Ghor Province

A Osama-run camp is reported to be in existence in Ghor province, where the pace of training activities has been increased.

Camps in Kandhar Province

A training camp for imparting training in light weapons exists in Kandhar. After training, the merçenaries are sent to Kashmir as well as to the battlefront to fight alongside the Taliban against NA.

Document 38

From *Knights under the Banner of the Prophet: Reflections on the Jihad Movement in Egypt,* by Ayman al-Zawahiri

Reproduced here are the title page and page 130.

[3.] International Pursuit

Since the fall of the Soviet Union, America's military superiority has enabled it to impose its will on many governments, and as a result of this control impose intelligence agreements on them, thus widening the influence of pro-American governments such as the Egyptian one in pursuing fighters [mujahedeen] in many countries. No doubt this has affected the flexibility of the jihad movement, but it is a new challenge faced by the

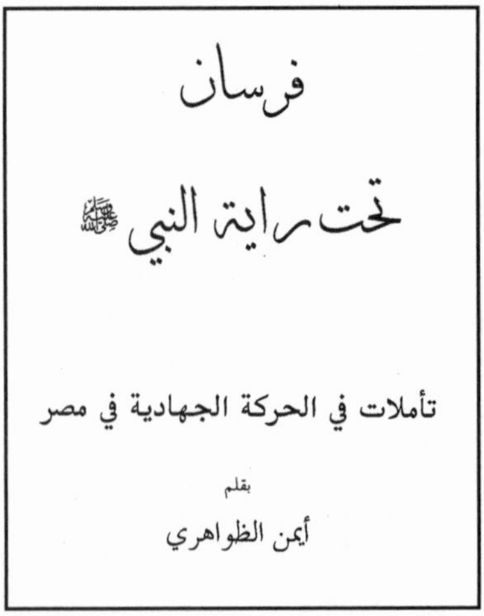
فرسان

تحت راية النبي ﷺ

تأملات في الحركة الجهادية في مصر

بقلم

أيمن الظواهري

movement: to include America as a target in the battle, as we shall see, God willing.

We should not forget to mention the Sharm el-Sheikh conference of March 1996, attended by the Arab countries—with the exception of Sudan, Iraq, Syria, and Lebanon along with America and Russia and a number of Western countries. The purpose was to agree on ensuring Israeli security from the attacks of the fighters. It was a sorry and humiliating sight, in the words of the [medieval] poet al-Mutanabi: "He who humiliates bears humiliation easily / Were he to be wounded in a hundred ways." The conference issued official decisions and secret agreements about intelligence cooperation in the service of Israeli security.

٣- المطاردة الدولية:

استطاعت أمريكا بتفردها بالتفوق العسكري بعد سقوط الاتحاد السوفيتي أن تفرض إرادتها على كثير من الحكومات، وكان من نتائج هذه السيطرة فرض الاتفاقات الأمنية على كثير من البلاد، وبذلك اتسع نفوذ الحكومات التابعة لها -كالحكومة المصرية- في مطاردة المجاهدين في كثير من البلدان، ولاشك أن هذا قد أثر على مرونة الحركة الجهادية، ولكنه تحد جديد واجهته الحركة الجهادية بما يكبحه وهو إدخال أمريكا كهدف في المعركة كما سنرى بإذن الله.

ولا يفوتنا هنا أن نشير إلى مؤتمر شرم الشيخ الذي عقد في مارس ١٩٩٦م وحضرته الدول العربية ـ فيما عدا السودان والعراق وسوريا ولبنان ـ مع أمريكا وروسيا والعديد من الدول الغربية، للاتفاق على تأمين إسرائيل من هجمات المجاهدين وكان المنظر في غاية الإهانة والإذلال ولكن كما قال المتنبي:

من يهن يسهل الهوان عليه ما لجرح بميت إيلام

وخرج المؤتمر بقرارات علنية واتفاقات سرية تدور حول التعاون الأمني لخدمة أمن إسرائيل.

Document 39

Training materials on the manufacture of atomic weapons

لقد تم شراء قنابل من المانياحيث صنعت في مدينة (فرنكفورت) لصالح العراق وعددها خمسة عشر قنبلة في نهاية عام 1990 واطلق العراق عليها اسم (الجمرة)
وقد كان يهدد بها اثناء حرب الخليج الثانية لما لها من قوة تدميرية حيث تحتوي تركيبتها على بعض انواع الاشعة , وتستخدم هذه القنابل في تدمير الانفاق وابار البترول , وعند تفجيرها تحدث فراغا هوائيا كبير يؤدي الى التدمير.

1- قنبلة وزن واحد كيلو غرام 1000 غ
قوة تدميرها لاتقل عن نصف قطر دائرة 500 م

2- قنبلة وزن خمسه كيلو غرام 5000غ
قوة تدميرها مضعفة عدة مرات

تم اخرج هذا القنابل الى دولتين مجاورتين للعراق بعد الحرب الاخيرة بمعرفة السلطات العراقية , وحاولو تسويقها الى عناصر المعارضة السعودية , يوجد سبعه منها في الاردن وثمانية في تركيا بطرف المافيا العراقية المتصله بالمخابرات العراقية .

شكل القنبلة مثلث ويكتب على جنبيها الاتي:

الجانب الاول color - red formlin
n-weight 1000
i-ndustrie - qqveck silber
germmany - frankfurt
p-1991-e1996
ce clissa

الجانب الثاني \ dangr
red mercvry 20 -20
% 9999\5
chmcal- s- rcification
beact - f-9-000
beact-ko-0001

الجانب الثالث \ n. 558210
camma0fs-0439
red 10 fn - sf 6 - 510
0714
flash - p- 100'026 grc
flash - ny19.

Document 40

Pages from what appears to be an engineering manual showing the different types of buildings, building materials, etc. This is significant in the light of the World Trade Center attacks.

النوع الثاني وهو الابنية ذات الاعمدة الزوايا المعدنية او الاسمنيته المسلحة عادة تكون هذه المباني ارفع من المباني بدون الزوايا ، الجدران الخارجيه لا تكون محملة بشيء كثير من الوزن وغالبا تكون من الاسمنت الخفيف ، تتكون الجدران من طوب خفيف مثبت مع بعضه بشيء من الاسمنت احيانا تكون الجدران مصنوعة فقط من الزجاج .

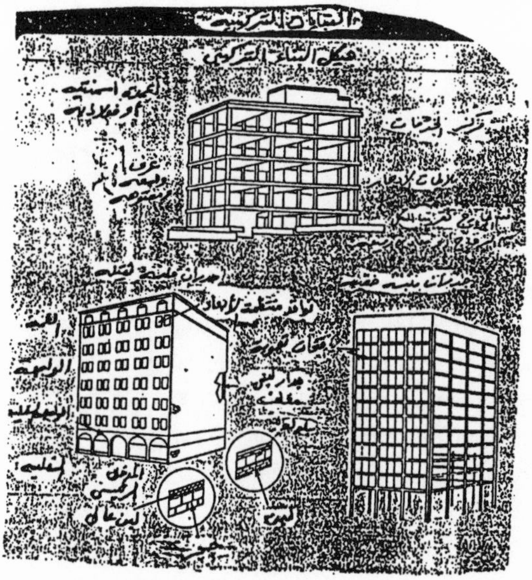

المواصفات الرئيسية للابنية

متوسط سماكة الجدار (سم)	الارتفاع (طابق)	مواد البناء	نوعية البناء
٧٥	١ - ١٠	حجري	بدون اعمدة .
٢٢	١ - ٣	طابرق	بدون اعمدة .
٣٨	٣ - ٦	طابوق	بدون اعمدة .
٢٠	١ - ٥	اسمنت مسلح	بدون اعمدة .
٢٢ - ٣٨	١ - ١٠	اسمنت مسلح	بدون اعمدة .
١٨	١ - ٣	اسمنت مسلح	بدون اعمدة .
٣	١ - ٥	خشب	باعمدة .
٣٠	٣ - ٥٠	حديد	باعمدة .
٢ - ٨	٣ - ١٠٠	حديد و اسمنت مسلح	باعمدة .

ب - ٥٢

Glossary

AIS	Armee islamique du salut
ANC	African National Congress
ARC	Advice and Reformation Committee
ASEAN	Association of Southeast Asian Nations
BKA	(German counterespionage service)
CERN	European Center for Nuclear Research
CIA	U.S. Central Intelligence Agency
DEA	U.S. Drug Enforcement Administration
DMI	Dar al-Maal al-Islami
DST	Direction de la surveillance du territoire
FBI	Federal Bureau of Investigation
FIS	Islamic Salvation Front [Algeria], Islamic Salvation Party
FLB	(Brittany liberation front)
FLN	National Liberation Front (Algeria)
FLNC	(Corsican liberation front)
FSB	(successor to KGB)
GIA	Armed Islamic Group
GIGN	Intervention Group of the National Gendarmes
IEFE	Instance exécutive du Front islamique du salut à l'étranger
IFOR	(NATO's multinational force)
IIF	International Islamic Front
IIRO	International Islamic Relief Organization
IMF	International Monetary Fund
INF	Islamic National Front (Sudan)
ISI	(Pakistan) Inter-Service Intelligence

KGB	(Soviet intelligence agency)
NATO	North Atlantic Treaty Organization
NGO	nongovernmental organization
NMD	national missile defense
NSA	U.S. National Security Agency
OIC	Organization of the Islamic Conference
ONDCP	Office of National Drug Control Policy
PAIC	Popular Arab and Islamic Conference
PDF	Popular Defense Forces (Sudan)
PFLP-GC	Popular Front for the Liberation of Palestine–General Command
PFNA	pulsed fast neutron analysis
PULO	Pattani United Liberation Front
RIMA	(French marine corps)
SCTIP	Police International Technical Cooperation Service
SPLA	Sudanese People's Liberation Army
UCK	Kosovo Liberation Army
UCLAT	Unit for Coordination of the Antiterrorist Struggle
UNCHR	United Nations High Commissioner for Refugees
WAD	Afghan Intelligence Service

Notes

Introduction

1 Mark Juergensmeyer, *Terror in the Mind of God: The Global Rise of Religious Violence* (Berkeley: University of California Press, 2000), 8.
2 "Jihad Is an Individual Duty," *Los Angeles Times,* August 13, 1998.
3 Juergensmeyer, *Terror in the Mind of God,* 10.
4 The Shia or Shiites are the second largest branch of Islam after the Sunnis. The Shia account for 10–15 percent of all Muslims.
5 The Islamist movement in Egypt is far from monolithic, however. There is a moderate wing forsaking violence for legitimate means that is trying to gain a share of power through the electoral process. Although Islamic parties are officially banned in Egypt, candidates with Islamist leanings made a good showing in the most recent (2000) parliamentary elections.
6 A "fatwa" in Islam is an opinion or ruling issued by a trained religious scholar on a matter of jurisprudence, most frequently in cases of disputed inheritance, marriage, and divorce. The scholar must base his opinion on the entire body of Islamic jurisprudence and not on an arbitrary opinion. However, his ruling is not legally binding; it carries only as much weight as the authority and reputation of the scholar issuing it. Since the Salman Rushdie affair, the word "fatwa" has come to be used in the Western media in the sense of a death decree, or more loosely in the sense of a declaration of "jihad."

1 / A Young Man from a Good Family

1 The original meaning of the word "jihad" in Islam means "struggle or striving" in the way of God, particularly the believer's struggle against his own baser inclinations. One form of jihad is the struggle to defend Islam and Muslims against aggression. This is considered a secondary form of jihad, according to a speech of the prophet Muhammad, who is reported to have said to his companions on returning from a military campaign: "This day we return from the lesser jihad (war) to the greater (self-control and betterment.)" The word "jihad" has entered the lexicon of the Western media in the sense of "holy war."

2 At the end of time, before the Day of Judgment, a man who is a descendant of the Prophet Muhammad is said to appear, bringing a reign of justice. This tradition is central to Shii theology, but contested by some Sunni scholars.

3 This family of large merchants was well connected among arms dealers; it was an intermediary in large contracts between France and the Middle East.

4 He has been on the throne since 1982.

5 According to Simon Reeve in *The New Jackals* (London: André Deutsch, 1999), about Osama bin Laden and Ramzi Yussef, this version is debatable; Salem is said to have died at the controls of a glider in Texas.

6 This episode was confirmed to me by Captain Paul Barril, one of the key participants in the counterterrorist operation.

7 Profilers are intelligence or police specialists who establish the portrait of a criminal in order to better define his personality and to be able to predict his actions. Like many American serial killers, Osama bin Laden has been the subject of this kind of study in the United States.

8 Yeslam bin Laden was born on October 19, 1950 in Saudi Arabia. He unsuccessfully attempted to obtain Swiss citizenship in late 2000.

9 General headquarters for American forces in the Gulf.

10 The BAC 111 is a twin-engine jet made by British Aerospace and able to carry 89 passengers for a distance of more than 3,500 kilometers. The Learjet is a small business jet that can carry seven passengers, with a range of 2,500 kilometers.

2 / From Riyadh to Peshawar

1 Personal communications to the author, Pakistan, from 1998 onward.

2 Reeve, *The New Jackals*.

3 Hekmatyar, born in 1948, had been a student in the faculty of sciences in Kabul. He settled in Pakistan in 1973, founded his party in 1976, and then joined the fight against the Soviets from Peshawar—he did not participate in battles against the Red Army—and became one of the dominant leaders on the Afghan political stage. Relying on support from the Pashtuns, he was very close to the Pakistani Islamists and benefited from Saudi donations. Having lost influence under the Taliban after 1994, he was active in the anti-Taliban resistance

4 The ISI, Inter-Service Intelligence, depends on the Pakistani armed forces. It is placed under the authority of the minister of defense. The service enjoys broad freedom of action and significant resources. It is very strongly implanted in the North West Province on the border with Afghanistan. The ISI has often been accused of complicity with regionally destabilizing activities along with the mujahedeen in Afghanistan and Kashmir. In the last several years, the aims of the ISI have not necessarily coincided with the government's objectives, except under General Zia. The ambiguity of the relationship between some Pakistani agents and bin Laden troubles Saudis and Westerners. Many Afghans have Pakistani papers through marriage or thanks to stolen documents.

5 Scott McLeod, "The Paladin of the Jihad" (May 6, 1996).

6 Wahhabism is an Islamic revivalist movement founded in the eighteenth century by Mohamed abdel Wahab and based on strict monotheism, a return to the precepts of early Islam, and puritanism. The movement became political with the conversion of Mohamed Ibn Saud, who established himself as the monarch of the Nejd and fought to drive out Ottoman and foreign influence. Wahhabism relied on warrior-preachers called the Ikhwan, or Brothers. In the twentieth century Ibn Saud, a successor of Mohamed Ibn Saud, succeeded in conquering the rest of the Arabian Peninsula and gaining control of the holy cities of Mecca and Medina, driving out their erstwhile rulers, the Hashemite family (currently kings of Jordan). In 1932 the kingdom of Saudi Arabia was created, with Wahhabism as the basis of its legitimacy. The Ikhwan, however, were eliminated by the new king because of the rigidity of their doctrine and their refusal to adapt to aspects of modernity. Wahhabism is the state religion of Saudi Arabia and Qatar. Another name for Wahhabism, preferred by its adherents, is the Salafiya movement, which gains its inspiration from strict adherence to the precepts set down by the earliest Muslims, or "those who came before," the literal translation of "Salafi."

3 / Exile in the Sudan

1 The Anglo-American intelligence services spoke at the time, among others, of a camp in Bilal near Port Sudan said to have served Afghans; another at Dinkola, harboring Egyptians and Algerians; a base at Ikli al-Aswat training Yemenis, Somalis, Moroccans, Kenyans, and Malians; a camp in Jedid al-Haq specifically dedicated to Palestinians from Hamas; and a final camp in Abu Rukhn for Afghans. According to Sudanese authorities, who acknowledged the existence of these bases, they were barracks for the PDF, the Popular Defense Forces, and journalists were invited to visit them.

2 Hezbollah is a Lebanese movement supported by Teheran with bases in the Bekaa Valley, Lebanon.

3 Gum arabic, the sap of a variety of acacia harvested almost exclusively in Sudan, is a substance used in the manufacture of soda and drug excipients. The largest consumer of gum arabic is the American food industry.

4 Illich Ramirez Sanchez, alias Carlos, was captured in Sudan on August 15, 1994 by the French secret service. See Roland Jacquard and Dominique Nasplèzes, *Carlos, le dossier secret* (Paris: Jean Picollec, 1997).

5 There had been nearly forty violent government overthrows, civilian or military, in the forty years preceding the arrival of al-Beshir on June 30, 1989.

6 The Sudanese national drink, brewed from hibiscus leaves.

7 According to some Muslim traditions, a series of "Mahdis," or spiritual guides, appear to guide Muslims throughout history.

8 "Sharia," an Arabic word meaning "the way," is the universal Islamic law that regulates all aspects of religious and social life, covering civil and family law as well as criminal and commercial law.

9 In 1989, the rebellion, a legacy of British colonialism, was made up of seven different movements that had never been able to establish a unified organization, the best known of

which was led by John Garang. Since 1998, six of these factions have normalized their relations with Khartoum and have entered into a process of pacification and democratization. Only John Garang's SPLA has remained aloof from negotiations.

10 The author attended and filmed this conference.

11 Ayman al-Zawahiri, born June 9, 1951 in a Cairo suburb, is from a prominent Muslim family (his uncle Fatha Azzam was the first general secretary of the Arab League) of graduates from al-Azhar University (the university of Islamic studies) in Cairo. He received a medical degree in 1974 and a surgical degree in 1978 from the University of Cairo. He settled in Afghanistan as a doctor, after being sentenced to a three-year prison term in 1981 at the trial stemming from the assassination of President Anwar al-Sadat, which had been carried out by the Islamic Jihad. Having become the head of the Egyptian Islamic Jihad movement, he is said to have met Osama bin Laden in 1985 and then to have joined him in Sudan in 1992 and 1993. He is now considered one of Osama bin Laden's contacts. Two of Osama's closest collaborators, Mohammed Aref and Abu Ubaidah al-Banshiri, come from the ranks of Islamic Jihad. Ayman al-Zawahiri, who uses two aliases, has several passports: Egyptian, French, Swiss (in the name of Ayman Othman), and Dutch (in the name of Sami Mahmoud al-Afnawi). He was sentenced to death on February 24, 1999, by the Supreme Military Court in Cairo, one of the 107 Islamists of the Islamic Jihad who were defendants in the trial known as the trial of the Albanians, because many of them had been extradited from that country. In 1998, he and Osama bin Laden established the World Islamic Front for Holy War against the Jews and the Crusaders. For Ayman al-Zawahiri, who said as much to several Islamist emissaries from London who had come to meet him, Osama bin Laden is a hero; he claimed that millions of Muslims would revolt if bin Laden were to be arrested and imprisoned in the United States or Saudi Arabia. He often names bin Laden the "new Che Guevara" in public.

12 This occurred in one of the attacks fomented by the Soviets in Pakistan to break the Afghan resistance. According to another version, Osama bin Laden was suspected of having had Azzam eliminated in order to take on his title of leader of the Afghan Arabs. Osama bin Laden denied that accusation in 1999, explaining that he had even warned Azzam to be on guard after the discovery of a bomb in a mosque in Peshawar (see document 7, proving the influence of Azzam).

13 This federal grand jury indicted Osama bin Laden on November 4, 1998, in the Southern District Court of New York for the murder of American nationals outside the United States, for conspiracy to murder Americans outside the United States, and for attacks against federal establishments causing death.

14 When he was questioned, Manduh Mahmud explained to investigators that he had traveled throughout the Muslim world (twenty countries in four years) in order to find a wife, and that he had come to Europe to buy a Mercedes.

15 The testimony of a Sudanese renegade, a member of one of the opposition parties, was refuted at the time. According to the information he had provided to several Western intelligence services, Sudan had begun constructing near Khartoum a military-industrial complex financed by Osama bin Laden, intended to produce chemical and bacteriological

weapons in cooperation with Russian, Chinese, Iraqi, and Iranian firms. According to this information, later disproved, these operations were managed by a company in Canada associated with Osama bin Laden.

4 / Among the Taliban

1 Interview with the daily *Al-Quds al-Arabi* (Jerusalem) on November 27, 1996. In the same interview, Osama bin Laden stated that the Saudi regime had put pressure on his family to have him return to Saudi Arabia, where his possessions and his passport would be restored provided he declared that King Fahd was a good Muslim.

2 One of these attempts is said to have happened in November 1995, as retaliation for the attack against the Saudi National Guard in Riyadh a short time before. It was said to have been an initiative of some Saudi officers against bin Laden.

3 Shiite Islam originated as a political movement supporting Ali (cousin and son-in-law of Muhammad, the Prophet of Islam) as the rightful leader of the Islamic state, hence the name "Shiat Ali," or the party of Ali. A civil war broke out between Muslims supporting Ali and those supporting another clan, the Umayyids, who eventually won. In the fighting Ali's son Husayn was martyred in 680 A.D. in Karbala (Iraq); this traumatic event is believed to have initiated the evolution into a religious formulation.

The early Shiites, a recognized, if often persecuted, opposition to the central government, soon divided into several factions. The majority of the Shiites today are Twelve-Imam Shiites (notably in Iran, Iraq, Lebanon, Saudi Arabia, Bahrain, India, and Pakistan). Others are Zaydis (in Yemen) and the Ismailis (in India, Pakistan, Syria, and Yemen). The central belief of Twelve-Imam Shiites, which notably sets them apart from Sunnis, is the occultation (or disappearance from view) of the twelfth Imam, or spiritual guide, believed to be a descendant of the prophet.

The religious authority of the Shiite clerics, as opposed to Sunni, is derived from their role as deputies of the absent twelfth Imam; they are as such the recipients of the *khums* religious tax, a source of substantial economic autonomy.

The Safavid dynasty in Iran adopted Shiism as a state religion, leading to the expansion of clerical involvement in private life. The attempt of the Pahlevi monarchy in the twentieth century to curtail the influence of the clerics strengthened clerical political militancy, and the Iranian revolution in 1979 brought Ayatollah Khomeini to power.

4 After 1989, the "boss" of the ISI, General Hamid Gul, organized networks for the recruitment and transport of Islamist fighters from Pakistan to Afghanistan. The number of men receiving "tourist" visas are estimated to have been seventeen thousand.

5 Afghanistan includes about twenty ethnic groups and about thirty languages. Within any particular ethnic group, different tribes may have divergent interests, making Afghanistan an extremely heterogeneous country.

6 In the spring of 1996, the Israeli airforce bombed civilian targets in Cana, causing 150 deaths. Ogaden is a region of Ethiopia claimed by Somalia.

7 Reported to the author by an associate of bin Laden.

8 Statement to the Urdu-language Pakistani newspaper, *Pakistan*, March 18, 1997.

9 This raid on Indian territory by an alliance of the Pakistani military and mujahedeen in

the contested region of Kashmir, which began on May 9, 1999, provoked violent military confrontations between India and Pakistan. The incident suggested that, considering the nuclear capability of the two countries and the tension between them, they were carrying on no negotiations. The risk of a nuclear war could not be excluded.

The tension between the two countries reached another crisis point on December 24, 1999, when an Indian Airlines Airbus en route from Katmandu to New Delhi was hijacked to Afghanistan. The hijackers demanded in exchange for their 155 hostages the release of a Muslim cleric, Massud Azhar, imprisoned in Jammu, Kashmir, since November 1994 for association with Harakat ul-Mujahedeen, among the most violent of Kashmiri separatist movements, with an office in Rawalpindi, Pakistan (see document 10). This organization had lost several militants in the American bombardment of the Khost base in August 1998. Azhar belongs to the Deobandi school, to which the Taliban also claimed affiliation. He was released in exchange for the hostages on January 7, 2000. According to some observers, this hijacking was sponsored by the Pakistani ISI. During the crisis, to the surprise of the Indians, the Taliban condemned the taking of hostages and cooperated with New Delhi with no conditions, not even asking for recognition. For some, this was evidence that the hijacking was a well-organized operation whose outcome was known in advance.

10 Considered the armed wing of the FIS, the AIS was established in the fall of 1993. This organization never assassinated civilians or foreigners.

5 / The Islamic Legion

1 Information given to the author by official sources in Israel.

2 "Qadassiya" comes from the name of an Arab victory over the Persians in 637 A.D., prelude to the Muslim conquest of Iraq, which put an end to the Persian occupation.

3 Massoud's position at the end of his life was very clear. He stated in an interview with the authors that terrorism was harmful to Islam, and that if he were to return to power, he would put an end to all terrorist activities in camps in Afghanistan, including those of Osama bin Laden. According to the leader of the armed opposition to the Taliban, tension in the region was due to the interventionist policy of Pakistan, which was running the show, driven by the ambition of becoming a major regional power. For that purpose, Pakistan needed to use Afghanistan as a strategic backup in case of a direct confrontation with India.

4 More than sixty Islamist newsletters, produced principally by Egyptian and Algerian militants, are published in London (see appendix, documents 20 and 21; Osama bin Laden himself signed a document opening an office in the English capital). A large number of these publications were financed until 1998 by Osama bin Laden and a Pakistani known as Kelim. In 1996 Osama bin Laden attempted to finance the Islamic Conference of London, which was canceled under pressure from the British government. During the conference, Osama bin Laden intended to call for a jihad in the Gulf, or more precisely, against Anglo-American interests. The conference had not found unanimous support in English Islamist circles; Azzam Tamimi, one of the leaders of the Muslim Brotherhood in England, believed that several Islamist movements were not in favor of holding the conference and would refuse to participate if it called for terrorist acts. Osama bin Laden in reality in-

tended to use this platform in Great Britain to call for the unification of Shiites and Sunnites and an alliance between Iran and the organizations of Afghan veterans. This Islamist plan was discovered through disclosures from organizations based in London.

5 Kamar Eddin Kherban left the Algerian armed forces in 1983 and joined the mujahedeen in Pakistan, where he took over leadership of the Afghan Algerians.

6 According to the Bin Laden Brotherhood, the Israeli Mossad was responsible for this assassination, and Osama bin Laden decided to give financial support to any fighter with a legitimate claim to belonging to Azzam's organization.

7 Between July 11 and October 17, 1995, the population of Paris was subjected to six terrorist attacks, the most deadly of which took place in the Saint-Michel metro station on July 25, causing seven deaths and injuries to 84. The attacks as a whole killed 9 and injured 198.

8 Relations of Osama bin Laden with Hamas date at least to 1994. At the time, bin Laden was already financing the Palestinian Islamic movement. Osama bin Laden had come up against some resistance from some Gulf nations and from Iran, which were suspicious of his taking control of the organization. In August 1997, he offered substantial sums to extremist elements of Hamas after 360 million francs collected by agents for the movement for the liberation of Palestine were frozen in the United States. This freezing of the fundamentalists' assets by the American authorities gave bin Laden the idea of using his financial means to recruit Hamas militants trained in commando actions to join his camps in Afghanistan—a fair exchange.

9 Before ceasing publication, this periodical regularly denounced the West and ferociously attacked France, against which it called for a jihad.

10 Kumander Abu Sayyaf, also known as Abubakr Janjalani, was born in 1963 in Isabela in a mixed Christian-Muslim family. He was a student in Saudi Arabia and Libya. He established the Abu Sayyaf group in the early 1990s and was killed in a police operation on the island of Basilan in December 1998. The price on his head was $375,000. The Abu Sayyaf group demands autonomous status for the Mindanao region of the southern Philippines. This terrorist movement, whose methods are closer to those of organized crime than of a revolutionary political group, took a group of twenty-one tourists from Europe, Asia, Lebanon, and South Africa hostage on the Malaysian island of Sipadan on April 23, 2000. The hostages were then transferred to the island of Jolo, 960 kilometers from Manila, where the terrorists have their base. The group is thought to number nearly a thousand well-armed men. On August 30, 2000, while in the midst of a process of freeing the hostages, the group seized an American and demanded the release of Ramzi Yussef, imprisoned in the United States for the 1993 attack on the World Trade Center.

11 Ahmed Rassem's links with bin Laden were proved after the arrest of al-Qaeda members in Jordan.

12 Yossef Bodansky, *Bin Laden, the Man Who Declared War on America* (New York: Forum Editions, 1999).

13 These accords, signed in Dayton, Ohio, under the leadership of the American mediator Richard Holbrooke, were nicknamed the Pax Americana agreements. They provided that Bosnia-Herzegovina became a sovereign state made up of the Muslim-Croat federation (51 percent of the territory) and the Republika Srpska (49 percent), not to be confused with the Serb Republic of Yugoslavia.

14 The UCK is the Albanian militia whose aim is the independence of Kosovo and unification with the Albanians in the neighboring countries of Macedonia and Albania. In 1998 the UCK included several thousand volunteers who had come from Switzerland and Germany.

6 / The Anti-American Crusade

1 The word "fatwa" is used here in the sense of a death decree or a declaration of "jihad."

2 It is interesting to note that nine months before the attacks in Nairobi and Dar es Salaam, several Western intelligence services, notably the American services, had been informed of an Islamist threat against American embassies in Africa. This information came from telephone conversations of an Egyptian, Mustapha Mahmoud Ahmed, recorded several months earlier.

3 The author has spoken with this journalist on several occasions (French publisher's note).

4 On October 21, 2000, Ali Mohamed entered a guilty plea to charges connected with the attacks.

5 This operation, using the code names Kenbom and Tanbom, after the countries in which the attacks took place, was the largest foreign deployment of the FBI in its history. The investigators questioned more than one thousand witnesses.

6 Al-Owhali was one of the authors of the attack on the Nairobi embassy. His photo had been taken in the camp in Khost during Osama bin Laden's press conference launching his fatwa against the Americans. Linked to Islamists in Algeria and Comoros, al-Owhali had promised the Algerians also to attack French interests in Nairobi (according to information I have received from well-informed Islamists).

7 According to the American indictment, al-Haj also used the following pseudonyms: Abdus Sabbur, Abd al-Sabbur, Norman, and Wada Norman.

8 Al-Banshiri was one of the presumed chief officers of al-Qaeda.

9 Some Islamists have spread the rumor that al-Banshiri did not drown in the accident.

10 Mohamed Atef belonged to bin Laden's inner circle.

11 According to the Yemeni secret services, his real name is Abdul Rahman Hussein Mohamed al-Safani. He is said to have been in contact, to get advice, with veterans of the network of Wadi Hadad, one of the PLO hard-liners at the time of Black September. Wadi Hadad recruited Carlos (see Roland Jacquard and Dominique Nasplèzes, *Carlos, le dossier secret* [Paris: Jean Picollec, 1997]).

7 / Target: Bin Laden

1 In July 2000, Jamal Ismail issued a limited printing of the text of an interview of bin Laden and al-Zawahiri.

2 The president to whom he refers was Bill Clinton, mired in the Monica Lewinsky scandal.

3 Mary Jo White was a specialist in the mafia and had already prosecuted several New York "families."

4 This source gave up his anonymity on February 6, 2001, during the trial of the bin Laden network in New York. Jamal Ahmed al-Fadl, a Sudanese aged thirty-four, told of his career

from a Brooklyn mosque in 1988 to his involvement in the jihad in Afghanistan. He revealed that the aim of the al-Qaeda organization was to establish the caliphate in all Arab countries. Under questioning by the prosecutor, Patrick Fitzgerald, al-Fadl said that he had made a vow of allegiance to "the emir" bin Laden in 1989; he was the third to sign the "bayat."

His testimony enabled the partial dismantling of the organization of the bin Laden movement, structured in finance, military, fatwa, and travel committees. The media committee was led by a militant known as Abu Moussa "Reuters," after the celebrated news agency. Implicated since the establishment of al-Qaeda, al-Fadl also revealed that the organization had moved to Sudan because there was no longer "much to do" in Afghanistan after the Russians left, and that in Sudan, close to the Arab world, the National Islamic Front that had just come to power was willing to help them.

8 / Osama bin Laden Confronts the Arab World

1 Contrary to common belief, Operation Desert Storm was not exclusively American. The allies, and countries friendly to the alliance, provided more than 245,000 men for the expeditionary force in Saudi Arabia and contributed $70 billion to the expenses incurred by the United States. Osama bin Laden and his sympathizers openly denounced the United States, which makes for an easy target, but they were aware that the consensus at the time was global because Saddam Hussein had endangered world oil supplies. See Thierry d'Athis and Jean-Paul Croizé, *La Guerre du Golfe* (Paris: Jean Picollec, 1991).

2 The Iraqi invasion of Kuwait began on August 2, 1990. American aid was immediate, although the implementation of the Desert Shield and Desert Storm military operations took several months.

3 Conversation with the author in London, November 1997.

9 / The Bin Laden Brotherhood

1 Seeking information from the public, the FBI set up a most-wanted list code-named Heroes to track down all criminals.

2 Sadat was assassinated on October 6, 1981.

3 An infirmity that, according to some interpreters of the Koran, could prevent Sheikh Omar Abdul Rahman from being an emir.

4 The information on attacks planned on airlines was the subject of a very urgent diplomatic cable from the French embassy in Washington on May 2, 1995.

5 Notably the interrogation by Egyptian prosecutors of Ahmed Ibrahim al-Sayed al-Najar at his trial in Cairo in September 1998 after his extradition from Albania.

6 Al-Najar was arrested and extradited on June 12, 1998. He was sentenced to death by the Egyptian Supreme Military Court and executed in late February 2000. Officially, he had been head of the Islamic Assistance Movement. He was also associated with Ayman al-Zawahiri. According to some analysts, his arrest led to the Nairobi and Dar es Salaam attacks in retaliation.

7 The attack against the American embassy in Beirut occurred on April 18, 1983 (16 killed and

120 wounded); against the American Marines headquarters on October 23, 1983 (239 killed); against the headquarters of the French contingent of the multinational force on the same day (74 killed).

8 En-Nahda (the Renaissance) is a religious movement whose ideology is inspired by the ideology of the Muslim Brotherhood.

9 Interview with the author, Peshawar, 1988.

10 Qossay is the assistant head of al-Khass, the Iraqi counterespionage service.

11 Saddam Hussein is a native of Takrit. He has surrounded himself with devoted supporters from that region.

12 According to others, on the contrary (see *Le Monde* of March 24, 2001), bin Laden played a "much more important role in internal Afghan affairs," thanks to his historic ties to the commanders of the anti-Soviet war. This is all the more the case because Arab fighters were increasingly involved in combat against the armed Afghan opposition. In return, Karachi's influence was slipping.

13 It is interesting to note that Tarik Aziz, one of Saddam Hussein's key ministers, is a Christian.

10 / Asian Fever

1 The Chinese province Xinjiang Uygur was a part of the Islamic Republic of Eastern Turkistan in 1933 and 1934.

2 The Hwei are descendants of Arab traders who settled in China. They are Muslims and number ten million.

3 Islam was introduced into China in the thirteenth century by Muslim merchants traveling on the Silk Road. Chinese Islam took root in the provinces of the center and the northwest: Yunnan, Sichuan, Gansu, Ningxia Hweizu, Shanxi, Qinghai, Anhwei, and Xinjiang Uygur.

4 The ASEAN organization comprises Brunei, Indonesia, the Philippines, Singapore, Thailand, and Malaysia.

5 The PULO was founded in India in 1968 by a group of intellectuals headed by Tengku Bira Kotanila. It was for a time supported by Libya, Iran, and the PLO. Other movements are also agitating for the secession of Pattani: the Pattani National Liberation Front, the National Revolutionary Front, and the United Front of Pattani Combatants.

6 More than half the Chechen capital was razed to the ground. Dozens of schools and hospitals, as well as the airport, were destroyed.

7 Since its withdrawal from Afghanistan, Moscow has been desperately attempting to protect its assets in the region as well as the Russians living there—an often highly educated population, which Moscow counts on to maintain its influence and counterbalance the rise of Islam. For example, 5 million Russians still live in Kazakhstan, 900,000 in Kirghizstan, 800,000 in Uzbekistan, and 50,000 in Tajikistan. Moscow thus intends to be in a position to resist the risk of destabilization caused by a possible fundamentalist contagion in Central Asia, a risk increased by the already existing drug traffic, with which the Russian mafia is broadly associated. Other possibilities have also been considered by Moscow, notably a Machiavellian negative politics aimed at fostering the emergence of radical

Islamic forces in certain republics in order to bring others back into Moscow's fold in return for some protection.

11 / The Bin Laden Network's Billions

1 According to another hypothesis, this missile traffic was in the hands of some officers of the ISI, who had the weapons purchased by intermediaries in order to sell them even more dearly to Osama bin Laden. For their part, the Taliban also traded missiles for chemical products such as acetic anhydride, necessary for the production of heroin. These transactions were sometimes fools' bargains, as the missiles were not always operational because of the limited life of some of their components, such as batteries that last for only two years. Osama bin Laden tried to get around the problem by hiring electronic engineers.

2 Bin Laden set up a special organization to manage his secret funds, the Islamic Salvation Foundation, whose initials evoked the FIS of the Algerian Islamists.

3 In developing countries, informal commerce or the informal economic sector is used to mean any economic activity that, although often very lucrative, is subject to no regulation and generally is not subject to taxation.

12 / Drugs and Terrorism

1 In the language of dealers and police, a "mule" is a smuggler of small quantities of drugs.

2 On September 12, 1994, former Pakistani prime minister Nawaz Sharif told the *Washington Post* that he thought the drug mafia in Pakistan had leadership in the highest organs of the state. The former head of government went so far as to accuse the former army chief of staff and the former head of the secret services. According to Sharif, these two former security chiefs had proposed to him a plan for heroin trafficking to cover military expenditures for the purchase of nuclear material such as plutonium.

3 *Zakat* is a certain amount of money every financially able Muslim, man or woman, must pay annually to support the poor, the needy, those in bondage or debt, recent converts, wayfarers, and the cause of God. It is calculated as 2.5 percent of money that has been in its owner's control for over a lunar year. Zakat is comparable to the tithe. It is one of the five pillars of Islam; the others are testifying (that there is no god but God and that Muhammad is his prophet); prayer; fasting during the month of Ramadan; and pilgrimage to Mecca once in a lifetime if the believer is physically and financially able.

4 Figures from the Observatoire Géopolitique des Drogues.

5 See the thorough article in *Le Point*, June 2000.

13 / Jihad's New Weapons

1 The trial, known as the trial of the Albanians because twelve of the thirteen other principal defendants were Albanian nationals, was one of the most important since the assassination of President Anwar Sadat in October 1981. The proceedings, the result of discreet cooperation between Egyptian and American services, concerned 107 defendants, 67 of

whom were tried in absentia. Nine were sentenced to death in absentia.

2 These gases belong to the family of organophosphates. The other major family of toxic gases is the fluoroacetates. These categories include industrial and agricultural products such as herbicides and insecticides.

3 During morning rush hour on March 20, 1995, five cars on three Tokyo subway lines were contaminated by small packages containing sarin gas, causing twelve deaths and more than five thousand injuries or serious illnesses. Several weeks after the attack, the Aum Shinri Kyo (Supreme Truth) sect, led by Shoko Asahara was identified as responsible for the attack. A few miles from Mount Fuji, investigators found a facility for the production of sarin gas.

4 The seed of the castor bean plant, which grows throughout the world, contains a toxin. The Bulgarian dissident Georgi Markov was assassinated on September 11, 1978 by the toxin, administered with an umbrella that had been prepared by the Bulgarian security services. The poison kills all living cells that it contacts. If it is inhaled, it causes necrosis of the lungs; if it is ingested, it poisons the liver and kidneys and causes internal hemorrhages. The poison acts within ten hours, and the first symptoms are vomiting, abdominal cramps, fever, and diarrhea. There is no treatment. Although it is not a mass bacteriological weapon, because of its natural origin, it is a toxin particularly suited for terrorism.

Afterword

1 Samuel Huntington, article in *Foreign Affairs* (summer 1993), and *The Clash of Civilizations and the Remaking of World Order* (New York: Oxford University Press, 1997).

2 Juergensmeyer, *Terror in the Mind of God*, 7.

3 *Newsweek,* October 20, 2001.

4 The Intifada is the outbreak of Palestinian rage and rebellion that started September 2000 in reaction to Israeli prime minister Ariel Sharon's provocation at the al-Aqsa mosque in Jerusalem, Islam's third holiest site.

5 Bruce Lawrence, speech to the National Humanities Center, North Carolina, November 1, 2001. He is the author of *Defenders of God* (San Francisco: Harper and Row, 1989) and *Shattering the Myth: Islam Beyond Violence* (Princeton: Princeton University Press, 1998).

6 In articles published in the Pakistani weekly *Dawn,* January through March 1999.

Index

Roland Jacquard is President of the Paris-based International Observatory on Terrorism and is Strategic Expert and Consultant on Terrorism to the United Nations Security Council. He is the author of a dozen books (in French) on terrorism and espionage, including *The Secret Files of Terrorism; The War of the Lie: A Secret History of Disinformation; Fatwa Against the West;* and *Carlos (the Jackal): The Secret Files.* Since the events of September 11, 2001, Jacquard has frequently been quoted as "a leading expert on terrorism" in *Time* magazine, where he wrote a piece about his discovery of the "Encyclopedia of Jihad."

We appreciate that Laura Dail, head of the Laura Dail Literary Agency, chose to bring this project to Duke University Press; we are also grateful for her wonderful spirit, good sense, and steady professionalism. Kathryn Nanovic-Morlet, former Managing Director of the French Publisher's Agency, was instrumental in helping us find our translator. Shannon Mullin and the Center for French and Francophone Studies at Duke University generously provided help with auxiliary translation. We are also grateful to Bruce Lawrence for his help and advice on this book, with special thanks for his suggestion that we contact Samia Serageldin.

Library of Congress Cataloging-in-Publication Data
Jacquard, Roland.
[Au nom d'Oussama Ben Laden. English]
In the name of Osama bin Laden : global terrorism and the bin Laden brotherhood / Roland Jacquard ; Samia Serageldin, consulting editor ; George Holoch, translator.
Includes bibliographical references and index.
ISBN 0-8223-2977-8 (cloth : alk. paper) — ISBN 0-8223-2991-3 (pbk. : alk. paper)
1. Bin Laden, Osama, 1957- 2. Terrorists—Saudi Arabia—Biography. 3. Terrorists—Afghanistan—Biography. 4. Terrorism—Religious aspects—Islam. I. Title.
HV6430.B55 J3313 2002 958.104'6'092—dc21 2001008513